The Science of Winning

A Random Walk Along The Road To Investment Riches

Burton P Fabricand

Oldcastle Books

FOR HEATHER

1995

Oldcastle Books, 18 Coleswood Rd

Harpenden, Herts, AL5 1EQ

Copyright © Burton P Fabricand 1979,1983,1995

First Published 1979

A CIP catalogue record for this book is available from the British Library.

I S B N 1 - 874061 - 42 - 4 The Science of Winning

Printed by The Guernsey Press

CONTENTS

PREFACE

It's no longer a sin to be rich. It's a miracle.

Message on the bulletin board of the First Christian Church, Galesburg, IL

Winning! There's a subject so close to our hearts and yet so far from our minds. Like the famous Egyptian horseplayer, Shudda Haddim, we find all kinds of explanations to account for winning performance after the fact, but few of us are aware of the deeper probabilities that hold the key to prediction before the fact. Hindsight is easy, but it is foresight that pays off. It has set the human race apart from all other species on earth and won for us dominance of a planet. It has built civilization upon civilization, each an elaborate preparation of the physical environment to secure the people's future needs. Now the competition exists among the people themselves, with the bulk of the rewards going to those able to see the future more clearly. Is it possible for us to sharpen our prescience and share more fully in the available wealth?

I have attempted in this book to formulate a general theory of winning. Many applications are touched on, and these will certainly enhance the quality of our foresightedness. But only two, pari-mutuel horse betting and the stock market, are treated in depth. In this era of ever-increasing taxation and inflation, they are among the few remaining areas where the average person may become rich by using deliberate, disciplined procedures.

For those readers familiar with my previous books, *Horse Sense* and *Beating the Street,* the winning systems presented here represent major improvements over the earlier ones in both profitability and ease of application. The success so many of you have enjoyed in the past will surely carry over into the future. I trust many others will join you.

This updated edition of my 1979 book, *The Science of Winning,* contains a new introductory chapter on the present status of my original and highly successful pari-mutuel and stock market systems from the point of view of chaos theory and symmetry. In addition, a brand new pari-mutuel betting system is presented in three appendices. It differs from the old mainly in its handling of the historical record and in its use of a simple algebraic format that removes the ambiguities of ordinary language. Other than the substitution of the new system, I see nothing in the book that needs changing. Its insight into the efficient-markets theory is more relevant than ever.

For those readers interested in applications of chaos and symmetry to other fields, I have appended a reading list to the new introductory chapter.

For my British and Irish readers, an additional appendix D, has been added that shows how to adapt the horse-betting system to wagering with the Tote or the bookmaker.

CHAOS, SYMMETRY AND PREDICTING THE FUTURE

An Updated Introduction to *The Science of Winning*

Beauty is in the eye of the beholder.
Margaret Hungerford, *Molly Bawn*

'Beauty is truth, truth beauty...'
John Keats, *Ode to a Grecian Urn*

Truth, like beauty, is in the eye of the beholder.
Burton P. Fabricand, *Abolish the Income Tax*

"The science of betting on horses is, as we shall see, as much concerned with people as with horses." That is the opening sentence of my book, *Horse Sense*, first published thirty years ago. It sets forth the central problem facing horse bettors in the pari-mutuel market and investors in all other financial markets as well. Horses, you see, don't have any money. Neither do stocks or bonds or any other financial instruments. Only people have money. Enriching yourself in these markets, therefore, can be accomplished only by getting other people's money! And that is never easy. Other people want your money just as much as you want theirs. Should you decide to become a market participant, you will be risking *your* money in the hope of rewarding yourself in the future with *their* money. The ensuing competition, I can assure you, will be fierce.

Predicting the future! And doing it better than the competition! That's the key to winning performance. It has been the dream of humankind since our earliest beginnings, and the methods employed to do so have been legion. The marketplace quickly disposes of false claims, however, and none but one need concern us here. That one is the latest and most successful attempt to read the future, and it is what the science of physics is all about.

In this introductory chapter, I wish to consider anew this ancient problem of prognostication, but in the context of two contemporary concepts vitally important in today's research, chaos and symmetry. Their application to free markets places the efficient-markets hypothesis, which underlies the methods described in this book, on a firm theoretical foundation. The implications for you, dear reader, and society as a whole are far-reaching.

How does physics work? Let us begin by looking in on the Apollo 8 mission, the first flight to the moon in 1967. Astronauts Frank Borman, James A. Lovell Jr., and William A. Anders are in earth orbit and about to risk their lives on the predictive power of Isaac Newton's Laws of Motion. Round and round they go, one orbit, two orbits, three orbits, all the while the computers here on earth busily solving and resolving the equations of motion, checking and double-checking flight paths and the effects of possible errors in the measurements of the spacecraft's position and velocity. Finally, at some point in time and space, they ignite their rocket engine briefly and blast off into a pre-calculated trajectory which, they believe, will lead them to a future rendezvous with the moon 250,000 miles away. Any miscalculation or observational error in their initial position or velocity could doom them to an eternity in space. All went well, however, and this first manned voyage to an extraterrestrial orb concluded successfully. Magic? Maybe. But certainly one of the innumerable triumphs of Newtonian physics.

Our space voyage epitomizes the doctrine of determinism: The present gives birth to one unique future, and that future can be ascertained through the application of known laws. So ordered and predictable was the Newtonian world picture that the great French scientist and mathematician, Pierre Simon de Laplace, could imagine his famous superman, who, given the present position and momentum of every particle in the universe, could compute the entire course of world history, past and future. This scientific ideal, so imaginatively developed in physics, exerted enormous influence on the social sciences where workers like Karl Marx, John Maynard Keynes and Sigmund Freud hoped for comparable progress by exploiting the same procedures. Alas, it was not to be, for the results have been disconcertingly dismal. And the reason is simply this: The world is much more chaotic than anybody thought even fifty years ago.

All through the era of determinism, people were well aware of the existence of unpredictably chaotic phenomena. Dice, roulette and horse races, for example, exhibit a decided absence of determinism. In games of chance, the present gives birth to many possible futures, not just one. A role of the dice may beget any whole number from "2" to "12", a spin of an American roulette wheel any whole number from "0" to "36" plus "00". The same multiplicity of futures occurs in the scientifically important problem of turbulence, which affects weather forecasting and airplane flights. But even more startling is the recent discovery that Newtonian physics itself, once the shrine of determinism, yields chaos. Moreover, it now appears that chaos is the rule rather than the exception, and the successes of determinism are limited to a small part of the real world.

How does chaos arise? Returning to the Apollo 8 mission, let us remember the blast-off point from earth orbit. The spacecraft's initial condition, its position and velocity at the time of ignition, must be accurately known and inserted into the Laws of Motion. Only then is it possible to compute a unique moon trajectory. Fortunately for the astronauts, a slight error in the measurements produces only a slight error in the trajectory, and the slight error can be neutralized by a mid-course correction. Here, then, is the magic of deterministic physics. From a knowledge of just three observables, the position and velocity of the spacecraft at some measured time, and Newton's equations, we can generate an infinite set of positional coordinates and velocities that define with great precision its future trajectory.

Chaos enters the picture when the future behavior of a phenomenon under study exhibits a sensitive dependence on initial conditions. Even unobservable differences at the start can generate vastly different futures and limit predictability. No matter how carefully we try to control the rolling of dice or the spinning of a roulette wheel, we shall find the outcome as uncertain as ever. Matters are a bit better in weather forecasting. Massive daily balloon launchings and weather satellites now provide the needed initial information on atmospheric temperatures, pressures and wind velocities. These data, when combined ith Newton's Laws of Motion and processed with high-powered computers, yield volution equations that produce valid forecasts for a few days more or less. Then the ensitivity to initial conditions (turbulence) nullifies them. It is much like the stream of moke from a steadily held cigarette. At first, the flow is smooth and predictable. But, ter a short time, it breaks up into unpredictably chaotic patterns.

When we look at the so-called "social sciences", the picture is more turbulent. ime evolutions here are notoriously complex and even limited predictability is absent. Vhy this should be is not hard to trace. Chaos dominates human relations because we live nd learn. Our expectations, desires and behavioral incentives are ever changing, and we e never the same system twice. Mathematically speaking, stationary probability stributions and linear equations rarely approximate reality. Moreover, the specification f initial conditions for us and our institutions, a goal of historical studies, may be humanly npossible. Is it any wonder, then, that the methods of deterministic physics have not orked in this area. Even Laplace's superman would find himself confounded by the scrutable ways of human beings and unable to foresee the chaotic consequences of their ell-intentioned initiatives.

Are we at an impasse? Is the future forever closed to us? Is there no way to edict a trajectory to other people's money? Not necessarily. After all, we do have iccessful businesses and social organizations which must defend themselves against the nexpected. And we must not forget all the life forms that have survived myriads of ture shocks. How does order emerge from what appears to be chaos? The answer lates to the methods used in this book, and it amounts to fighting chaos with chaos.

An omniscient God could, I suppose, program each of His creations for survival by iticipating every random cruelty that a hostile environment might inflict on them. That e did not do it that way may be due to the excessive space and power demands of the cessary computing mechanism. Instead, He chose a self-perpetuating scheme of ngoing random mutation that flooded the world with the widest possible variety of life rms. Those that fit best into some ecological niche survived and multiplied, their imbers regulated by the prodding forces of the environment. The others faded into olivion. This dynamic process wrests order from chaos and selects from the multitude e few winning species. We call it evolution.

Chaos plays a similar role in protecting us from disease-bearing bacteria and ruses. Once again, it is conceivable that the immune system could have been so ogrammed to repel not only all existing invaders but all future mutations as well. But ture chose otherwise. The body's response to invasion is the generation of a wondrous sortment of randomly shaped molecules. The attachment of just one of them to an vader earmarks it for destruction or elimination and signals the body to manufacture odigious quantities of that one unique molecule. Production ceases when the threat is moved. The use of chaos is primary not only in the origin of winning species but also in eir preservation from random attack.

From chaos created, in chaos living. That is how our early ancestors perceived e world. Having little foreknowledge of what to expect, they could depend on nothing ore than the evolutionary implants necessary for survival. There preexisted no treasure ouse of information, no elaborate programs and no godlike individuals to guide their forts at improving their lot. They could combat chaos only with the means that nature provided, through the randomly wrought personalities and talents of a large number of fellow creatures, each free to seek in his or her own way that which is the better. Although most of them performed about average and survived, an unforeseen few succeeded in breaking new paths. Advances in the arts and crafts, inventions, new ideas and innovative processes erupted as random events in space and time. Each success added new information, after steadily shortening time lags, to the race's store of knowledge. Each success further facilitated the production and marketing of the necessities and niceties of life and raised the standard of living. These self-organizing transformations from chaos to order continue to this day. They are the essence of Adam Smith's "invisible hand": The greatest prosperity for all comes about when each and every individual has a maximum of freedom to decide upon and pursue his or her own best interests. This sophisticated principle is the basis of capitalism.

In the financial markets of concern to us, each individual investor engages all other investors for the money at stake. But, if chaos reigns supreme in dealings among people, the future is equally mysterious to everybody. There is, therefore, equal opportunity for all, and nobody can expect to do better than average. Equality of opportunity, it must be understood, does not translate into equality of reward. Although most market players will be average performers, an unforeseen few will do much better - these are the lucky ones - and a few unforeseen unfortunates will do much worse. Furthermore, past performance gives no hint as to future performance. A market of equal opportunity is known as an efficient market.

Out of this seeming chaos, there emerges a remarkable symmetry. Scientific symmetry, I hasten to explain, probes deeper than but includes our commonplace notion of it. It has played a crucial role in modern physics ever since Albert Einstein stressed its importance in his special theory of relativity, introduced in 1905.

A system possesses a symmetry if we can operate on it in a way that leaves something about the system unchanged. Displacing this book from one position to another is an example of a symmetry operation because it does not alter the book or its contents. Another is the rotation of a ball about a diameter because it looks the same before and after. If I reflect the letters A, H, I, M, O, T, U, V, W, X and Y in a mirror, they look identical to the originals; the other letters do not possess this reflection symmetry. If, in an equal opportunity market, I interchange any market participant with any other person in the world, the replacement can be expected to perform much like the person replaced. In other words, the market sees the two players as identical in so far as their expectation is concerned, and we have an interchange symmetry. This symmetry is the basis of all random walk models in both the natural and social sciences.

A symmetry often indicates the presence of what is known as a "conserved" quantity, some system parameter that remains fixed or invariant until the symmetry is broken. Under displacement symmetry, "momentum" is conserved. This conservation law allows our spacecraft to move along forever with unchanged velocity as long as no stopping force is brought to bear. Under rotational symmetry, "angular momentum" is conserved. This conservation law forces the earth's rotational axis to point fixedly at the North Star and permits ice skaters to turn themselves into whirligigs. Reflection symmetry leads to conservation of "parity", which is of great importance in the quantum theory of physics and chemistry. These are just three of the great conservation laws that prove so useful in predicting the future behavior of real-world systems.

Interchange symmetry in the marketplace gives rise to a conservation law of information: There exists no information, what I term "privileged" information, that enables one market participant to have a higher expectation than any other. No one of us knows more than all of us, it might be said, and market prices generally reflect all information extant at any given time. To beat the chaos of interchange symmetry and perform better than average, a person must gain possession of privileged information. The distinguishing features of such information are randomness and exclusivity. It cannot be inferred from present knowledge and it must be accessible to relatively few people in order to retain its value. Otherwise, it becomes part of the general knowledge with everybody partaking of it. Quite naturally, the acquisition of privileged information is the goal of most market players. And, quite naturally, it is very hard to come by, for it has a very fleeting existence. Almost always, by the time you and I are tipped onto something good, it is too late. Too many people know about it and market prices have long since discounted the information.

In my 1965 book, *Horse Sense*, and my 1969 book, *Beating the Street*, I discovered a market asymmetry by showing that not only did privileged information indeed exist in financial markets, but that it could be accessed and utilized by knowing people. Information was divided into two categories, historical and late-breaking. It is the historical part that is built into market prices and, in itself, is not helpful in achieving better-than-average performance. Late-breaking information, on the other hand, makes itself known unexpectedly and is discounted by the market only after a time lag. By comparing the two, profitable systems of investment in both the stock market and the pari-mutuel market were developed. The results have been impressive. In the stock market, my main interest, an investment fund that I manage has appreciated 80-fold over the last twenty years, far exceeding any average. In the pari-mutuel market, correspondents have reported up to a 30% return on investment.

But, as I indicated earlier, nothing ever stays the same when people get involved. My stock market system, which is based on surprising earnings reports, has been adopted (without acknowledgment, I might add) by nearly all investment services, professional fund managers and serious investors. The financial news media have even caught on and feature "better-than-expected" and "worse-than-expected" earnings. As a consequence, it is not as easy as it once was to make money in the stock market. The market has moved back toward chaos, i.e., equal opportunity for all investors. That is not to say that privileged information has disappeared completely, but it is now more likely to be discounted by the time you and I learn about it. Despite these reservations, I firmly believe that the stock market should be played only by the methods described in this book.

The pari-mutuel market has been similarly affected by the absorption of knowledge. The reported returns on *The Science of Winning* system had decreased to just above break-even as of 10 years ago. That is still a notable performance in the face of rising pari-mutuel "takes". I suspect matters are worse now, for the great popularity of exotic betting has extracted a huge amount of money from the win pools and shifted it to the exotic pools. Much of this money would in former times have been placed on long shots, causing underbetting of the favorites. Today, the situation appears reversed; the data point to overbet favorites, a considerable handicap to the old system. Whatever, something new is called for and it appears in the appendices to this book. The results are again impressive, better than a 50% return on investment. But, possibly because of the increased efficiency of the market, the frequency of betting is less than one race in five.

Coping with chaos through individual freedom and initiative, I should remark in closing, runs counter to today's conventional wisdom. Central planning by big central governments is the order (or disorder) of the day. And our financial and consumer markets, the vehicles for wringing order out of chaos, have been adversely affected. They are besieged by hordes of politicians, judges, scholars, reformers, lawyers, media mavins, economists and other social scientists, all of whom convinced they can do better by predicting the unpredictable and planning the unplannable. Their intentions may be noble. They usually are. We all like to do good, don't we? But, fulfilling noble intentions in the real world is fraught with difficulty and danger. Reality is not as simpleminded as these elitists project it to be. Again and again, they discover "truth" in random patterns of experience - what "chaosticians" call noise - and rationalize their findings with self-serving plums plucked from the ingredient-rich puddings of human history and literature. Always, they associate themselves with the benevolent despot or benign dictator who knows the formula for doing good as opposed to the wicked tyrant or despised businessperson who does evil. Invariably, they picture themselves as Plato's philosopher-kings in communion with the Supreme Good and Ultimate Truth, superior beings who will fashion the State according to the eternal nature of things and human freedom be damned. Ordinarily, the marketplace quickly perceives their pervasive twaddle for what it is and ignores it. But not when the authority of law is invoked to enforce it. And there's the rub, for a lot of bad government hides behind noble intentions.

Mistaking noble intentions for knowledge and wisdom, lawmakers the world over pave "the road to hell" with vast arrays of regulatory and operational agencies, costly monoliths that compromise a society's freedom to adapt to and exploit "the slings and arrows of outrageous fortune." Even God did not presume to mandate our responses to a chaotic future in the way most of our laws do. The effects on our unplannably efficient markets have been marked. Taxes and fees, rules and regulations, all have taken their toll. In financial markets, there are lowered returns on investment and higher than necessary costs of capital; in consumer markets, excessive prices of goods and services; and, for the world as a whole, stifled economic growth and reduced expectations for our standard of living. Communist countries stand as fearful monuments to the deleterious effects of government interference in the marketplace. Even America, an upstart nation whose unfashionable policy of almost no government and no taxes during its first 100 years begat in that time the greatest country in the world with by far the highest standard of living ever attained, has seen the growth of government slow her economic expansion to a crawl, and worse may be in store. Not for naught did Henry David Thoreau, American naturalist and author of *Walden*, echo Adam Smith when he wrote in *On the Duty of Civil Disobedience* (1849): "I heartily accept the motto, 'That government is best which governs least'; and I should like to see it acted up to more rapidly and systematically. Carried out, it finally amounts to this, which also I believe - ' That government is best which governs not at all.'"

Further reading (also see the list in the main text)

Ekeland, Ivar, *The Broken Dice and Other Mathematical Tales of Chance*, University of Chicago Press, Chicago 1993.

Fabricand, Burton P., *Abolish the Income Tax: A New and Rigorous Inquiry into the Wealth of Nations*, D.P.A., Box 956, Mt. Dora, Florida 32757, 1985.

Fabricand, Burton P., *Symmetry in Free Markets*, in *Symmetry 2 - Unifying Human Understanding* (ed. Hargittai, I.), Pergamon Press, Headington Hill Hall, Oxford OX3 0BW, UK and Elmsford, NY 10523, 1989.

Ford, Joseph, *What is chaos, that we should be mindful of it?*, in *The New Physics* (ed. Davies, P.), Cambridge University Press, Cambridge 1989.

Nicolis, Gregoire, *Physics of far-from-equilibrium systems and self-organization*, in *The New Physics* (ed. Davies P.), Cambridge University Press, Cambridge 1989.

PART I
THE RANDOM WALK IN SCIENCE AND SOCIETY

1
THE PROBLEM OF WINNING

The gods did not reveal from the beginning
All things to us; but in the course of time
Through seeking, men find that which is the better.
But as for certain truth, no man has known it,
Nor will he know it; neither of the gods
Nor yet of all the things of which I speak.
And even if by chance he were to utter
The final truth, he would himself not know it;
For all is but a woven web of guesses.

Xenophenes

We are all gamblers. We must all combat as best we can the "slings and arrows of outrageous fortune," ignorant to a degree of what blind chance has in store for us, uncertain as to what actions to take in the present to achieve some future goal. For the most part, these encounters with probability take place largely on the intuitive level. A person drives a car feeling that the chances of a fatal accident are negligibly small. Rarely does he figure that 50,000 deaths occur on the highways of this country each year out of a population of 200 million, so that he has roughly 1 chance in 4,000 of losing his life in the next year from this cause. And should the thought arise, he would rationalize away his fears by thinking his excellence as a driver precludes any dire consequences. It would not occur to him that he might be participating in a random walk process in which a coin having 3,999 chances in 4,000 of coming up heads for life and 1 chance in 4,000 of coming up tails for death is flipped for each member of the population. Usually, our notions in commonplace situations stand us in good stead, and we may expect to do about average, which in the case of the human race means survival with plenty of room to spare. Our goal in this book, however, is more ambitious. To attain better-than-average performance in the myriad competitions of our daily lives, to understand how it comes about, that is our aim. To achieve it, we must render more precise our ideas of reality.

In any undertaking possessing a multiplicity of possible future outcomes—and that includes, as we shall see presently, all operations in the real world—there is a certain risk and a certain reward attached to each end result. The estimation of these two attributes motivates all activity, or the lack of it. Because their analysis can become enormously complicated, we shall initially consider risk and reward in some simple games of chance. This approach to probability offers several advantages: (1) the risks are easily calculated; (2) the rewards are well known; (3) all possible future outcomes can be foreseen; and (4) they are realized in a short time. Some or all of these benefits must be given up as our study broadens to include the more complex games exemplified by the public markets in which we as human beings participate. The natures of the pari-mutuel betting market, the stock market, and the market-organized society undergo examination to assist us in the determination of the expectations, the risks, and the rewards each of us may anticipate as we perform in the game of life. Finally, the prerequisites for better-than-average performance in the arena of the marketplace are taken up and applied to the development of two systems of investment, one in the pari-mutuel market and the other in the stock market, that will assuredly place many readers of this book on the road to riches.

I should perhaps stress at the outset the unique approach to winning adopted in this book. Of prime importance is the "efficiency" of the marketplace: Do market prices (the odds on horses in the pari-mutuel market and the prices of securities in the stock market, for example) afford to all participants equality of opportunity? If such turns out to be the case, the market is termed "strongly efficient" and nobody, be he expert or novice, can expect anything other than average performance. Only to the extent that a market deviates from strong efficiency is it possible to beat the averages. Unfortunately for system builders, the pari-mutuel and stock markets are strongly efficient to a high degree of approximation, and both provide excellent examples of Adam Smith's conception of the operation of a free market. Observe the flashing odds on the totalizator board at the race track or the changing prices of stocks on the ticker tape. It marks the beginnings of wisdom in a person when he appreciates the uncanny accuracy with which these numbers predict the future outcomes of current ventures. Any system purporting to better-than-average performance that ignores this vital characteristic of free markets is doomed to failure from the start. To be worthwhile, a system must furnish better estimates of future probabilities than does the marketplace, which itself makes a superlative job of it. Here is the seemingly insoluble task that must be faced before superior performance can be achieved. To my knowledge, only the methods presented in this book attack the problem successfully.

It should not be inferred that equality of opportunity is identical to equality of reward. The people sitting around a roulette table in a gambling casino all have equal opportunity, but they realize very different rewards, and it is impossible to predict who wins, who loses, or who breaks even. Both from practical and theoretical considerations, the old doctrine of determinism is no longer tenable. It appears as if God plays dice with the world and, perforce, thrusts us into uncertainty, into a reality where cause and effect are obscurely related. A given event may have many possible consequences and itself may arise from many possible causes. We are compelled out of ignorance, frustration, and desperation to assign probabilities to possible future outcomes and past causes. The weatherman tells us there is a 50-percent chance of rain tomorrow, meaning that present meteorological conditions have in the past led to rain on 50 percent of the following days. Actuarial tables tell us that male babies in this country have a 50-percent chance of living to be seventy years old, which reflects the observation that half of all men die before that age. Even the act of observation itself, on which all knowledge is based, is beset with doubt since no two people's sense impressions are quite the same. Only in this century have scientists recognized fully the uncertainty inherent in knowledge and developed guidelines for determining its reliability. Man's quest for certainty has turned into an exploitation of probability theory and statistics in all fields whose content deals with quantitative relationships—physics, chemistry, biology, engineering, business, economics, sociology, medicine, and political science, to mention but a few. We shall learn about the methods being so effectively applied and direct them toward achieving our goal of better-than-average performance.

2
DOING THE RANDOM WALK

THE
NORMAL
LAW OF ERROR
STANDS OUT IN THE
EXPERIENCE OF MANKIND
AS ONE OF THE BROADEST
GENERALIZATIONS OF NATURAL
PHILOSOPHY ♦ IT SERVES AS THE
GUIDING INSTRUMENT IN RESEARCHES
IN THE PHYSICAL AND SOCIAL SCIENCES AND
IN MEDICINE AGRICULTURE AND ENGINEERING ♦
IT IS AN INDISPENSABLE TOOL FOR THE ANALYSIS AND THE
INTERPRETATION OF THE BASIC DATA OBTAINED BY OBSERVATION AND EXPERIMENT

W. J. Youden

Imagine yourself playing this game. Draw a line on the ground twenty paces long and stand at its midpoint. Flip a coin. If it comes up heads, take one pace to the right. If it comes up tails, take one pace to the left. Repeat after each step. Where will you be after, say, ten flips?

This is the problem of the random walk (in one dimension), first solved by James Bernoulli almost 300 years ago. Its importance lies in the fact that so many of the phenomena around us appear to behave in just this manner. Brownian motion, discovered in 1827 by the Scottish botanist Robert Brown, is perhaps the most famous example. Brown noted that, viewed under a microscope, small particles, like bits of pollen, glass, wood, and rock, executed an unceasing jiggling motion when suspended in water. All efforts to understand this example of perpetual motion failed, and it went unexplained until 1905, when Albert Einstein likened Brownian motion to a random walk and was able to predict the future positions of the particles in a statistical sense. That is, he could calculate how many particles would be a certain distance from their starting points at some future time, but not where any designated single particle would be. Einstein pictured the particles as undergoing a constant bombardment by the molecules of water, which are in turn receiving their impetus from the thermal energy of the surroundings. Every so often, there is an imbalance in the number of molecular "kicks" on opposite sides of the particle of sufficient magnitude to displace it an observable distance. Einstein's work not only provided a description of vitally important diffusion processes, but offered as well the most convincing proof up to that time of the existence of atoms and molecules.

Unbeknownst to Einstein, his remarkable research had been anticipated by some five years by Louis Bachelier. Unbelievably, Bachelier had derived many of the same results, not for Brownian motion, but for the changes in stock prices on the Paris stock exchange over a period of time. It appeared as if the stock market and Brownian motion were closely related to each other and to the random walk. Of course, the forces knocking stock prices about are imbalances in buy and sell decisions rather than molecular collisions, but the effects seemed the same.*

The implications are far-reaching. Is the world, from the tiniest of its particles to the affairs of men, at the mercy of fluctuating forces whose application is ultimately decided by the flip of a coin? Does intelligence and ability count for naught? Answers are not easy. The more closely a phenomenon approximates the random walk, the more probable it is that most participants will fare about average. For people in a true random walk situation, equal opportunity is guaranteed; the simpleton will likely do as well as the expert. However, deciding where, when, how, and to what extent random walk behavior applies is difficult, as we shall see.

The adoption of the random walk model for Brownian motion and the stock market bespeaks of our inability to apply the basic laws of physics to these events. In our ignorance, we choose the model as a representation with which we can work to predict results. If the forecasts fit the facts as we observe them, we consider the model a good reflection of reality. It is then assumed that the model is derivable from the laws, could we but work out the step-by-step details.

Let us examine the random walk more closely and try to discover those of its characteristics that relate to happenings in the real world. Suppose we play the game described at the start of the chapter and flip an unbiased coin ten times. Because the coin is just as likely to come up heads as tails, we feel instinctively that our final position will not be far from our starting position, at the midpoint of the line. Of course, we may end up anywhere from ten paces to the right of the start to ten paces to the left. (With one caveat: Since the coin is flipped an even number of times, we must finish an even number of paces from the midpoint.) At the end of ten flips, we mark our position in Figure 2-1 with an *x* above the line, and then repeat another ten flips, again marking the result. In this manner, a histogram is constructed that exhibits the frequency with which each position along the line occurs at the end of each set of ten flips. Alternatively, ten coins may be flipped at once and the net number of heads or tails tallied. Figure 2-1a illustrates the shape of the histogram after 100 experiments of 10 coin flips. For comparison, a second set of 100 flips of the same 10 coins is also shown (Fig. 2-1b).

---

*Louis Bachelier, "Theorie de la Speculation" (Paris: Gauthier-Villars, 1900).

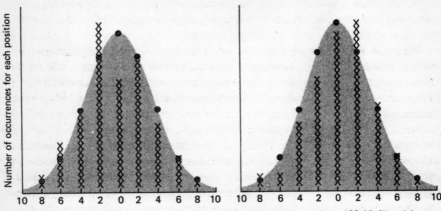

a. and b. Number of steps from start at the end of 10 flips of the coin in 100 10–flip trials

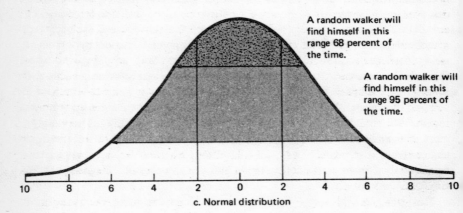

c. Normal distribution

Figure 2-1. The Results of Random Walk Experiments

These histograms are known as probability or frequency distributions since they indicate how many times a given position along the line appears out of the total number of trials. Thus, position "zero" occurred 17 times out of 100 trials in the first histogram and 24 times in the second. For a very large number of trials, much larger than 100, the shape of the distribution will assume the form shown by the smooth bell-shaped curve, which is known as the normal or Gaussian distribution. According to it, the "zero" position is most likely and will occur 246 times out of every 1,000 10-flip trials, a probability of 24.6 percent. The "two" positions, to the right and left of zero, will each occur 205 times out of 1,000 trials, a probability of 20.5 percent. The least probable is the "ten" position, 1 occurrence in 1,000 trials for a probability of 0.1 percent.

What are the distinguishing features of this random flipping that may have parallels in such natural phenomena as Brownian motion and the stock market? First, each flip of a coin is independent of every other. Regardless of what the coin came up previously, the chances for heads and tails in future trials remain unchanged. In other words, nature has no memory (at least in this case) of past events. Some people dispute this assertion, arguing that after a run of heads, tails become more likely. Strange to say, no theoretical disproof of their contention is possible. Of themselves, logic and mathematics can tell us nothing about actual physical phenomena. They are merely tools used to deduce the consequences of hypotheses intended to describe an event. In the example of coin flipping, once the probabilities for heads and tails are assigned, the mathematical theory of probability enables us to predict the future behavior of the coin. But suppose the true probabilities are not known, as they are not for any real-world coin. No amount of logical reasoning suffices to depict the subsequent results of coin-tossing. It is now the business of the scientist to do anything he can to come up with a hypothetical model of probabilities for heads and tails when the coin is flipped. He then uses the theory of probability to infer the consequences of his model and compare them with the actual experimental results obtained by flipping the coin. If the theoretical deductions agree with the experimental results, the model is thought to have a high degree of validity. The weight of empirical evidence in coin-flipping experiments is on the side of fixed, unchanging probabilities of heads and tails. There can, however, be no appeal to an omniscient, ultimate authority on the identity of the true and assigned probabilities for any real coin.

Translating the idea of independent trials to Brownian motion assumes that each shock undergone by the jiggling particles is unconnected with earlier ones. The picture gains plausibility when it is considered that each water molecule is far less massive than the Brownian particle, and, consequently, each single collision of molecule and particle cannot of itself affect the latter's position. A huge number of molecules acting in concert is needed to affect the position of the particle, so that all memory of past single collisions is erased. A comparable model of the stock market implies the independence of successive price changes of a stock, or, to put it another way, the fact that a stock went up in price today has no effect whatsoever on its performance tomorrow. To draw an analogy with the Brownian collisions, the random confluence of a number of buy and sell decisions, arrived at individually, causes movement in the price of a stock.

The second feature of the random walk is the stationary character of the probability distribution—the probabilities for the final displacement of the random walker after ten coin flips do not change with time. Thus, he will have a 24.6-percent probability of ending up on zero, a 20.5-percent probability on two, and so on in all future experiments. Note the similarity of the two histograms in Figure 2-1a and b. Their resemblance to each other and to the normal distribution (Fig. 2-1c) can be expected to increase with the number of trials. Although the normal distribution is widely approximated in physical measurements, some random phenomena may exhibit differently shaped stationary distributions.

Third, most random walkers will end up near their starting point. This most likely end result is called the *expected* or *mean* or *average* value for this particular random walk. Other mean values are possible, as we shall see. If we have a large number of people performing the coin tossing experiment, it can be predicted from the properties of the normal distribution that 68 percent of them will finish fewer than four steps from the "zero," or mean, position and 95 percent will be six or fewer steps away (see Fig. 2-1c). Only 1 in 100 walkers will find themselves more than eight steps from zero. Put another way, any given random walker has a 68-percent chance of finding himself after ten flips on the "zero" or "two" positions to the right and left, a 95-percent chance on any of the positions between and including zero and six, and less than a 1-percent chance of being more than eight steps away from where he began.

I have introduced here the important property of the random walk known as the *standard deviation*, the probability that experimental observations on phenomena subject to random influences fall within certain limits. Thus, one standard deviation denotes those limits on our line, the "two" position to the left and the "two" position to the right, between which 68 percent of the outcomes of the random walk experiment will fall. Two (more precisely 1.96) standard deviations determine the limits between which 95 percent of the outcomes occur, and 2.56 standard deviations the limits between which 99 percent of the outcomes occur.

In our random walk experiment, the use of an unbiased coin was assumed. Any tendency of the coin to come up heads rather than tails, or tails rather than heads, will change both the mean and the shape of our histograms. A coin biased toward heads, for example, might give a frequency distribution for our random walk that looks like Figure 2-2. All even steps to the right and left of our starting point are still possible. But the most likely result is now six steps to the right, and ten steps to the right is more probable than ten steps to the left. If the number of flips were increased to twenty, the curve would regain its symmetry about the mean. It is obvious that knowing our coin is vital to the prediction of the future outcomes of a random walk experiment.

Let us use our knowledge of the mean and standard deviation to determine

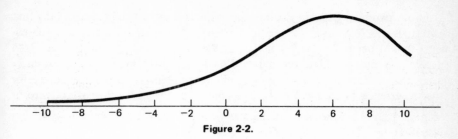

Figure 2-2.

whether or not a coin is biased. Because most coins are apt to have nearly equal chances of turning up heads or tails when flipped, we first hypothesize that the coin is unbiased—that is, that heads and tails are equally likely to turn up—and proceed to observe the results of 100 flips. On the basis of a fair coin, we expect a result somewhere near 50 heads. But how close to 50? Since innumerable random factors enter into the final outcome of a head or a tail, there should be some spread around 50 in line with the standard deviation. There is a deduction in probability theory that we shall find most useful:

$$s.d. = \sqrt{Npq}$$

where N is the number of trials, p the probability that a head results, and q the probability that a tail results based on our model of the coin. In this example, therefore, the standard deviation $s.d. = \sqrt{100 \times .50 \times .50} = \pm 5$, meaning that if the coin is unbiased, we should obtain between 45 and 55 heads in 68 percent of our 100-flip experiments, between 40 and 60 heads in 95 percent of our experiments, and between 37 and 63 heads in 99 percent of our experiments. Fifty-two heads is a very likely result and no reasonable person should find cause for thinking the coin is biased on the basis of this experiment. At the same time, other models, such as one assigning a probability of 51 percent for heads, cannot be rejected.

How many heads are sufficient for evidence of bias? There can be no hard and fast line of demarcation, and scientists have learned how to handle situations like this only after long experience. On the basis of this experiment, any model other than that of an unbiased coin would be rejected unless more than 60 heads or fewer than 40 heads were obtained in the 100 flips. Two standard deviations is usually taken as the dividing line. Even so, in 5 out of 100 100-flip experiments, using an unbiased coin, we can expect to see more than 60 or less than 40 heads. To narrow the uncertainty, each experiment should use more flips. In a 10,000-flip experiment, $s.d. = \sqrt{10000 \times .50 \times .50} = \pm 50$, so that flips of a fair coin should result in 5,000 $\pm$ 100 heads. In proportion to the expected number of heads from an unbiased coin, the range about the mean is considerably narrowed and any bias shows up more readily.

In our two histograms in Figure 2-1a and b, zero occurred 17 times in the first 100 trials and 24 times in the second 100 trials. Assuming the coin was unbiased, zero should occur 24.6 times in 100 trials. Are the results "unexpected"? To decide, we must calculate the standard deviation in the number of occurrences using the same formula of the preceding section. Now, p is the probability for the occurrence of zero and q the probability for the nonoccurrence of zero or $(1 - p)$. Therefore,

$$s.d. = \sqrt{100 \times .246 \times .754} = \pm 4.3$$

This figure is interpreted by saying that there is a 68-percent chance that the number of occurrences of zero in a 100-trial experiment will fall within one standard deviation of the mean, between the limits 24.6 + 4.3 and 24.6 - 4.3, or between 28.9 and 20.3 occurrences, and a 95-percent chance of its occurring within two standard deviations of the mean, between 24.6 + 8.6 and 24.6 - 8.6, or between 33.2 and 16.0 occurrences. The occurrence of zero 17 times in one of our experiments is, therefore, "expected." A psychic claiming that powers of psychokinesis enable him to influence the results of the coin flips so that zero will not come up as frequently as predicted by the random walk theory would not be believed if zero occurred 17 times in 100 trials. If, however, zero resulted 170 times in 1,000 trials, he would be taken seriously. For now,

$$s.d. = \sqrt{1000 \times .246 \times .754} = \pm 14,$$

and two standard deviations = 28, so that the "expected" number of occurrences of zero is 246 ± 28. Since 170 lies outside this range, the result is unexpected. (There could, of course, be other explanations.)

Sums of random events—the individual coin flips, for example—form stationary probability distributions. Therefore, if the displacements of the Brownian particles, which are caused by the sum total of many single collisions with water molecules, and the price changes in stocks, which arise from the sum total of many individual buy and sell decisions, do show distributions of stationary character, it is evidence in favor of their essential randomness. However, the reverse is not true: the existence of such a pattern does not constitute a sufficient proof of randomness. A devious observer, as a counter example, could fudge results so as to obtain a spuriously stationary distribution.

3
THE RANDOM WALK
IN THE REAL WORLD

The scientist is astonished to notice how sublime order emerges from what appeared to be chaos.

Albert Einstein

In order to apply random walk concepts usefully to measurements in the real world, proper sampling of a phenomenon is essential. Each empirical curve in Figure 2-1, for example, exhibits just 100 samples of ten coin flips each from a total population of all possible sequences of ten coin flips, which number 1,024 or 2^{10}. (There are two possible outcomes for the first coin, heads or tails; two for the second coin; two for the third; and so on. The total number of sequences of H and T is then $2 \times 2 \times 2 \times 2 \times 2 \times 2 \times 2 \times 2 \times 2 \times 2 = 2^{10}$.) One possible sequence is HHHHHHTTTT; another is TTTTHHHHHH; and a third is HTHTHTHTHH. Although different, each of these sequences will land the random walker two steps to the right of zero. Now we may comprehend the underlying reason for our instinctive feeling that the random walker will most likely end up at the starting point: The number of possible distinct sequences comprised of five heads and five tails (which land the random walker at the start) is greater than the number of sequences for six heads and four tails or four heads and six tails, which in turn is greater than the number for seven heads and three tails or three heads and seven tails, which in turn is greater than the number for eight heads and two tails or two heads and eight tails, and so on. If each sequence has the same chance of being selected as a sample, the random walker will then trace out histograms similar to those in Figure 2-1.

Here is the basic requirement to be satisfied by random walk parameters such as the mean and standard deviation of a set of observations on real-world phenomena if they are to have meaning. Sampling must be random, each sample from a total population having the same probability of being selected as any other. Any deviation from random sampling as a result of bias in the observational process will yield samples whose means and standard deviations fluctuate in an unknown manner from sample to sample. Nonrandom sampling permits a person to prove anything he wishes by simply selecting those samples fitting his preconceived notions; such a practice constitutes one of the most flagrant misuses of statistics. As Stephen Leacock observed, "In earlier times, they had no statistics, and so they had to fall back on lies. Hence the huge exaggerations of primitive literature—giants or miracles or wonders. They did it with lies and we do it with statistics; but it is all the same."

A measurement in an experimental science, especially when the subject is inanimate, can usually be taken as a random sample from a total population of all possible measurements. It must not be supposed that all the possible measurements yield the same value even though they are thought to be meticulously carried out by competent people. Consider for a moment the room in which you are now sitting. What is its floor area? You might like to think there exists one true value for this parameter. But what is it? Who knows it? If 1,000 people carefully measure the area, there will be many different answers. Plot them as in our random walk histogram and you will get something close to the normal distribution. There are random influences operating in all measurement processes which tend to produce differences in results. The mean of the 1,000-measurement sample is taken as the number closest to the "true" answer, whereas the spread of the normal distribution (the standard deviation) tells us something of the uncertainty inherent in this number. More precisely, the mean of the total population of all competent measurements (which, by definition, is the "true" value) will with 95-percent probability fall within two standard deviations of the sample mean.

Some further examples of randomness will prove useful.

Radioactivity

The fundamental uncertainty inherent in atomic processes was demonstrated in the early years of this century by Nobel Prize-winning physicist Ernest Rutherford (1871-1937), the first man to realize the ancient alchemists' dream of the transmutation of one element into another. Radioactivity results when the nucleus of an atom spontaneously disintegrates, ejecting nuclear particles or gamma rays in the process. In a famous experiment, Rutherford sampled the number of α particles emitted in the disintegration of the radioactive element polonium in some 2,608 time intervals each of 7.5 seconds duration. Figure 3-1, a histogram of the particle counts, shows the number of time intervals containing 0, 1, 2, 3, . . . , 10 or more α particles.

This is a stationary distribution related to the normal distribution and is known as a *Poisson distribution*. To account for it, Rutherford was forced to assume that each polonium atom has a small and uniform probability of exploding, so that in a 7.5-second interval some fraction of the original polonium atoms disintegrate. Just which particular polonium atoms are destined to explode cannot be determined; only the overall number of exploding atoms given by the histogram can be known. This is the random walk; the probability of

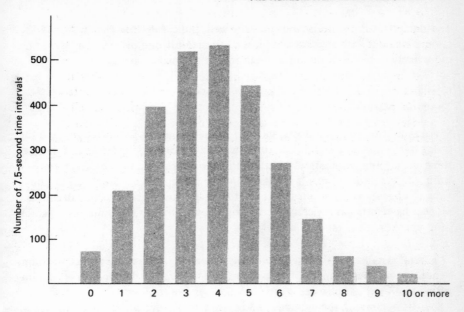

Figure 3-1. Number of α Particles Emitted by Polonium Nuclei in a 7.5-second Time Interval

disintegration replaces the probability for heads and tails. Not until 1928 was Rutherford's hypothesis put on a firm theoretical basis by the new quantum theory.

Flying-bomb Hits on London During World War II

This example illustrates the tendency of the untrained observer to view randomness in terms of patterns that supposedly may be used to predict the future. During World War II the city of London underwent a bombardment from flying bombs launched from continental Europe. The south of London was hit by a total of 537 bombs, and most people believed in a tendency of the points of impact to cluster. To check this belief, the entire area was divided into 576 smaller units each of $\frac{3}{4}$ square kilometer and the number of hits in each area was recorded as follows.*

Number of hits	0	1	2	3	4	5 and over
Number of areas	229	211	93	35	7	1

---

*The figures are from a paper by R. Clarke in *Journal of the Institute of Actuaries*, 72 (1946), as quoted in William Feller, *An Introduction to Probability Theory and Its Applications* 2d ed. (New York: John Wiley, 1957), p. 150.

The data fit a Poisson distribution very well, indicating that each area had the same probability of a hit as any other. An area hit one or more times was no more likely to be hit in the future than was an untouched area.

The Stock Market

A random series of numbers, like the particle counts of radioactivity and the flying-bomb hits on London, can often trace out short-term patterns in time that some people find meaningful in attempting to predict the future. An interesting form of this illusion manifests itself in the stock market. Much of the huge volume of research done on the character of the stock market since Bachelier's pioneering efforts has concerned itself with demonstrating the similarity of stock price changes to the random walk:*

a. Statistical correlation techniques have convincingly revealed the correspondence of the price changes of stocks to the coin flips of the random walk, indicating that the price changes are independent of one another;

b. Histograms of the number of occurrences of percentage price changes of stocks for each percentage price change invariably resemble the normal distribution. The graph in Figure 3-2 shows a typical example, where the daily percentage price changes of a stock were observed over a period of years.

Thus, price changes satisfy the random walk criteria and are, presumptively, a series of random numbers.

Now, if the price changes of a stock or the average of a group of stocks is transformed into the actual price level, what results is the typical price-time chart shown in the daily newspapers. As an example, the Dow-Jones Average for 1967 is shown in Figure 3-3. In this graph appear two of the many chart formations used by some investors as a tool in what is called *technical analysis*, the object of which is to predict the future course of the stock market. The pattern on the left is the "head-and-shoulders top" and the one on the right the "double top." Both are known as reversal patterns and are believed by technicians to indicate the end of an upward movement in stock prices. If, however, the price changes generating these patterns are random, the predictive power of the patterns is nil. It is interesting to note that random-number tables have been used to simulate a series of fictitious price changes and that, when these are

---

*See R. A. Brealey, *An Introduction to Risk and Return from Common Stocks* (Cambridge, MA: MIT Press, 1969).

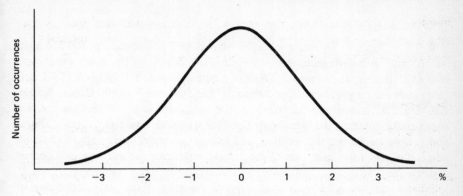

Figure 3-2. Daily Percentage Price Change

transformed into a price-time graph, the characteristics of actual market charts appear, including many of the patterns employed by technical analysts.

In sampling human populations, considerable and often unpredictable difficulties are encountered. Although sampling problems will not bulk large in subsequent chapters of this book, it is instructive to consider them in some practical measurement applications that affect all of us.

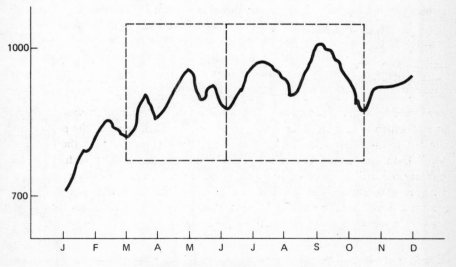

Figure 3-3. Dow-Jones Average for 1967

Polling

In 1936, *Literary Digest*, a magazine that ceased publication in 1937, mailed out 10 million ballots seeking to determine the winner of the presidential election of that year. It received 2,376,523 returns, of which 1,293,669 (54.4 percent) indicated a preference for Alfred M. Landon over Franklin Delano Roosevelt. On the basis of this sampling of the electorate and the fact that it had successfully forecast the winner in the four previous contests, *Literary Digest* confidently predicted the election of Landon. Actually, Roosevelt received 60 percent of the votes cast, one of the largest majorities in American presidential history.

What went wrong? If this were a random sample of the total population of voters, we should expect the sample to reflect the unknown intentions of the electorate in much the same way that a set of 100 coin flips approximates the normal distribution, as shown in Figure 2-1. We could then assume that 54.4 percent represents the probability of a voter preferring Landon and calculate a standard deviation for the sample—s.d. $= \sqrt{2376523 \times .544 \times .456} = \pm768$—and interpret this figure by saying that any random sample of 2,376,523 voters would have a 95-percent probability of containing 1,293,669 ± 1536 votes for Landon (two standard deviations). This range corresponds to a percentage range of 54.37 to 54.50, which we expect includes the true but unknown percentage for Landon in the electorate as a whole. Therefore, Landon is our pick.

The trouble stemmed, of course, from the nonrandom method of sampling, which turned out to overrepresent those voters with high incomes. Although such biases did not preclude some correct predictions, as in the four previous elections, they invariably lead to fiascos sooner or later. Even the huge size of the sample failed to compensate in the slightest for the effects of nonrandomness.

(Thinking in terms of our random walk histogram in Figure 2-1, suppose we did not know that the total population of ten coin flips forms a normal distribution. The polling problem would then be equivalent to asking what percentage of the total population of ten coin flips lands a random walker on his starting point, knowing that our sample showed 24 zeros in 100 ten coin flips. Assuming 24 percent of all sequences of 10 coin flips lands the random walker on zero, the standard deviation of our sample would be $\sqrt{100 \times .24 \times .76} = \pm4.3$. We then estimate that the actual percentage in the total population is in the range 24% ± 8.6%. The figure for the normal distribution is 24.6 percent. If we use the histogram with 17 zeros, our range would be 17% ± 7.5% and our estimate somewhat faulty. Conservative people use ±2.56 standard deviations for a range, so that there is a 99-percent chance of the total population parameter falling within the estimated range. At the same time, there is less certainty about the exact location of the population parameter.)

In 1948, the pollsters ran into a problem of nonresponse, which was not faced by the *Literary Digest* poll. The Gallup poll, on the basis of a final canvas involving about 3,000 interviews with what it called a "scientifically" selected sample of voters, proclaimed the election of Thomas E. Dewey over Harry S. Truman by a substantial margin. Other polling organizations made the same prediction, some even more confidently. However, Truman won by a small margin. A major reason for this failure of the polls was the treatment of a substantial group of voters who had not made up their minds when interviewed. In the preceding three elections, including that of 1936, similar methods had accurately predicted the result, although not the margins of victory. The nonresponse problem is one that is difficult to handle and frequently leads to disastrous consequences when ignored in practice.

Life Insurance

Life insurance companies base their operations on mortality tables, which are frequency distributions showing the number of people at each age in the total population who are alive at each subsequent age. The figures are based on past population samples. Although the distributions are not normal, they are roughly stationary, there being a slight drift to increased longevities over the years. From the tables, the companies can predict very accurately the number of people at any given age who will be alive 1, 2, 3, . . . years in the future, although they cannot tell any particular person how long he will live. (The analogy with Brownian motion should be clear.) By setting premiums accordingly, the companies can assure themselves of having enough money in any year to cover the payments to beneficiaries, the costs of doing business, and to secure a reasonable profit.

Smoking and Cancer

In 1954, a preliminary report of an extensive statistical study by the American Cancer Society purported to reveal a relationship between smoking and cancer.* Initially, 187,766 men fifty to seventy years of age were classified according to their smoking habits. Twenty months later a determination was made of which men had died and from what causes. Deaths from lung cancer were about nine times higher for men smoking one or more packs of cigarettes per day than for nonsmokers.

---

*E. C. Hammond and D. Horn, "The Relationship between Human Smoking Habits and Death Rates," *Journal of the American Medical Association* 155 (1954): 1316–28.

Controversy over the finding arose from indications of nonrandomness in the sample. The percent of smokers in the sample was less than that in the comparable portion of the population of the United States, and the death rate from all causes for the sample was about 30 percent below the corresponding US rates. Even the heavy smokers in the sample showed a lower death rate from cancer than the corresponding US rate. (In 1953, deaths from cancer for the total population averaged 144.7 per 100,000 people.) The possibility of substantial selectivity in the sample reminded some statisticians of previous incidents in medical statistics that had proved fiascoes and prompted them to suggest models which could produce the observed results without the existence of any cause-and-effect relationship between smoking and cancer.

Testing of Drugs

Suppose that a new vaccine gives promise of preventing cancer and it is decided that a test of its effectiveness is indicated. Assuming that the difficult but common-sense questions of cost, safety, administration, and diagnosis have been satisfactorily answered, how should such a test be conducted? Ideally, two random samples would be drawn from the population, one of which would be given the vaccine and the other a placebo. (For simplicity, I will ignore refinements such as stratified sampling, or using samples that are relatively homogeneous with respect to age, race, or some other parameter.) The incidence of cancer in the two groups over the next year would then be determined to see if a significant difference arises.

Ordinarily, the incidence of cancer in the two groups would be different even if the vaccine were ineffective. So the question becomes: What is meant by a "significant difference"? Suppose that each of the two random samples comprise 100,000 persons and the incidence of cancer cases in the control group (the one given the placebo) over the next year is 150, a rate of incidence in good agreement with that of the total population. The probability of an unvaccinated person getting cancer in the next year is then $p = 150 \div 100,000$ or 0.15% or one chance in 667. In a random sample of 100,000 persons drawn from the total population, we should expect with a 95-percent probability 150 ± 2 s.d.'s cases of cancer, where s.d. $= \sqrt{100000 \times .0015 \times .9985} = 12.24$, or 150 ± 24.5 cases. Thus, if the incidence of cancer in the vaccinated group were 125 or less, we should have valid evidence that the vaccine is effective. Should the incidence of cancer in the vaccinated group be 175 or more, the vaccine might then be looked upon as a cause of cancer. A number of cases between 125 and 175 would lead to the conclusion that the vaccine was ineffective. The Salk polio vaccine was tested in a similar manner.

In conclusion, it should be reemphasized that chances for better-than-average performance depend on the extent to which a phenomenon deviates from random walk behavior. In a random walk situation, such as the game of coin-tossing, no special talent of any kind will help one person outdo the next. However, deciding whether or not the random walk model applies can be difficult. Trial independence and the stationary character of the frequency distribution must be exhibited. And even then, there can never be complete assurance that somebody will not happen along and establish a causal relationship among events previously thought to be random.

4
RISK AND REWARD

For a deeper understanding of human nature, the game's the thing.

Marvin B. Scott

By the middle of the seventeenth century, gambling had become immensely popular in the fashionable circles of French society. Large sums of money, personal honor, and possessions were staked on dice, cards, roulette, and many other games of chance. So much was involved and so little was known that many people of the time felt the need for a deeper understanding of what was going on. One such person was the Chevalier de Méré, an ardent gambler and a close observer of the gambling scene. De Méré had a problem, now known as "De Méré's paradox." He had determined to his own satisfaction that the chances of rolling at least one ace in four throws of a die were the same as the chances of rolling at least one double ace in twenty-four throws of two dice. Yet, in actual games, he incurred steady losses on this bet, for, as he was quick to perceive, the rolling of one ace in four throws of a single die occurred slightly more than half the time, whereas the rolling of at least one double ace in twenty-four throws of two dice occurred less than half the time. After having puzzled in vain over the difference between what he thought should happen and what actually did happen, de Méré turned for help to the great French scientist, mathematician, and philosopher, Blaise Pascal.

From what strange and unexpected directions the great advances come! Pascal took an immediate interest in the whole subject of gambling. In Pascal's studies and those of Fermat, Bernoulli, and d'Alembert, the mathematical theory of probability had its beginnings. Almost every mathematician of note furthered its development, and, today, not only is it a major and active branch of mathematics in its own right, but it lies at the heart of all science. One might say that a subject becomes meaningful only when it is firmly based on probability theory.

Let us start with a game of coin-tossing to develop some needed concepts. Call the toss correctly and you win a dollar. Call it incorrectly and you lose a dollar. How much will you have won or lost after, say, ten flips? Of course, this is just the random walk problem again. Only now, instead of taking paces to the right and left, you are gaining and losing capital with each toss. If we agree to omit consideration of those rare times when the coin leans upright against a piece of furniture or disappears into a crack in the floor, there are two possible outcomes, heads and tails. The risk, assuming the coin is unbiased, is a 50-percent chance of losing on each toss, what is known as a fifty–fifty chance, or an even money bet, or 1 chance in 2 of losing, or a probability of 1/2 of winning and a probability of 1/2 of losing on each toss. The reward is the gain of one dollar if you win and the loss of one dollar if you lose.

You know instinctively (and you can see from the graphs in Chapter 2) that playing this game is a waste of time. At the end of a number of flips, you will probably have won or lost very little, if anything. Putting it more technically, your *expectation* of gain is zero. *Average performance* here means little change in starting capital. This is not to imply that lucky streaks are ruled out. There is, for example, 1 chance in 100 (a probability of 1 percent) for a person starting out with $10 to win $1,000 by making $1 bets on the flip of a fair coin, and, conversely, 99 chances in 100 (a 99-percent probability) of ruin, which means he loses his $10 before attaining the $1,000.

The concept of average performance is defined concisely by the expectation, which is given by a simple formula from probability theory:

$$E = P_1 o_1 + P_2 o_2 + \cdots$$

E is the expectation of gain, the P's are the probabilities of the various possible outcomes, and the o's are the rewards for each outcome. In the coin tossing game, there are two outcomes, a correct call of the flip or an incorrect call, each with a probability of 1/2. The rewards are, respectively, a gain of a dollar and the loss of a dollar. Therefore, $E = 1/2 (+\$1) + 1/2 (-\$1) = 0$. On average, over a number of games, a person may expect his money to fluctuate in value around what he began with. His expectation is zero, or, in other words, his capital will in the future perform a random walk about the starting amount, neither increasing nor decreasing.

The game of roulette affords another simple instance of risk and reward. As played in the United States, a rotating wheel is divided into thirty-eight slots numbered from 1 to 36 plus a 0 and a 00. Eighteen numbers are red and eighteen are black, while the 0 and 00 are a third color. A ball is rolled around the outer rim of the wheel and eventually drops into one of the slots. One possible wager is on red or black, which returns a profit of one dollar for each one dollar risked. What is the gambler's expectation? If he bets on red, there are eighteen ways of being right (the eighteen red numbers) and twenty ways of being wrong (the eighteen black numbers plus the 0 and 00). His winning probability is, therefore, 18/38 and his losing probability 20/38. Substituting in the formula for the expectation, $E = 18/38 (\$1) + 20/38 (-\$1) = -2/38$ of a dollar, or $-5.3¢$. The negative sign indicates loss of capital. These are the house odds that a gambler must buck. He may expect to lose 5.3 cents out of every dollar bet, or 53 cents on every ten red-black bets at the roulette table. A random walk histogram of ten-bet trials will now center on the point .53 to the left (minus) of zero rather

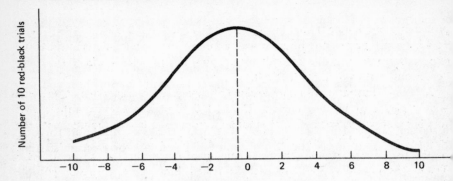

Figure 4-1. Dollar Return after Ten Red-Black Bets at Roulette. The mean is a loss of 53 cents.

than on the zero mark. The number of steps to the left of zero at the end of ten trials increases at the expense of those to the right. It is now more likely that a gambler will end up to the left of zero, for a loss, than to the right, for a profit. Lucky streaks are also far more unlikely; there is only 1 chance in 10,000,000,000,000,000,000,000,000,000,000,000,000,000,000 (10^{43}) of running $10 into $1000 on this kind of wagering.

Another habitual roulette bet is to risk one dollar on any one of the thirty-eight numbers. The reward for being right is an enticing profit of thirty-five dollars, but it is the expectation that is important. The probability of success is now 1/38 and the probability of failure 37/38. Hence, $E = 1/38\,(\$35) + 37/38\,(-\$1) = -2/38$ of a dollar, the same as for the red-black bet.

A more complicated game of chance, and one of the most popular, is craps. It is played with two dice and, as played in casinos, offers many betting opportunities. We shall consider only the line bet, where the gambler wins if the roller of the dice wins and loses if the roller loses. The roller wins in any of the following circumstances: a 7 or 11 on the first roll (a "natural"); a 4, 5, 6, 8, 9, 10 on the first roll (the roller's "point") followed by the point turning up again in subsequent rolls before a 7 turns up. If the roller shoots a 2, 3, or 12 on the first roll he loses ("craps out"). The reward for winning is one dollar for a one-dollar bet. To calculate the expectation, we need to know the probability of winning, which is obtained in the appendix to this chapter and shown to be 0.493. Therefore $E = .493\,(\$1) + .507\,(-\$1) = -.014 = -1.4\mbox{¢}$. A loss of only 1.4 cents per dollar bet is to be expected. With the possible exception of blackjack, this is the best casino game to play. Although the expectation is negative, it is less so than any other game. The gambler will lose over the long run but at a slower rate.

In casino craps, it is also possible to bet against the roller. Providing all conditions were unchanged, such a bet would have a positive expectation since the probability of winning is now $1 - 0.493 = 0.507$ and $E = .507\,(\$1) + .493\,(-\$1) = +1.4\cent$. Unfortunately, the house is well aware of the probabilities and shifts the expectation into negative grounds by denying the gambler a win if the roller "craps out" with a 3 on the first roll.

As a final illustration of a simple game of chance, we consider one of the most widely played of all, the numbers. The trick is to pick in advance a three-digit number that will be selected later at random from the 1,000 possibilities between 000 and 999. At this writing, the number used in New York is the last three digits of the pari-mutuel handle (the total amount of money bet) at Aqueduct Race Track. The reward is $500 for each $1 risked. Since there are 1,000 possible outcomes and only 1 way to pick the number correctly, the probability of winning is 1/1000 and the probability of losing is 999/1000. $E = 1/1000\,(\$500) + 999/1000\,(-\$1) = -499/1000$ of a dollar, or an expected average loss of almost 50 cents per dollar bet. This is perhaps the worst game of all to play, except for the government lotteries. The lure of the big payoff obscures the confiscatory nature of the game.

Leaving aside emotional considerations of excitement, tension, and the thrill of winning that make games of chance worth playing for many people, the expectation defines a figure of merit. Those games for which it is positive will be termed *favorable*, and those for which it is negative, *unfavorable*. Favorable games include savings accounts, bonds, and, as we shall demonstrate, common stock investments. Unfavorable games consist of almost all casino games, horse racing, lotteries, sweepstakes, and the numbers. In the former type, *all* players are more likely to win than lose, with the proviso that loss of initial capital before attainment of the final goal has a non-zero probability. In the latter type, a player is almost certain to lose all the money he cares to risk if he persists in playing. The public, in its great wisdom, intuitively thinks about these two groups in a less technical manner, which, nonetheless, reflects the sharp difference between them. Favorable games are considered quite respectable—indeed, our society relies heavily on them for capital formation—whereas unfavorable games have an air of illegality and immorality about them, even though many now receive government sanction.

Why, it may be asked, does a person engage in an unfavorable game? To answer in the language of utility theory,* a wealth-seeking person undertakes those actions that maximize his utility, which is a measure of psychic gain. Suppose an investment opportunity presents itself offering a fifty-fifty chance of increasing or decreasing one's capital by $100; the expectation of gain is zero. A risk-lover

---

*See O. Morgenstern and J. von Neumann, *Theory of Games and Economic Behavior*, Rev. ed. (Princeton: Princeton University Press, 1953).

will make the investment, a risk-averter will not, and a risk-neutral person will be indifferent. Or we may say that the risk-lover's utility increases in making the investment, the risk-averter's utility decreases, and the risk-neutral person's utility remains the same. Under most circumstances, people prefer to avoid hazards in this uncertain world and make the decisions among those having a given expectation that entail the least risk. In unfavorable game situations, it seems, some people derive increased utility from the excitement of participation notwithstanding their negative expectation and the accessibility of favorable but dull games like savings accounts.

As we proceed to the more complex problems of the real world, the calculation of the expectation becomes hopelessly difficult. Even the possible outcomes cannot be delineated with clarity. In the estimation of risk and reward, people must be guided by the knowledge and experience accumulated over the million years of man's existence on earth. This vast store of information, constantly evolving, continually tested, always growing, is the basis of decision-making under uncertainty. Its assimilation is the process of education; its mode of application establishes the quality of life. It offers comfort and hope to those desiring a quiet, secure, average existence, and it offers opportunity to those few inspired individuals who seek to enlarge it. We wish to study this body of information, to assess its character, to evaluate its determinations of expectation in the real world, and to comprehend the conditions necessary to exceed its expectations.

APPENDIX TO CHAPTER 4: HOW TO CALCULATE THE WINNING PROBABILITY FOR CRAPS

To calculate the probability of winning in craps, we must find the probability for each way of winning and add them all up:

1) A 7 on the first roll
Since there are thirty-six possible outcomes for the roll of two dice and six ways to shoot a 7 (1, 6; 6, 1; 2, 5; 5, 2; 3, 4; 4, 3), this probability is 6/36.

2) An 11 on the first roll
There are two ways to make 11 (5, 6; 6, 5), so the probability is 2/36.

3) A 4 on the first roll followed by another roll of 4 before a 7 comes up
The probability of a 4 is 3/36. This probability must be multiplied by the probability that the roller shoots another 4 before he shoots a 7. All other numbers are now immaterial. Since there are three ways of shooting a 4 and six ways of shooting a 7, the probability of making a 4 before a 7 is 3/9 or 1/3. Therefore, the probability of making a 4 point is 3/36 × 1/3 = 1/36.

4) A 5 on the first roll followed by another 5 before a roll of 7
The probability of a 5 is 4/36, while the probability of shooting a 5 before a 7 is 4/10. Therefore, the probability of making a 5 point is 4/36 × 4/10 = 1.6/36.

5) A 6 on the first roll followed by another roll of 6 before a roll of 7

The probability of a 6 is 5/36, and the probability of making a 6 point is 5/36 × 5/11 = 2.2727/36.

6) 8, 9, or 10 on the first roll followed by a repeat roll of the same number before a roll of 7

These probabilities are the same as those for 6, 5, and 4 respectively.

Adding up all the probabilities of winning gives us the probability of winning a line bet:

$$p = 6/36 + 2/36 + 1/36 + 1/36 + 1.6/36$$

$$+ 1.6/36 + 2.2727/36 + 2.2727/36$$

$$= 17.7454/36 = 49.3\%.$$

5
THE EFFICIENT - MARKETS HYPOTHESIS

Nasreddin Hodja, a famous Turkish folk philosopher, was seen one day sitting by a lake casting yeast upon the waters. A passerby asked what he thought he was doing. "Trying to turn a lake of water into a lake of yoghurt," answered the wise one. "But that's impossible," said the passerby. "Yes," said Hodja, "I know it's impossible. But supposing it weren't?"

Turkish folk tale

Perhaps the best way to crystallize the difficulties inhibiting better-than-average performance is to examine the possibilities for doing so in two relatively simple games of chance, roulette and blackjack (or 21, as it is sometimes called). First, we consider roulette and its associated expectation, which sets the standard for average performance. According to our expectation formula, only if we are able to augment either the probabilities or the rewards for favorable outcomes can better-than-average performance be realized. However, this path is dubious since the risks appear to be mechanically fixed by the nature of the wheel and the rewards are determined by the operators of the game. Presumably they are not in business to give away their money in excessively generous pay offs. What about systems that vary the size and frequency of the bets? Forget them! No matter which one is employed, the successively allowed bets form a sequence of independent trials each with the same unchanged probability for success. The painful expectation of the gambler is precisely equal to what it would have been had he bet every time (Doob's martingale theorem). Such naive approaches as doubling up on bets after each loss on a red-black bet until a win occurs or betting red after a string of blacks are doomed to failure. ESP? Psychokinesis? No valid evidence of better-than-average performance by people supposedly blessed with those powers has ever been presented, and certainly not in connection with roulette. We would appear to be in a cul-de-sac from the very start.

But, fortunately or unfortunately, reality is a great deal more complex than the simple calculations of probability theory would have us believe. In our model of roulette, we assumed the probability of the ball falling into any given slot to be 1/38, which, when plugged into the theory along with the reward, yielded a negative expectation. Based on this picture, we would expect each number o the roulette wheel to come up on average once in every thirty-eight games after many thousands of spins. Suppose, though, that the probabilities for each number are not known, as they are not for an actual rotating roulette wheel in a gambling casino. All mechanical devices are to some degree imperfectly constructed, so it is very likely that the probabilities are not all equal to 1/38. If this be the case, no amount of logic and mathematics in themselves can then describe the behavior of this real-world object. Probability theory is unable to say anything until the right probabilities are fed in. Once this is done, however, the theory becomes the proper tool for predicting the future.

Proponents of the biased wheel model insist that the probabilities of certain numbers are great enough to produce a positive expectation. To gain an idea of the effect of a wheel imbalance, suppose the probability of number 7 were 2/38 instead of 1/38. The expectation of a bet on 7 would then be $E = 2/38$ ($35) - 36/38 ($1) = + 34/38 of a dollar, or a profit of eighty-nine cents for every dollar bet, a fantastically large return.

Now the argument is joined on proper grounds. Based on their knowledge of roulette—details of the manufacture of the mechanism and probability theory—the people running the casino have decided that a probability of 1/38 for each number is a close approximation to the true but unknown value. In keeping with this opinion, they have set the reward for winning sufficiently low to guarantee a negative expectation for their customers and a positive expectation for themselves, which enables them to cover the costs of doing business and secure in addition a reasonable profit on their investment.

Whose conception of reality is correct? Every once in a while, someone makes a serious attempt to make money at roulette. In the hope of uncovering evidence of bias, the would-be winner always begins by charting in the form of a histogram the frequencies of occurrence of all the numbers. To illuminate the problems encountered, suppose we too proceed in this manner and ask what can be expected in the way of frequency distributions of the numbers from a perfectly symmetrical model wheel and from a real one. Will it be possible to detect a deviation between the two sets of results? If not, then the model of a theoretically perfect wheel well represents reality as far as we are concerned and there is no hope of better-than-average performance.

Let us record the results from thirty-eight roulette games. If the wheel were perfect, each number could be expected to occur once (the probability for each number times the number of games, or 1/38 × 38 = 1). Of course, there will be a dispersion in the frequencies of occurrence about 1 given by the standard deviation. Since the standard deviation $= \sqrt{38 \times 1/38 \times 37/38} = 1$ approximately, we can expect a variation of two standard deviations about the mean, or 1 ± 2. Thus, any given number may turn up from zero to three times in a set of thirty-eight games without furnishing evidence of bias. Only if a number occurs four times

will suspicions of a wheel imperfection receive some sanction. Caution is still de
manded because we expect 5 percent of our thirty-eight numbers (about two o
them) to occur more than three times based on the meaning of the standard de
viation. However, should another thirty-eight-game test result in four or more
appearances of, say, number 7, the evidence for wheel asymmetry would indeed
be strong. The probability of 7 is very likely around 4/38, which would make
wagers on 7 immensely profitable.

Needless to say, such large deviations from perfect symmetry would be in
stantly recognized by the casino operators. Their business is based on a fair whee
(although crooked ones do exist), and they would take immediate steps to rec
tify matters. Possibly a small deviation might escape notice. A probability fo
some number of 1.06/38 (106 occurrences in 3,800 games) rather than 1/38 i
needed to make the game even, while a probability of 1.11/38 gives the playe
the same advantage the house enjoys in a game with a perfect wheel. Unfortu
nately, to detect an asymmetry of this tiny magnitude would require observa
tions on the behavior of the same roulette wheel for many thousands of games
If the probabilities shift during the period of measurement either from norma
wear and tear or actions by the house, the test is vitiated.

Two of the conditions for better-than-average performance now come int
clearer focus, to wit, a conception of reality deeper than the competition an
the time, effort, and ability to implement it. Recapitulating, we first assessed i
our quest for superior performance the expectation set by the marketplace. Thi
value was judged to be faulty on the grounds of imperfections in mechanical de
vices and a new expectation was formulated. The two expectations were the
tested against each other by observing the behavior of a roulette wheel. If statis
tically significant deviations from the model postulated by the marketplace ar
observed, better-than-average performance may be achieved by wagering on thos
numbers having the greatest expectation. In essence, we must always pit ourselve
against conclusions reached by knowledgeable people on the basis of an existin
body of information. The likelihood of error should never be underestimated.

In the early 1960s, mathematician Edward O. Thorp devised a profitable sys
tem for playing blackjack, the eventual dissemination of which threatened for
time the very survival of casino gambling, since blackjack is probably the mos
popular and lucrative of all house games. What he discovered was a faulty assign
ment of probabilities to the future outcomes in blackjack.* The model of realit
on which those probabilities had been based assumed a constant deck of fifty-tw
cards and made no allowance for the diminution of the deck as the game pro

---

*Edward Thorp, *Beat the Dealer* (New York: Vintage, 1966).

gressed. With probabilities calculated for a diminishing deck, Thorp was able to devise strategies leading to a positive expectation in what had appeared to be an unfavorable game.

Armed with his newfound knowledge, Thorp proceeded to put his theories to the test. Card dealers, who at first scoffed at the lucky newcomer, became by degrees increasingly bewildered and frustrated. The consternation of casino managements mounted as funds drained from their coffers, until, finally, Thorp was barred from playing. Disguises and changes of venue no longer sufficed once dealers caught on to the style of play. The respite was short lived. With the publication of Thorp's book, hordes of expert blackjack players descended on the gambling palaces seeking quick fortunes. Was there any way out of the quandary? By now, the house experts understood that Thorp's system had exploited a deficiency in their knowledge of blackjack, and they frantically sought a remedy. Their very existence jeopardized, the casinos changed the rules to ensure a negative expectation for the players based on the new probabilities. But one problem led to another. Under the altered rules, play at the blackjack tables fell off sharply, obliging a return to the old ones. Multiple decks dealt from a shoe were next introduced, making it harder for players to "case" the deck, a prerequisite for profitable operations. More frequent shuffling made the Thorp system more difficult to apply, although it slowed the game down considerably. Winning players were vigorously excluded or taken care of by nimble-fingered dealers. Needless to say, this modern-day gold rush was effectively detoured. As of this writing, matters have come full cycle. The original rules are still in force and blackjack is again played in many places with one deck dealt and shuffled by hand. Adjustment to the new market conditions has been completed and equilibrium prevails. Casino profits are increasing, blackjack is more popular than ever, yet Thorp's work remains as valid as before. When is a good system for beating the averages not a good system? Confronted with this apparent paradox, I let the reader draw his own conclusions.

Our two examples suggest a division of markets in financial risk into categories that reflect the state of knowledge governing the behavior of their participants.* Those markets which fully reflect all existent information at all times so that the probabilities of future outcomes are accurate and well-known to any interested person we shall term *strongly efficient*. Some people prefer the term *equitable* for these markets since all participants have equal opportunity and the same expectation. Strict random walk behavior holds and better-than-average

---

*E. Fama, "Efficient Capital Markets: A Review of Theory and Empirical Work," *Journal of Finance*, 25 (May 1970): 383–417.

performance is excluded. In particular, no information exists which benefits a small group of insiders or experts. The roulette market fits this description in the absence of any evidence to the contrary. Certainly, the operators of the game feel no pressure to change the rules and no threats to their solvency from any system, with the consequence that roulette continues to be played now as in the past. (It might be contended that strong efficiency does not apply to roulette since the operators of the game are exploiting their patrons. Such an argument goes beyond the limits I have imposed on our deliberations at this juncture. Suffice it to say here that a determination of utility received by those patrons and the fairness of return on the casino's investment must be made in a larger and more diffuse market.)

If we admit the possibility of information available to a group of people small in relation to the total number of participants in the market, we have a *semi-strongly efficient* market. The favored few have gained monopolistic access to significant information at crucial points of time and are thereby able to raise their expectations above the norm. Because of the inequity, this type of market is more inefficient than the strongly efficient market. The blackjack market was an excellent example of semi-strong efficiency until Professor Thorp published his system.

The final category is the *weakly efficient* market, which takes into account historical data but adjusts to increments in the store of knowledge available to the public only after a time lag. During the period of adjustment, the market is more or less inefficient and knowledgeable people enjoy advantages over others. In contrast, the strongly and semi-strongly efficient markets are defined so as to adjust instantaneously to freshly published information. We are led to the concept of a *relaxation time*, the period necessary for new information to be incorporated into the world's body of knowledge. Physicists and engineers have long used the term to indicate the time needed for a system parameter to achieve a certain value after the application of a stimulus. Different weakly efficient markets have different relaxation times, but only very rough values can be estimated from the rudimentary state of today's knowledge. It took about ten years for the blackjack market to adapt to new ideas. Over this interval, the glaring inefficiency originally apparent has been steadily reduced, bringing the expectations of all players much closer together.

Because relatively few people have the ability to master the intricacies of advanced blackjack systems, the market must be regarded as somewhat inefficient. Whether or not it is now profitable, the game can most assuredly be played so as to minimize losses. In this respect, better-than-average performance by expert players is a part of blackjack. As more and more people learn to play the game correctly, this inefficiency may tend to vanish. Possibly, the ever greater diffusion of knowledge tends to make market efficiency, like entropy, increase with time.

We are ready to broaden our concept of "game" to include any activity in which blind chance plays a part in the outcome. Since nothing in this world is certain but death and taxes, an element of risk enters into everything we do, and everything we do, therefore, may be conceived as some appropriate game of chance. Thus far, conditions in some relatively simple but narrow betting markets have been described in terms of expected returns and the body of information leading to a determination of equilibrium expected returns. In these markets, the expectations of the players are determined by the judgment of a small group of people who operate the casinos. We turn now to an operation so complex as to defy rational analysis, but one in which the public as a whole, acting on the basis of a huge amount of information, is asked to apply its knowledge to the calculation of the probabilities of future outcomes and their associated rewards. Let's see how well it does.

6

THE NATURE OF THE PARI-MUTUEL BETTING MARKET

A horse! a horse! my kingdom for a horse!

Shakespeare, *Richard the Third*

We're off to the races, to examine the nature of pari-mutuel wagering. In so doing, we are able to extend our previously developed concepts to the behavior of a large group of people and still retain the advantages associated with the analysis of the simpler games of chance. That the racetrack is an almost ideal laboratory for the study of market mechanisms under institutional conditions has been largely ignored until recently. Yet, here we have a microcosm of society struggling to combat as best it can its own unique set of problems and uncertainties. Here are thousands of diverse individuals with easy access to enormous amounts of data trying to see what the future holds in store. Their problem is everybody's: to determine the probabilities and rewards of the possible future outcomes of an event, in this instance a horse race. How each fares depends on the state of the betting market: If it is strongly efficient, all racing fans have the same expectation; if it is not, those with the more realistic probability estimates will do better than their compatriots.

Conventional wisdom has it that horseflesh is unpredictable, that the pari-mutuel betting market is inefficient. Adherents of this view point out that horses are capable of all sorts of antics—refusing to break, rearing, leaving the course, throwing riders, stumbling—and subject to many infirmities such as bucked shins and broken legs. True, but hazards exist everywhere in the real world. Despite its uncertainties, a horse race is not nearly as intricate as other social, economic, and political phenomena. Gross inefficiency at this level of complexity would challenge the confidence we have in our ability to manage the institutions on which civilization depends.

In the games considered earlier, the probabilities are mechanically fixed—by the wheel mechanism in roulette, by the shifting values of the unplayed cards in blackjack, by permutations and combinations in the ideally simple numbers game—and are known to a high degree of approximation by the operators. If you gamble in these games, you are willing to pay for the privilege by accepting a return less than necessary to break even over many bets. It's you against the house, and the odds are strongly against you.

At the races, the situation is somewhat different. A person wishing to bet on a horse buys a certificate from the race track on which is printed the details of the transaction, identification of the horse chosen, the amount staked, the date, the number of the race. The track collects all the money wagered and puts it into a pool, from which it deducts a certain percentage known as the "take" (usually between 15 and 20 percent) as a commission for itself and for the state. When the race is over, it redeems the winning certificates with the money remaining in the pool. Unlike the casino, it acts merely as a broker, taking neither any interest in the outcome of the race nor any part in determining risk and reward. It cannot lose and, consequently, does not care even if a favorable horse betting system comes along. The track and state always get their "take" from the top of the pool, while the rest of the money is merely redistributed among the bettors. This circumstance is of major importance to the system builder, since it admits the possibility of a favorable betting method that does not threaten the very existence of the house.

Who then fixes the expectation of each horse bettor? Against whom does he compete? Nobody other than all his fellow racegoers taken as a body, their collective opinion on the winning chances of each horse versus his. Just as in roulette, the "true" probabilities are unknown so that each racing fan must estimate for himself the winning probability of a horse and decide whether or not the return is worth the risk of his money. To aid him in his deliberations, he has at his disposal an array of historical data on the past races of the horses, expert opinions, track and weather conditions, weights carried, shoes, latest workouts, equipment, jockeys, trainers, breeding, and the totalizator board (the "tote"), which displays the latest odds and money bet on each horse. As each person reaches a decision and makes his bet, there emerges a consensus that reflects all the uncertainties of a horse race as visualized by the crowd. This is the key piece of information, for what the public is thinking specifies the reward. The game of horse betting is concerned as much with people as with horses.

Always, in any attempt at winning, a determination of the expectation of the average player must be the first step. Only in this context can results be judged for above-average performance. Befitting the greater complexity of the pari-mutuel betting market, its expectation becomes harder to calculate and requires a more thorough knowledge of how to express what we don't know (in this case the expectation) in terms of what we do know or can measure, a discipline known as elementary algebra. In order not to interrupt the continuity of presentation, I have relegated the algebraic details to the appendix of this chapter and give here the expectation formula for pari-mutuel betting:

$$E_i = \frac{P_i}{p_i} (1 - f) - 1$$

E_i is the bettor's expectation when betting on horse i, P_i is that horse's true (and unknown) probability of winning, p_i is the winning probability of horse i as estimated by the public, and f is the percentage "take." Now we see that a bettor's expectation hinges upon the percentage of money deducted from the pool and the public's estimate of the win probability of a horse compared to the true probability. If these two probabilities of winning are equal ($p_i = P_i$), $E_i = -f$ and bettors can expect to lose on average f cents for every dollar bet, or between fifteen and twenty cents, depending on the state. This is much greater than the 5.3 cents per dollar bet loss in roulette and makes the game very unfavorable, providing of course that the public is correct in its probability estimates. Merely to break even ($E_i = 0$), a racing fan would have to estimate winning probabilities 15 to 20 percent more accurately than the betting public.

The strongly efficient market in pari-mutuel wagering may now be defined as one in which the expectations of all players, no matter which horse they bet, are the same—that is, all the E_i's are equal to $-f$ cents. In this type of market, the public's probability estimates equal the true probabilities of winning for all horses. All bettors, from hunch-playing housewives to expert handicappers, can expect average performance, a loss of f cents for every dollar bet. This is random walk behavior again, with a mean of $-f$ cents. A bettor's capital may fluctuate wildly after only a few bets because the swings between winning and losing are enormous. When he wins, he may net several hundred percent on his investment (a win on a 2-to-1 bet represents a gain of 200 percent); when he loses, there is a loss of 100 percent. After many bets in this kind of market, the return will settle down to a loss of f cents per dollar bet. It should be noted that any demonstration of inefficiency in the market must be accompanied by a system enabling better-than-average performance.

We proceed to an analysis of pari-mutuel results in order to find out to what extent the public's probability of winning estimates approximate the true probabilities. Extensive data compiled on races run in the United States and the United Kingdom will be utilized. Figure 6-1 presents the results of 10,000 races run at American thoroughbred tracks over the years 1955 to 1962. The 93,011 horses are grouped according to the dollar odds at which they started and the corresponding probabilities of winning as determined by the public. (The dollar odds represent a bettor's profit for every dollar risked should his horse win. They are related to the horse's probability of winning as shown in the appendix to this chapter). The "true" probability for each group is taken equal to the win-

Figure 6-1. Comparison of True Winning Probabilities with the Winning Probabilities Determined by the Public, 1955 to 1962

Dollar Odds	Public's Probability (percent)	True Probability (percent)	Number of Horses and Winners	Expected Number of Winners ±2 s.d.'s	Expectation per Dollar Bet (in cents)
0.40–0.55	56.9	71.3	129–92	73 ± 11	+3.4
0.60–0.75	50.2	55.3	295–163	148 ± 18	−7.1
0.80–0.95	44.9	51.3	470–241	211 ± 22	−3.8
1.00–1.15	40.6	47.0	615–289	250 ± 25	−2.4
1.20–1.35	37.1	40.3	789–318	293 ± 27	−8.1
1.40–1.55	34.1	37.9	874–331	298 ± 28	−6.1
1.60–1.75	31.5	35.5	954–339	301 ± 29	−4.8
1.80–1.95	29.3	30.9	1051–325	308 ± 30	−10.5
2.00–2.45	26.3	28.9	3223–933	848 ± 50	−6.5
2.50–2.95	22.8	23.0	3623–835	826 ± 50	−13.5
3.00–3.45	20.1	20.9	3807–797	765 ± 50	−11.0
3.50–3.95	18.0	18.6	3652–679	657 ± 46	−11.6
4.00–4.45	16.2	16.1	3296–532	534 ± 42	−15.3
4.50–4.95	14.8	15.5	3129–486	463 ± 40	−10.6
5.00–5.95	13.2	12.3	5586–686	737 ± 50	−20.1
6.00–6.95	11.4	11.0	5154–565	588 ± 46	−18.0
7.00–7.95	10.0	9.9	4665–460	467 ± 41	−16.4
8.00–8.95	9.0	8.2	3990–328	359 ± 38	−21.8
9.00–9.95	8.1	8.2	3617–295	293 ± 33	−14.7
10.00–14.95	6.5	6.0	12007–717	780 ± 54	−20.7
15.00–19.95	4.7	4.0	7041–284	331 ± 35	−26.4
20.00–99.95	2.5	1.4	25044–340	626 ± 50	−54.0
			93011–10035*		

Source: Adapted from Burton P. Fabricand, *Horse Sense: A Rigorous Application of Mathematical Methods to Successful Betting at the Track* (New York: McKay, 1976), p. 34.

*The number of winners exceeds 10,000 because of dead heats.

ning percentage of the horses and is found by dividing the number of winners by the number of horses for that group. In the next-to-last column are the expected number of winners, based on the assumption that the public's probabilities are correct, and a range about this number equal to two standard deviations. The last column presents a bettor's expectation in terms of money won or lost per dollar bet if one dollar were staked on each starter in the group.

The win percentage in each group is only an approximation to the true probability, one that grows more accurate as the sample size increases (the law of large numbers). For all groupings, the win percentage adequately represents the true probability for our purposes.

It is immediately evident that the public's probabilities are close to the true probabilities, as demanded by the strongly efficient market hypothesis. And here is the underlying reason why bettors lose at the races. Closer examination, however, reveals an underestimate of the true probabilities at short odds and an overestimate at long odds. In terms of the expectation, we find less of a loss at short odds and more at long odds. Are the differences statistically significant? If so, there is a departure from strong efficiency.

To check, let us assume the public's probability is the true probability and compare the number of winners to be expected on this basis with the actual number of winners in each of the odds ranges. This expected number of winners is shown in the fifth column of Table 6-1 and is obtained by multiplying the public's probability by the number of races in that odds range. For example, in the 5/1 odds range (dollar odds from 5.00 to 5.95), the public's probability of 13.2 percent times the total number of horses, 5,586, equals 737. From our study of the random walk, we should understand that in any sample of races, there is a range of possible values around this number of winners (the mean) that may result when selecting horses from a sample of this size. If another sample of 5,586 horses off at 5/1 were chosen, we expect with a 95-percent probability that the number of winners will fall within 2 standard deviations of 737, providing $p_i = P_i$. (One standard deviation in this case equals $\sqrt{5586 \times 0.132 \times 0.868} = 25$). Therefore, should the actual number of winners fall within the range, we take the public's probability as equal to the true probability. For those groups where the actual number of winners falls outside the range, the public is assumed to err in its judgment of winning probabilities.

For horses starting at dollar odds between 2.50 and 10.00, the actual number of winners falls within the anticipated range, and the equality of the public and true probabilities is substantiated. However, deviations from the strongly efficient market hypothesis arise for dollar odds less than 2.50 and greater than 10.00. There is too little betting on favorites (the horses on which the public wagers the most money and which start at the lowest odds) and too much on longshots. This demonstrated inefficiency in the market enables a bettor to perform above average simply by betting on the favorite in every race. In this 10,000-race sample, such a person would have lost only about nine cents per dollar bet compared to the expected loss of fifteen cents, the take being 15 percent at the time. In contrast, wagering on longshots (odds longer than 20 to 1) would have netted a substantial loss of fifty-four cents per dollar bet. Obviously, the favorite is the best bet at the track. A similar conclusion was reached in a study of over 1000 races by *Fortune Magazine* (September 1975).

Is the pari-mutuel betting market weakly efficient? On the basis of historical data, do some people have more favorable expectations than the average f cents loss per dollar bet? An answer may be obtained if we look at the records of the public handicappers, those brave souls who publish their forecasts of the winners in each day's races. These experts in most cases make their selections the day be-

Figure 6-2. Public Handicappers' Expectations for Four Samples

Public favorites	−10.8¢	−6.6¢	−9.2¢	−7.5¢
Reigh Count	−16.5	−16.0	−14.6	−12.1
Armstrong	−14.3	−14.9	−12.9	−14.7
Sharpshooter	−18.6	−17.6	−14.7	−13.2
Hermis	−15.0	−15.5	−18.7	−14.8
Handicap	−15.4	−18.2	−20.9	−17.3
Sweep	−15.9	−18.5	−19.0	−16.4
Trackman	−16.4	−15.7	−18.0	−12.8

Source: Adapted from Fabricand, *op. cit.*, p. 36.

fore the race and always in advance of the betting, so that they have no knowledge of the public's opinion and must rely solely on the past performances of the horses to make their decisions. Their expectations as computed from four different 5,000-race samples over the period 1955 to 1962 are shown in Figure 6-2, along with the expectations of the favorite player. The take during this time was 15 percent.*

It is evident that the expectations of these expert selectors are near average, indicating that their wide knowledge of horse racing is of little help in securing better-than-average performance. All historical data must be adequately factored into the betting by the public. That is what we look for in a weakly efficient market: equal expectations for all participants based on historical data.

I might include among the experts the modern electronic computer, since many people are of the opinion that this complex apparatus will be able to find a valid system for picking horses. There are two things to keep in mind always when dealing with computers: the first one is GIGO—garbage in, garbage out; the other that a computer is dumber than anybody. It is ridiculous to think that a computer, through an examination of the historical factors entering into horse racing, can better the performance of a crowd of knowledgeable people or that it can come up with a bright idea for better-than-average performance when the user cannot. All computer-based selection methods utilizing old records have been and will be exercises in futility.

Further support for weak efficiency is supplied by a sample comprising all races run at British tracks in 1973.[†] Here also are exhibited the underestimation of the probabilities of winning of favorites, overestimation of the chances of longshots, and comparable accuracy in forecasts between the public and experts.

---

*To the expected loss of the take must be added an additional loss known as "breakage." It arises because the racetrack does not pay off at the exact dollar odds but only to the next lower dime. Thus, dollar odds of $2.19 become $2.10, for example. This practice adds approximately 1 percent to the take.

[†]Jack Dowie, "On the Efficiency and Equity of Betting Markets," a paper presented to the 2nd Annual Conference on Gambling, Lake Tahoe, Nevada, 1975.

There have been attempts to attribute the too-little wagering on favorites and the too-strong wagering on longshots to risk-loving bettors having a decided preference for low-probability, high-return bets. Dowie's work, however, indicates that the probability estimates of the professional handicappers are afflicted with the same defect. Although the experts may be risk-lovers as well, a more likely explanation lies simply in the inadequacies of the historical record that prevent more accurate forecasting. There are significant late news breaks not properly discounted in the betting. The present pari-mutuel market is not semi-strongly efficient, and above average performance is easily attainable; profitable performance is something else again. Do the late-changing odds contain in their makeup unexploited information which renders profitable operations possible? We return to this question in Chapter 9.

The most striking feature of public behavior at the racetrack is the spectacle of each person wholeheartedly pursuing his own self-interest in a free market. No social, economic, or political barriers obstruct his efforts to arrive at the many decisions under uncertainty upon which he is called to make. Indeed, the rules of the game encourage the formulation and diversity of opinion through the circulation of all available information and through providing for full public expression of all points of view. Communication is implemented, first by the publication of the historical records of the horses and the forecasts of the experts and, second, by the "tote" board, which exhibits all opinions in the form of the odds against each horse winning. "It were not best that we should all think alike; it is difference of opinion that makes horse races," according to Mark Twain. How remarkable it is to find the thousands of diverse opinions of thousands of diverse people clashing, interacting, and modifying one another in such a way that the final consensus is a closer approximation of the truth than that of any single individual! How extraordinary to watch the public determining winning probabilities so accurately, and doing it in a manner whereby the horses voted most likely to succeed do best.

We may look on a horse race as an experiment designed to investigate the dynamics of a free economy, wherein every individual tries his utmost to secure as large an income as possible. The racetrack, like government, lays down the rules of the game and for its services extracts a tax from its patrons, the "take." Except for the market inefficiencies observed for favorites and longshots, equal opportunity prevails for all. There is no implication, it must be emphasized, of equal reward for all. The return received by bettors from wagers on horse races are parts of sums of random events (horse races) that lead as in the random walk to a stationary probability distribution, in this case some shape similar to the

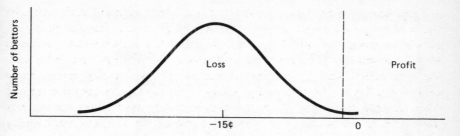

Figure 6-3. Reward per Dollar Bet Received after Many Wagers

normal curve centered on -15 cents per dollar bet. Over a number of races, many horse players will lose less than the mean 15 cents per dollar bet and many will lose more. A very few in the righthand wing of the curve may even turn a profit. But there is no predicting for any single bettor where on the curve he will end up in another sample of races. Note the spread in the results of the expert handicappers in the 5000-race samples.

We shall return to this question of the allocation of income by a free market. Does it represent the best possible distribution? Can other more restrictive markets improve on it? Do we have in horse racing a pristine illustration of Adam Smith's mystical principle of the "invisible hand," whereby each individual, in freely pursuing his own selfish ends, achieves the greatest good for all?

APPENDIX TO CHAPTER 6: HOW TO CALCULATE THE EXPECTATION FOR WINNING AT THE TRACK

Let us calculate the expectation of a horse bettor.

$$E_i = P_i o_i + (1 - P_i)(-\$1)$$

The formula is the same as before, only now E_i is the expectation of a gambler wagering on horse i, P_i its true (and unknown) probability of winning, o_i the reward if it wins, $(1 - P_i)$ the probability that it loses, and $1 the stake. By factoring, the expectation may be put in a more convenient form for our purposes.

$$E_i = P_i(o_i + 1) - 1$$

The term o_i is identical with the odds to a dollar against horse i winning the race, or the dollar odds, for short. If horse i is at odds of two to one (2/1), its winning will net backers a profit of two dollars for every one-dollar bet. If the odds are even (one to one), the profit for winning is one dollar for every dollar bet.

The odds are set by the opinion of the crowd on the winning chances of each horse in the race. They are related to the money bet according to the equation

$$o_i = \frac{M - m_i - fM}{m_i}$$

where M is the total amount of money wagered on all the horses in the race, m_i is the money bet on horse i, f is the percentage of the win pool deducted for the track and state commissions, and fM is the total monies siphoned off the top. The numerator is simply the amount of money in the pool available for return as a profit to those people who bet on horse i (total amount bet less the money bet on horse i less the money taken by the track and state). Dividing this quantity by the money bet on horse i gives the profit for each dollar bet should horse i win.

The odds may be related to the probability of winning p_i assigned by the public to horse i, which is simply the money bet on horse i divided by the total in the win pool:

$$p_i = \frac{m_i}{M}$$

This is not the unknown true probability of winning denoted by capital P_i. Introducing the public's probability into the odds formula yields an expression relating it to the odds:

$$o_i + 1 = \frac{1 - f}{p_i} \quad \text{or} \quad p_i = \frac{1 - f}{o_i + 1}$$

Finally, substituting for $(o_i + 1)$ in the expectation provides us with the desired relationship:

$$E_i = \frac{P_i}{p_i}(1 - f) - 1$$

Later, another expression for the public's probability estimates will be needed. Since it is certain that one of the horses must win, the probabilities sum up to 1:

$$p_1 + p_2 + p_3 + \cdots = 1$$

or, using the above expression for p_i:

$$\frac{1 - f}{o_1 + 1} + \frac{1 - f}{o_2 + 1} + \frac{1 - f}{o_3 + 1} + \cdots = 1$$

$$1 - f\left(\frac{1}{o_1 + 1} + \frac{1}{o_2 + 1} + \frac{1}{o_3 + 1} + \cdots\right) = 1$$

Writing S for the quantity in the parentheses,

$$1 - f = \frac{1}{S}$$

and

$$p_i = \frac{1}{o_i + 1} \div S$$

This equation gives the public's probabilities in terms of the dollar odds on all the horses in the race. Assuming the public's probabilities equal the true probabilities, the expectation may be written

$$E_i = \left[\frac{\frac{1}{o_i + 1}}{S} \right] (o_i + 1) - 1 \quad \text{or} \quad E_i = \frac{1}{S} - 1$$

This form of the expectation will be used later.

7
THE NATURE OF
THE STOCK MARKET

Speculation . . . is the self-adjustment of society to the probable. Its value is well-known as a means of avoiding or mitigating catastrophes, equalizing prices and providing for periods of want. It is true that the success of the strong induces imitation by the weak, and that incompetent persons bring themselves to ruin by undertaking to speculate in their turn. But legislatures and courts generally have recognized that the natural evolutions of a complex society are to be touched only with a very cautious hand. . . .

Oliver Wendell Holmes

The unparalleled advantages of cooperative effort in the search for food and shelter, long incorporated in the genes of many species of life, must have been recognized soon after the descent from the trees and led our ancestors to the adoption of rules of social behavior that most effectively implemented these pursuits. Civilizations arose in many different guises to impart a measure of stability to the shifting sands of the future. Gradually, imperceptibly, the life-style progressed from a level of bare subsistence to one of relative abundance. Man learned to produce in excess of his immediate needs and accumulate the surplus for later consumption by himself and others. Greater productivity was achieved with the introduction of specialization, and with it a system of barter to facilitate the exchange of commodities among hunters, artisans, and farmers. The invention of money enormously enhanced trading opportunities by making feasible the deferred exchange of goods and services. In effect, money became both a call on the future output of producers and a convenient method of storage. So flexible did this medium of exchange prove to be that it was possible for a new class of enterprising men to employ their savings in support of workers building roads, bridges, and ferries, from the use of which they hoped to exact tolls for future income. When advancing technology rendered practicable projects of a scope beyond the means and abilities of a lone entrepreneur, it was but a step to the notion of multiple ownership. Funds were raised by selling shares of common stock, which represented proportional ownership in an enterprise and were transferable. Perhaps the earliest examples of the modern corporation were the Muscovy Company (chartered in 1555) and the Dutch East India Company (chartered in 1602), which built tall ships at great cost, stocked them with expensive cargoes, and depended on astute captains to exchange domestic surpluses for foreign goods and gold on a favorable basis. The

Industrial Revolution encouraged the formation of many new corporations to finance costly new factories and machinery. Originally awarded by governments only rarely and by special acts of king and legislature, corporation charters have in the last century been granted to almost anyone for almost any purpose. Over the last hundred years in the United States and other countries, elaborate marketing facilities have sprung up to assist business in the raising of money. Literally billions of dollars worth of new securities are offered each year by both new and old corporations through investment bankers to millions of venturesome investors, all of whom risk present savings in the hope of receiving future income benefits. This truly sophisticated development effectively channels their small savings into a single powerful stream, which, when properly managed, spawns the production and expansion of the many enterprises on whose output our lives depend. This is the game of investment. Where successful, the financial rewards to the investors are exceeded only by the immense benefits to the public in the form of cheaper production, greater variety, and more widespread distribution of goods and services.

Those countries that have encouraged free enterprise and the unregulated allocation of savings by individuals enjoy the highest standards of living ever attained. So sensational have been the results that even Karl Marx, the chief critic of capitalism, paid tribute to its colossal productive forces, to "wonders far surpassing Egyptian pyramids, Roman aqueducts, and Gothic cathedrals." A consensus of decisions by millions of small investors furnishes the extraordinary solutions to the fundamental economic problems facing every society past and present: What should be produced? how much? by whom? and for whom? In a fine example of natural selection, capital flows to those businesses that in the eyes of the public most efficiently produce what the public wants and is drained away from inefficient corporations manufacturing obsolete products. The reward to the investor for the very considerable risks he assumes is a greater proportionate share of the output of goods and services, more money when he is successful, and a loss of capital when he is unsuccessful. Stock prices are critical. If they are perversely or randomly related to the future earnings prospects of companies, natural selection cannot operate, and the effectiveness of the stock market as an allocator of resources would be nil.

What is the expectation of an investor in stocks? How efficient is the market? What are the chances for better-than-average performance? Let us try to discover the answers to these questions.

The arenas of the game of common stock investment are the floors of the various securities' markets such as the New York Stock Exchange. Here are maintained ready markets to which corporations floating new securities and individual investors wishing either to buy or sell may come. A person buying the stock of some company thinks that the return on his money, from price appreciation and dividends, which are cash payments out of profits made to stockholders, less brokerage commissions of about 2 percent may be greater than the return available elsewhere. A person selling a stock thinks he can do better either in another stock or in some other investment instrument. In the marketplace for stocks, the opinions of these two groups of people continually clash, interact, and modify one another until a price level for a stock is reached at which there are about as many shares being bid for as being offered. What the investing public is trying to do is to decide on a price for a stock that adequately reflects the risks involved in securing a good return on the investment. Each passing moment, the risks are evaluated and reevaluated by someone in the light of any new information that arises, and the market price of each stock will fluctuate with each revelation. The thoughts of millions of people concerning the prospects of the many businesses upon which our society relies are mirrored in the market quotations on the financial pages of the daily newspapers. What fantastic complexity! What unfathomable, unmeasurable forces underlie each of the numbers!

Our initial problem is the measurement of expected return for common stocks. Matters are not so easy here as in the simple games of chance considered earlier because the outcomes now are contingent on the length of time stocks are held. We must express the expectation in a way that standardizes the holding time in order to compare the returns from stocks owned for varying intervals. For this purpose, the compound interest formula serves, the same one used by your bank to compute the interest paid to you on your savings account. We shall reduce the return on all stocks to an interest rate (denoted by r in what follows) that tells us the rate a bank must pay on the principal in a savings account to arrive at a final total after a time of deposit equal to the time the stock is held. (Details on the use of the compound interest formula are given in the appendix to this chapter).

Now we proceed as follows to determine an investor's expectation when buying stock: (1) Pick a stock at random; (2) pick a purchase data at random and note the price; (3) pick a later sale date at random and note the price; (4) using the compound interest formula, compute the interest rate r; (5) repeat the same procedure over and over again; (6) display the data in the form of our random walk histogram, with the number of steps to the right and left replaced with values of r. The resulting graph is a frequency distribution showing the number of holding periods for stocks that yield a given rate of return r, whereas the random walk histogram showed the number of times a certain number of steps to the right or left of the starting point occurred after ten tosses of the coin. The expectation is given by the usual formula

$$E = p_1 r_1 + p_2 r_2 + p_3 r_3 + \cdots$$

where p_i is the probability that a holding period yields a return of $r_i\%$ per year compounded annually and the o's have been replaced by r's. The number of holding periods yielding $r_i\%$ divided by the total number of holding periods in the sample equals p_i.

Carrying out the above procedure for all stocks and all time periods over stock market history would be an endless task. However, a good random sampling of the total stock population has been published using the 1,715 common stocks listed on the New York Stock Exchange during the interval from January 1926 through November 1960. The results are shown in Figure 7-1. For the 1,715 stocks, 56,557,538 holding periods, varying in monthly intervals from one month to the full thirty-five years covered by the study, went into the graph. The most likely return is between 8 and 12 percent per year compounded annually, as evidenced by the pronounced peak at this value. Away from the peak on either side, the number of holding periods decreases fairly smoothly toward zero. For 78 percent of them, a profit was shown, indicated by the white area of the graph; in 22 percent, a loss occurred, shown by the shaded area. A rate of return in excess of 5 percent appeared in over two-thirds of all the holding periods, a figure larger than that obtainable from savings accounts during that time. Nearly one-fifth of them had a return greater than 20 percent per annum compounded yearly, a rate that will double an investment in under four years. The return from one-half of the holding periods exceeded 9.8 percent, this being known as the *median* return. In only 3,045 periods was the investment wiped out altogether. The

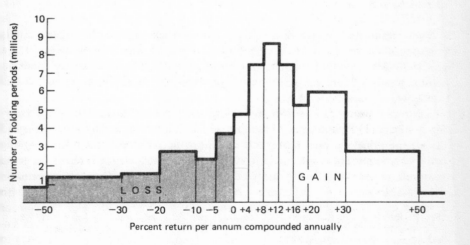

Figure 7-1. Rates of Return on Common Stocks Listed on the New York Stock Exchange, 1926 through 1960, Using All Possible Monthly Holding Intervals from One Month to Thirty-five Years

expectation calculated from the data is +9 percent. An extension of the research to the year 1976 revealed no significant alterations of the results.*

This later study contrasts the average return over the past half century of various investment instruments with the inflation rate. United States Treasury Bills[†] averaged 2.4 percent compounded annually over this period, almost exactly equal to the 2.3-percent inflation rate. An investor content with just keeping up with inflation, a zero real rate of return, might keep his money here. Constantly lurking in the background, however, is the Internal Revenue Service, which requires taxes to be computed on income tax returns without the benefit of adjustment for inflation. Their intrusion turns a zero real rate of return into a negative one. Over shorter periods, the equality vanishes. From 1926 to 1932, the T-bill return was 2.7 percent while the annual rate of inflation was a negative 4.4 percent, yielding a real rate of return on T-bills of 7.1 percent. In the decade from 1941 to 1951, on the other hand, the T-bills returned only 0.6 percent compared to a high 5.9 percent for the inflation rate, yielding a negative 5.3 percent real return. And the IRS, of course, insisted on its share of that 0.6 percent return.

The rates of return on long-term government and corporate bonds were lower than for common stocks, and, not surprisingly, the volatility of the returns was less. Adjusted for inflation, the average return on governments was 1 percent and for corporates 1.7 percent, both figures before the IRS took its cut. None of these other types of investment came close to matching the 6.9 percent real rate of return for stocks.

The measurement of the returns on common stocks suggest the possible outcomes available to an investor who bought blindly at any time between 1926 and 1976. Most likely, he would have chosen stocks and holding periods giving returns near 9 percent per year compounded annually. Sometimes, much higher yields would have been obtained—some people made fortunes—and sometimes much lower, even to a complete loss of capital. The worst losses took place during the Depression; almost a 50-percent loss of capital was taken by the average investor for stocks owned outright if he bought in September 1929 and sold in late 1932. Such catastrophic losses, while unlikely, are always possible even in a favorable game. Many "safe" savings accounts also disappeared over this period.

---

*See R. Ibbotson and R. Sinquefield, *Stocks, Bonds, Bills and Inflation: The Past (1926-1976) and the Future (1977-2000)* (Charlottesville, VA: Financial Analysts Research Foundation, University of Virginia, 1977).
[†]Treasury bills are one means the federal government utilizes to finance its short-term debt They are notes that mature in thirteen, twenty-six, and fifty-two weeks from date of issue. The Treasury Department usually offers new bills every week on a discount basis, the difference between the selling price and the price at maturity being the return on the investment.

So consistently high are the rates of return that it is small wonder to find that common stock investments have enjoyed widespread popularity in the past. The public has instinctively known all along that the stock market is a favorable game, one that yields a return substantially in excess of the inflation rate and greater than can be achieved in savings accounts and bonds.

How is it possible, many ask, for the great majority of investors to realize such high investment profits? Who loses? To answer these questions, let us consider first of all a simple model, a stock market sealed so that money can neither enter through the purchase of stocks nor leave through the sale of stocks and the payment of cash dividends. For every investor buying shares and putting money into the market, there must be an investor selling shares and withdrawing an equivalent amount of money from the market, and any dividends are immediately reinvested. In this kind of stock market (what is known as a zero-sum game), every investor who wins a dollar has a counterpart who loses a dollar, exactly as in a game of coin-tossing. If we make the model a little more realistic by allowing for brokerage commissions and taxes on transactions, the stock market becomes, in a manner analogous to the pari-mutuel market, an unfavorable game since there is a continual drain of money into the hands of brokers and government.

The real stock market, however, is not insulated from the economic environment, and there is a continual inflow and outflow of funds as it competes with all other forms of investment for the public's savings. As each individual investor seeks to maximize utility, a fluctuating consensus of decisions shifts money from one type of asset to another in a kind of Brownian movement. Financial assets, such as stocks, bonds, and bank accounts, and real assets, such as real estate and collector's items, all claim a share of the investor's dollar. Overall, we still have our zero-sum game and no appreciation in value, unless there is a growth in savings over the years and a relative scarcity of assets. Here is the fundamental reason why stocks have proved to be such good investments for the great majority in the past: the money from savings earmarked for investment in the stock market has grown faster than the supply of stock. A growing economy is rooted in growing savings, and the stock market reflects the prospects for future growth. It is the preferred channel for directing flows of money into the creation and expansion of the means of production, and its importance in a capitalist society can hardly be overemphasized. Should the growth of savings be curtailed by excessive taxation, the stock market could no longer function as an allocator of funds, and, as happens with dismaying results in many countries, government bureaucrats take over.

If people investing blindly can do so well, how do the experts perform? We get one hint from an item in *The New York Times* 16 August 1967: "A member of the Senate Banking Committee sought to prove today that it is possible to pick a portfolio of stocks that would do better than most mutual funds simply by throwing darts at the New York Stock Exchange list. Senator Thomas J. McIntyre, Democrat of New Hampshire, reported to the committee that he had done just that, and gotten better investment results than the average of even the most growth-oriented mutual funds. A hypothetical $10,000 investment made 10 years ago in the senator's dart-selected stocks would be worth $25,300 now." A mutual fund is an organization that collects money from people and invests it for the purpose of capital growth from appreciation and dividends. The fund managers spend full time investigating and analyzing investment opportunities and so, presumably, should be able to invest the fund's money in those stocks apt to do best. Senator McIntyre was raising questions about the charges that mutual funds impose for managing their investors' money. He tried his experiment, he told the committee, after fund managers had disputed the testimony given earlier by Paul Samuelson, now a Nobel Laureate in economics, that a random selection of stocks would yield investment results as good as or better than those achieved by the funds. The *New York Times* article concluded with the observation that spokesmen for individual mutual funds made no serious attempt to answer the senator, though several jokingly offered him a job.

But is it a joke? Do we have another example of a game in which the public is at least as good as the experts in forecasting possible outcomes? Let us examine the record of the experts more closely as exposed in the performance of mutual funds.

1927-1935: "It can, then, be concluded with considerable assurance that the entire group of management investment companies proper (as opposed to the sample here studied) failed to perform better than an index of leading common stocks and probably performed somewhat worse than the index over the 1927-1935 period. . . ." This statement is from "The Statistical Survey of Investment Trusts and Investment Companies," based on a compilation by the Securities and Exchange Commission staff.* The results following are derived from *Security Analysis*, a book which has enjoyed a wide reputation in investment circles.

1934-1939: The overall gain in asset value of the six largest companies averaged out to 53.7 percent including dividends paid out. Standard & Poor's 420 Stock (index) showed a 66.6-percent increase and only one of the funds exceeded this figure by achieving 70.6 percent.

1940-1949: In this period the same six companies had an average gain of 129 percent in asset value including dividends, compared to 97 percent for Standard & Poor's 420 Stocks.

1951-1960: The performance of fifty-eight companies over this ten-year pe-

---

*As quoted in B. Graham, J. Dodd, and S. Cottle, *Security Analysis* 4th ed. (New York: McGraw-Hill, 1962), p. 740.

riod, assuming that all distributions are reinvested in the (investment) companies' shares at the end of the year in which made, averaged to a gain of 221 percent, more than tripling the initial capital. But Standard & Poor's Composite Index of 500 common stocks showed a gain of 322 percent, almost 50 percent better than the average of the funds. This figure was exceeded by only three of the fifty-eight companies.

I quote Graham, Dodd, and Cottle: "These results do not appear to us to be as satisfactory as they should be. They suggest that the investment companies as a whole—and practicing security analysts as a whole—might well reexamine their basic approaches to both the selections of common stocks for purchase and the decision to sell 'less satisfactory' holdings."*

Matters have not improved since. In the period from 1958 to 1967, the average return per annum compounded annually for 146 funds was 10 percent, the same as for each of the Dow-Jones Averages of industrial, rail, and utility stocks.†
And in the ten years ending 31 March 1976, the net asset value of the average mutual fund was up 46 percent, far behind the 60-percent gain in the Dow-Jones Industrial Average. Both figures allow for reinvestment of dividends.

Arguments about expert performance continue to this day. Most professors of economics and finance in the universities and the Security and Exchange Commission believe the changes in stock prices are generated by a random walk process. They produce all kinds of evidence refuting claims of performance superior to the market averages by the expert managers of other people's money (OPM). They point to the similarity between the graph shown in Figure 7-1 and the normal distribution, and they demonstrate a lack of any significant correlation in successive price changes of stocks, implying that today's price change tells us nothing about tomorrow's. (We noted earlier that a stationary distribution, in this instance the returns from stocks over different time periods, and independence of trials are characteristic of random walks). It should be mentioned that histograms of returns on stocks deviate from the normal distribution to a small extent in that too many returns cluster about the mean, too few appear a moderate distance from the mean, and again too many returns lie in the wings. In Figure 7-1, 77 percent of the observations occur within one standard deviation of the mean compared with 68 percent in a normal distribution.

All in all, the evidence argues cogently for the validity of a random walk model of the stock market with a mean return of 9 percent. It would appear extremely unlikely for any investor, expert or novice, to outperform the market averages on the basis of historical data, such as patterns of past price changes used in

---

*Ibid., p. 741.
†Fabricand, Beating the Street (New York: McKay, 1969), pp. 38–40.

"technical" analysis and the status of individual companies, industries, and the economy used in "fundamental" analysis. Evidence to the contrary is lacking, a somewhat unusual situation in economics. The market in stocks is weakly efficient to a very high degree of approximation and discounts old news fully. Until somebody is able to demonstrate a statistically sound method of beating the averages, this conclusion must be maintained by any reasonable person. Interestingly enough, in recent years fund managers have themselves shifted goals from better-than-average performance to merely matching the averages.

The question arises, as to how rapidly the weakly efficient market in stocks reacts to news. What is its relaxation time? Only a small though rapidly growing volume of work has been done on this point. The best evidence at this time indicates that the market is not semi-strongly efficient; there is late-breaking news that can be utilized for better-than-average performance. The stock market partakes, as might be expected, of the same character as the pari-mutuel market. Later, we shall see how to take advantage of late news.

Appendix to Chapter 7: How to Calculate the Rate of Reward in the Stock Market

The compound interest formula shows the amount of money A your account is worth if P dollars are deposited for n years at a yearly rate of interest $r\%$. Here, r is the interest rate per year compounded yearly, which simply means that in any given year after the initial deposit, you are paid a dividend of r dollars for every $100 on deposit, which amount includes the original deposit plus all interest accumulated in subsequent years.

$$A = P(1 + r)^n$$

Although savings banks usually compound interest over shorter time spreads than a year, we shall express the rewards from stock investments in terms of the interest rate compounded yearly. Thus, suppose we buy 100 shares of the American Telephone and Telegraph Company (Telephone, for short) at a price of $55 per share and sell it one year later for $60 per share. What is our reward? The original investment is $5,600 ($5,500 for the cost of the stock plus an assumed $100 for the commission). On the sale of the stock one year later, we receive $6,000 less the $100 commission plus $380 in dividends paid by the company, or a net of $6,280. Substituting these figures into the formula,

$$6280 = 5600(1 + r)^1$$

$$r = 0.12 \text{ or } 12\%$$

Every dollar invested in Telephone is worth $1.12 one year later. If the stock went down in price and was sold at $50 per share one year later, our final money total A = $5000 − $100 (commission) + $380 (dividends) = $5280. The formula becomes

$$5280 = 5600 (1 + r)^1$$

$$r = -0.06 \text{ or } -6\%$$

There would have been a loss of 6 cents for every dollar invested.

8
THE EFFICIENT-MARKETS SOCIETY

The best jockey hinders the horse the least.

Eddie Arcaro

Striving to maximize his utility, Everyman pursues in his own way the goals he thinks best. Displaying an infinite diversity of behavior, he undertakes those activities of work and play, consumption and saving, that afford him the highest degrees of personal satisfaction. As he moves from childhood through school and into the real world, he finds himself facing steadily intensifying challenges for the things he desires. On average, he attains a level of achievement commensurate with the energy, knowledge, and talent he brings to bear on his chosen activities. Sometimes his lot falls above this level, and sometimes below, as Lady Luck in the guise of the random walk decides the ordering. Should he fail to do his best, there will always be others waiting to take his place and reduce his status. At the same time, the very uncertainties of the marketplace offer him great incentives for extraordinary achievement, whatever the field of endeavor. Usually between the ages of thirty-five and fifty, he senses the exhaustion of his potential for advancement, the full realization of which precipitates a psychological crisis leading either to an acceptance of his condition or a change of goals and life pattern to ensure future growth. At birth, his die is cast. What he amounts to, by what arts and accidents he attains his niche in life, no one can predict. As Mark Twain put it, "Among the three or four million cradles now rocking in the land are some which this nation would preserve for ages as sacred things, if we could know which ones they are."

Imagine now an efficient-markets society where, as in the examples of the racetrack and the stock market, a sufficient number of people have acquired the requisite knowledge and experience to make all markets efficient. It is a living organism whose metabolism comprises the sum total of all the decisions made by millions of people during the course of their daily lives. Fads and fashions ebb and flow on the unpredictable tides of public opinion; great advances spring from the most unexpected quarters; goods and services sell at prices set in the marketplace; Everyman earns a recompense accorded by the judgment of the job market and is free to spend it as he sees fit. The distribution of income in such a society, like the outcomes in our random walk experiment, conforms to a sta-

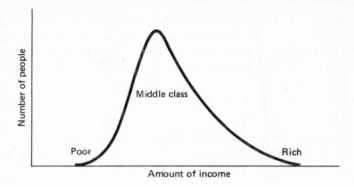

tionary distribution similar to the normal curve. In one tail of the spectrum are the few people with very high earnings, in the other the unfortunates who share the fate of Job. Most find themselves in the great central maximum of average income, what has become known as the middle class. In countries like the United States where the efficient-markets society is reasonably well approximated, the graph appears to be skewed toward higher incomes. More individuals appear in the upper middle class than would be the case under a normal distribution. The mean or middle class, however, connotes a high standard of living indeed when compared with those of the past and those that exist in most other countries today. How much ability, how much luck, figures in Everyman's success? Who can say? Who can pretend to understand? There are a few like Isaac Newton who were endowed at birth with a great brain, and there are others who were endowed with a great fortune. "My income doesn't descend upon me like manna from heaven," wrote Joseph Medill Patterson in *Confessions of a Drone.* "It can be traced. Some of it comes from the profits of a daily newspaper, some of it from Chicago real estate, some from the profits made by the Pennsylvania and other railroads, some from the profits of the American Tobacco Company. . . .

"It takes to support me just about 20 times as much as it takes to support an average working man or farmer. And the funny thing about it is that these working men and farmers work hard all year round, while I don't work at all."

The ubiquitous normal distribution displays what may be the fairest attainable division of income consistent with the highest standard of living for all. It is characteristic of an efficient market-organized society which makes possible more than ever before equality of opportunity. Although there may be excesses of reward at one end, like Joseph Medill Patterson, and appalling poverty at the other, it is certainly preferable to distributions similar to what I call the "poor" distribution that prevails in so many countries today, where the few live very

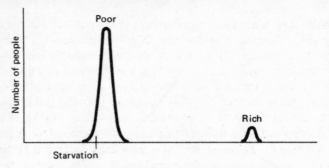

Figure 8-2. "Poor" Distribution of Income

well and the many not far from bare subsistence. The dream of utopians, communists, and socialists is the "Robin Hood" distribution—equality of reward rather than equality of opportunity. The above-average income earned by productive people is confiscated and transferred to the less productive element, so that everybody is located at the mean. Whether or not such an egalitarian distribution is desirable I do not know; whether or not it is realizable while still maintaining the average near that of efficient-markets societies is something for others to demonstrate if they can. "We live, not as we wish to, but as we can."—Menander. The recent evidence is startling: Compare, if you will, the economic booms of the 1920s in America, France, and Italy, where huge tax cuts were engineered by Coolidge, Poincaré, and Mussolini, with the stagnancy of Great Britain, where nothing was done to relieve the public of the steep progressive tax burden imposed during World War I. Compare the meteoric ascendancy of the post-World War II economies of capitalistic West Germany and Japan with the sluggishness of socialist England and communist Russia.

Crucial to the winning ways of capitalism is the small investor operating in a free environment. In a stochastic process reminiscent of the condensation of water molecules on atmospheric particles to form raindrops and the agglomera-

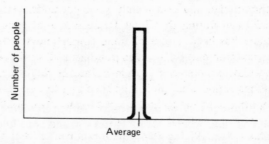

Figure 8-3. "Robin Hood" Distribution of Income

tion of galactic dust into stars and planets, capital tends to accumulate about people in varying degrees as a result of their labor and investments. What a person may do with his excess monies, profits, savings—call it what you must—depends on the framework in which he operates. In a collectivist society, his wishes are neither respected nor trusted and his wealth is taxed away to be spent supposedly more wisely by politicians and bureaucrats. At the opposite end of the scale is the efficient-markets society wherein optimal competitive conditions are maintained and each person is encouraged to amass to the limit of his abilities those financial and real assets he desires. Winners there are aplenty; but far from causing deprivation to others, these concentrations of wealth spark a vigorous exploitation of ideas and resources for the benefit of everybody. The Brownian movement of Adam Smith's "invisible hand" is subtle and mysterious, but its effectiveness has proved itself time and time again over hundreds of years. We have gotten an inkling of its workings earlier, and although the racetrack may be too simple an example from which to extrapolate to great social and economic structures, the same cannot be said of the stock market, which reaches into almost every facet of life and is an integral part of society. The excellence of the public's judgment in estimating the probability of things to come, which underlies the great difficulty one encounters in performing better than average at the races and in the stock market, surely carries further to other institutions. We might note in passing that the last two world leaders, England and the United States, are democracies whose people choose leaders best able to look after their interests. In the arts, a strong case can be made for public superiority in the recognition of great works by contrasting the experts' critical response at the time of their introduction with the usually very rapid public acceptance of them. Indeed, the noted pianist and musical commentator, Abram Chasins, devoted a whole radio program to a demonstration of just this point. In his opera *Die Meistersinger von Nürnberg*, Richard Wagner has his principal character Hans Sachs proclaim the necessity of submitting the rules of composition and performance of the Mastersingers' guild to public review once a year.

Since 1929, the efficient-markets society has come under incessant attack for its imputed breakdown during the Great Depression that ended the euphoric Coolidge era. There has been a general trend toward more restrictive societies with ever higher taxation and inflation as politicians all over the world eagerly embraced the speculative theories of economist John M. Keynes, which advocated government spending rather than individual spending to cure our economic ills. In view of its importance to the techniques put forth in this book, I must devote a few words to a defense of the efficient market.

The Coolidge tax cut of 1924 ignited a great bull market that carried stocks to lofty peaks never before reached. Despite claims to the contrary, these were not

wildly speculative gains, for the period saw a phenomenal growth in the nation'
capital stock, its means of production. And with product prices *falling*, real out
put was increasing even faster. Far from being exorbitantly overpriced in 1929
the stock market was in its accustomed position of being exactly where it should
have been. By every reasonable expectation, economic growth should have con
tinued, as it was to do many years later. Unfortunately, what happened was un
reasonable in the extreme.

Looking backward from the vantage point of somewhat more knowledge o
the efficient market and much better statistical data, we can now assess those
traumatic years, and, indeed, a consensus of expert opinion seems to have crystal
lized. The devastation wrought by the Great Depression arose not from any mal
function of the efficient market, but from an abysmal performance on the par
of the governmental monetary authorities (the Federal Reserve Board) tha
resulted in a one-third contraction of the country's money supply when ar
expansionary policy was desperately called for.* Monetary policy is little under
stood by most people, but hardly by the stock market, which waits with baitec
breath for the weekly release of the money supply figures every Thursday. Money
is the lifeblood of an economy, and too much or too little can foul the intricate
workings of the marketplace. During the Great Depression, the sharp monetary
cutback occasioned a severe case of economic anemia. Money was leached from
savings, from investments, from businesses, and simply dematerialized. Not only
was there not enough for future growth, there was not even enough to meet pay
rolls. Unemployment soared, companies and banks failed, and millions became
impoverished. Not until late in 1932 did the Federal Reserve Board initiate ar
expansion of the money supply, and when it did, business and the stock marke
responded in quick order, only to be thwarted from a full recovery by massive
interference from a newly burgeoning federal bureaucracy under President Frank
lin Roosevelt. The Depression lengthened into World War II, a time when the
exigencies of war demanded the mobilization and encouragement of our produc
tive resources and a return to the efficient market. The postwar boom year
followed.

Question? Were the business panics and depressions of the past the result o
failures of the efficient market, or were natural fluctuations of the economy, te
be expected on the basis of the random walk model, exacerbated by the inept
ness of government in adjusting the money supply judiciously? The question
demands an answer before our free economy, and those in many other parts o
the world, are tinkered to death by misguided legislative overkill. "The road te
hell is paved with good intentions."—Karl Marx

*See Milton Friedman and Anna Schwartz, "The Great Contraction," in *A Monetary His
tory of the United States 1867-1960* (Princeton: Princeton University Press, 1963), ch. 7.

9

BEATING THE AVERAGES

Having thus exposed the far-seeing Mandarin's inner thoughts, would it be too excessive a labour to penetrate a little deeper into the rich mine of strategy and disclose a specific detail?

Ernest Bramah, *Kai Lung Unrolls His Mat*

Can Mr. Average expect to perform better than average in any of the manifold activities of life open to him? Yes, but only if he is in a position to take advantage of a market inefficiency. Some illustrations: The average physician can expect greater rewards than his counterpart in another profession because the present value of the future income stream in the field of medicine is the highest of all. The Communist Party in Russia is an elite club, membership in which assures greater-than-average success. The average American fares better than the average citizen of most other countries. These inefficiencies arise from arbitrary decisions to limit the free flow of people into areas of maximum return and are part of the explanation behind the eagerness of people to enter these select groups. But aside from his job, to which he must devote his greatest effort, Mr. Average is unlikely to attain average performance by professional standards. His avocations, therefore, represent ways of maximizing utility outside his major occupation, with income playing a minor role. So the question becomes: Is there an easier way? Is there an escape from the routine and drudgery of a day-in-day-out job in favor of something more exciting and glamorous? Is it possible to augment income to an above-average level?

The answers lie in the character of the markets in which Mr. Average participates. A deviation from strong efficiency must be exploited by anyone hoping for better-than-average performance. However, the recognition and correction of an inefficiency in a market is a rather rare event, one that leads to a new invention or a new way of doing things or a new system of thought that reveals the future more clearly than before. These are achievements by gifted individuals fortunate enough to be in the proper place at the proper time. They are not in the purview of Mr. Average; if they were, he could hardly be considered average. His only chance, then, is to operate in a weakly efficient or semi-strongly efficient market. (He cannot hope for superior performance in a strongly efficient market.) If the market is semi-strongly efficient so that news is instantaneously discounted, he must have access to significant inside information on a continuing basis, which again implies that Mr. Average is not average. We are left perforce with the prerequisite that Mr. Average, in order to perform better than average, must do so in a weakly efficient market. He must somehow adopt a system for predicting the future that depends on freshly brewed information to which the market adjusts only after a time lag. All other avenues are closed.

A medical research worker, testing the effect of a new drug on cancer in chickens, was overjoyed to find that it seemed to cure in a high percentage of cases. Word of his success quickly spread, and he was invited to address a medical convention. In his talk, he described the drug, his techniques, and finally his results. These he reported as follows: "An amazingly high percentage of the chickens, one-third of them, showed a complete cure. In another third, there seemed to be no effect, and, er . . . the other chicken ran away."

Fortunately, much medical research has progressed far beyond this low estate. However, the anecdote does point up the ever-present difficulties in evaluating any model of reality. There are systems! and systems! and more systems! From Newton's System of the World to dialectical materialism, from relativistic quantum theory to psychoanalysis, from absolute truths to the latest gambling system, all claiming a close correspondence with reality. Outright chicanery, abuses of statistics, and improper sampling procedures abound. How do we separate the wheat from the chaff? How do we tell which represent significant additions to the pool of knowledge and which do not? Certainly, a mere accounting for past happenings, although important, is not nearly sufficient. Ideologues easily pluck from the ingredient-rich pie of experience their theses-serving plums. We must look to the future, for here is where a system must justify its claim for the attention of reasonable men. It should state clearly and unambiguously a recipe for others to test, by means of which the future may be revealed from measurements in the past and present, and it should display its conclusions in a statistically sound manner. Failure to satisfy these criteria will surely lead to fiascoes for those risking their lives on new medical procedures or their money on get-rich-quick schemes.

We are now prepared to learn about two systems operable in the weakly efficient pari-mutuel betting market and the stock market. They will show how to take advantage of late-breaking information to realize not only better-than-average performance but profitable operations as well. Both markets offer the investor the highly significant benefit of complete indifference on the part of other people to the extent of monetary gains. No matter how much he wins, the investor's path to possible riches will not be obstructed by arbitrary changes in the rules of play, strong-arm tactics, or other roadblocks set up by competitors threatened with the loss of their capital. Furthermore, these two areas are among the very few left where meaningful profits may be realized, and even these may disappear before too long because of government tax policies.

From our discussion of public wagering at the races, we recall that the post favorites, the horses which have received the most money at the close of betting, are not bet as strongly as they should be for equality of return with the other choices. This inefficiency in the market led us to infer the existence of information not included in the historical record that enables a bettor to do better than average by merely wagering on the favorite in each and every race. The pari-mutuel market is thus weakly efficient, and there is late-breaking news in at least some races not fully appreciated by all fans. In the system to be presented, I intend to show that (1) races with underbet favorites can be segregated from the others, (2) wagering on the favorite in these races yields a positive expectation, and (3) the second and third choices in certain races may be profitably bet. It must be remarked that this system is notably superior to the one published previously in my book *Horse Sense*.

In the case of stocks, controversy currently rages over the question of weak efficiency, mainly, I believe, because of faulty procedures and conclusions adopted by writers in the field. Cogent evidence against the semi-strongly efficient hypothesis will be introduced along with a system for picking those stocks apt to do best in the future. Since this game is favorable from the outset, it entails less risk than encountered in the pari-mutuel market.

The key to profitable operations in a weakly efficient market is surprise. Late-breaking news by definition must be surprising or it is not news at all. It must report happenings that take place unexpectedly, meaning their occurrence is not implied with a high degree of probability by previous events in the historical record. During the confusion occasioned by the surprise, good investments should abound. Examples, one from each of our two markets, serve to illustrate the common basis of our two systems, which will be described in detail in subsequent chapters.

In horse racing, surprising information, if such exists for some race, is reflected in the closing odds against each horse winning. Consider the following race, known as the Garden State, one of the richest stakes races for two-year-olds at distance of $1\frac{1}{16}$ miles, held at Garden State Park in New Jersey, 4 November 1961. For any handicapper with a modicum of skill, it was obviously a race between just two horses, Donut King and Crimson Satan. Both horses had very easily won tune-up races the week before at Garden State Park at the same $1\frac{1}{16}$-mile distance, under identical weights, and in almost the same time. Two weeks earlier, Donut King had won the 1-mile Champagne Stakes at Belmont Park, defeating the fourth-finishing Crimson Satan by two lengths under level weights. On the historical record, Donut King seemed to be the superior horse, and most professional handicappers picked him to win. Yet the racetrack crowd made Crimson Satan a strong 6/5 favorite with Donut King the second choice at 8/5.

I remember vividly the surprise I felt at the information conveyed by the odds. To many bettors, a wager on Donut King must have looked like money found. But beware! This kind of obvious situation is to be approached with caution. Something had happened, invisible though it was to average bettors like myself, that caused the odds to shift in favor of Crimson Satan. In view of the chronic underbetting of favorites, I make the assumption that races like this are the ones responsible for the better-than-average return on favorites. There is too much betting on the second choice for the wrong reasons transparently revealed in the past performances and consequently too little betting on the favorite; the public is making an error. Whether or not the favorites in such races are underbet enough to yield a positive expectation can be decided only by recourse to sufficient amounts of data in a way we shall shortly discuss.

Crimson Satan won the race by two lengths over Donut King. The next week the newspapers carried a story about the doubts expressed before the race by a leading trainer over the condition of Donut King's legs, an opinion later vindicated. Here was the hidden information that had caused the shift in the betting toward a more realistic appraisal of the win probabilities. Late news like this appears to be an important component of the considerations leading to the establishment of the closing odds in many races. Probably the most crucial data about a race not carried in the published record is the physical condition of the horse since its last race. Information on workouts, which is carried in the *Daily Racing Form*, is incomplete and often unreliable; owners and trainers, however, are aware of significant changes in a horse's condition through close observation of workouts, feeding habits, general health, condition of legs, and the blowout (a short, limbering up exercise given many horses before the race). Their opinions diffuse into the betting picture and in many instances bring about surprising situations.

The utility of owning stock in a company derives mainly from its future earning power, there being little artistic or sensory satisfaction connected with its possession. A potential investor, therefore, must make some estimate of the future earnings of a corporation and then decide before buying how the rate of return on the investment compares with that available elsewhere. His expectation is the same as that available to all other investors, if we agree that the buying price reflects everything that is known at the moment about the company's prospects. This is the strongly efficient market hypothesis.

Now suppose there is a sudden change in these prospects, possibly from a great oil discovery or a surprisingly high report of earnings. Both pieces of news will spark an upgrading in the outlook for future earnings and bring about buying that raises the price of the stock. Those advocating the strongly efficient market hypothesis insist that the price will react to the news instantly and completely, affording an investor no opportunity to take advantage of the information. Those advocating semi-strong efficiency will allow to some price adjustment from insider buying before publication of the news. Doubters argue for the existence of a non-zero time constant, which, if true, would enable an investor to do better than average by buying on the news release.

A case history will help clarify the chain of events. On 21 January 1971, Fred J. Borch, chairman and chief executive officer, told a news conference that the fourth quarter 1970 profits and sales of the General Electric Company set records for any quarter in its history. He estimated that earnings rose to a few cents over $1.80 per share, far above the $1.25 range expected by all financial analysts. That day, General Electric stock closed at a price of $100\frac{1}{8}$, up from $96\frac{3}{8}$ the day before. On January 22, trading in General Electric did not begin until the afternoon because of an avalanche of buy orders and a lack of sell orders. (The New York Stock Exchange is an auction market, where for every buyer at a given price there must be a seller. There is no negotiation.) Buyers and sellers were finally matched at a price of $103\frac{3}{4}$, up more than 3 percent from the close of the previous day.

Did this price fairly reflect the surprising news development? How does one decide? The only way, of course, is to compare the price action of the stock with the market as a whole over some future time interval. And that is what we shall do for some 1,500 stocks. As will be described more specifically in Chapter 13, quarterly earnings estimates for these companies were compared to the actual earnings reported at the end of the quarter. If the weakly efficient market hypothesis is valid, those stocks reporting earnings surprisingly higher than the estimate should outperform the market averages in the near future; those stocks reporting surprisingly low earnings should underperform the market. We shall learn that purchases of those stocks reporting surprisingly high earnings enables the individual investor to decisively beat the averages. In the case of General Electric, by the time of the next earnings report three months later, the stock was at 120, far outpacing the market averages.

Surprisingly bad news has the opposite effect. Then there is a lineup of sellers and few buyers, usually causing a precipitous drop in the price of the stock. Again, adherents of semi-strong efficiency maintain that the bad news is instantaneously discounted.

"Well," you might object, "if semi-strong efficiency is not valid, how come the experts don't know it? It all sounds simple enough. Why don't the money managers immediately jump on a stock like General Electric when it reports higher than expected earnings and with the huge amounts of money under their control wreck all chance for better-than-average performance?"

Samples of expert opinion on the startling earnings announcement of General Electric appeared soon afterward in the comments of several leading financial analysts quoted in the *Wall Street Journal.* "GE is a high quality stock, but I would lighten holdings on any further advance. I think the turnaround in such operations as nuclear, jet engines, and time-sharing will all have been completed within two years ... and after this swing, a slowdown in earnings growth is possible."*

Other analysts concurred. Many, while bullish about the long run prospects for General Electric, could not see much more price appreciation for the present. What these analysts failed to recognize was that the investing public was just as aware as they were of the possible slowdown in earnings growth for the company a few years hence and this potentiality had already been factored into the price. There was nothing new here. But the earnings report revealed unsuspected profitability that could not have been discounted in the price. This was news! As it was, the *Wall Street Journal* article drove the price of the stock down to 98 before it began its big rise.

Most economists and financial experts in the universities, it is safe to say at present, hold the semi-strongly efficient markets model to be a good representation of the stock market. They base their belief on research of a kind now described.† Earnings estimates for the coming year were generated by an econometric model for a sample of several hundred firms. These yearly projections were then compared with the actual reported earnings one year later and the price action of the stocks before and after the annual report recorded. It was shown that those stocks of companies reporting higher-than-projected earnings indeed outperformed the market averages, but that most of the price rises had been anticipated and occurred prior to the release of the annual report. Consequently, those investors buying on the news release of annual earnings realized only insignificant profits. Completely ignored in the model is the fact that there are at least three indications in the year preceding the annual earnings announcement that earnings are going to be better than expected, the quarterly earnings reports. And herein lies the fallacy of this type work. For if the annual report is better than expected on the basis of a forecast made one year earlier, the surprise is bound to have been reflected in one of the earlier quarterly reports. In addition, other pieces of information on a company's performance surface during the year, such as interviews with officers and press releases. Therefore, an investor buying for reason of an unexpectedly good earnings report issued at the end of a quarter will get in on much of the rise that occurs before publication of the annual earnings. In this sense, Ball and Brown confirm the research reported here. Furthermore, the use of an econometric model to predict earnings is, in my

---

Wall Street Journal 27 January 1971, p. 31.
†R. Ball and P. Brown, "An Empirical Evaluation of Accounting Income Numbers," *Journal of Accounting Research* 6 (Autumn, 1968): 159–78.

opinion, an exercise in futility. It can hardly be as accurate as the forecasts of financial analysts in close touch with reporting companies. And since these models do so very poorly in predicting the economic future, why believe their earnings projections?

Whenever a stock does report surprisingly high earnings, there is almost always a lineup of buyers. There is also a rush to sell on surprisingly low earnings. Many people know, and have known for a long time, that the moment to buy and sell on surprising information is immediately. But, it seems, not enough people know it. Professional money managers are in a unique position. Even if they disagree with semi-strong efficiency, they cannot move in and out of stocks easily in a short time; their holdings are much too large for quick trades. Furthermore, the universe of stocks from which they make their selections is very limited, generally comprising only those companies with large amounts of stock outstanding. Because the fraction of stocks reporting surprising earnings is small compared to all stocks, the number of stocks so reporting in the universe of the manager will be even smaller. Timely investments in these stocks cannot have much affect on the performance of portfolios containing large investments in other securities.

The weakly efficient market concept does not appear to be limited to the pari-mutuel and stock markets, but may pervade many other areas of speculation. For the benefit of those of my readers interested in constructing systems based on this idea, I mention the last two of the rare instances in which I have gambled in other fields. In June 1975, while participating in the Second Annual Conference on Gambling at Harrah's on Lake Tahoe, Nevada, I chatted at length with an inveterate baseball bettor. I endeavored to instruct him in my concept of the efficient market, but to no avail; he was convinced of his superiority to the odds-makers in judging the outcomes of the games. To demonstrate his prowess, he predicted that the next day's game between Cincinnati and Atlanta was certain to be won by Cincinnati and that we should bet the following morning when the casino windows opened. Although I have little interest in baseball, I was curious and pressed him for his reasons: Cincinnati has its best pitcher starting against a mediocre Atlanta hurler; Cincinnati's powerhouse hitting should easily account for a large number of runs; Atlanta had been playing badly recently whereas Cincinnati is threatening to walk away with the pennant even at this early stage of the season. He was obviously an expert on baseball, so I asked him what I consider the crucial question: "What do you think the odds should be?" So certain was he of the outcome, he did not want to say at first; but after some consideration he answered, "5/2 on Cincinnati." Risking $5.00 in order to win $2.00 was in his mind a fair bet on Cincinnati. When we entered the betting chamber the next day, the odds favored Cincinnati as expected, but, surprisingly, at a low 5/8, which meant that a risk of only $3.20 was necessary to win $2.00. My newfound acquaintance turned ecstatic and, despite my protestations that something was fishy, proceeded to wager $100.00 on Cincinnati. With the similarity of this betting situation to the Donut King-Crimson Satan race in mind, I bet a modest $20.00 on Atlanta at odds of 7/5, so that my profit would amount to $28.00 in the event of an Atlanta victory. It seemed inconceivable to me that the odds-makers were less knowledgeable than my expert friend. The discrepancy between the two views on what the proper odds should have been indicated to me the existence of late-breaking information favorable to Atlanta of which my friend was unaware and which was, because of bettors like him, not fully discounted in the betting. Atlanta won 5 to 1.

The other speculative venture took place at the Third Annual Conference on Gambling at Caesar's Palace in Las Vegas, in December 1976. After checking in, I wandered into a betting establishment along The Strip and regarded with surprise the odds on the Los Angeles-Dallas football game scheduled to start within the hour. It was one of a series of playoffs leading to the Superbowl. Dallas was a three-point favorite, to me a surprisingly small margin. As with baseball, I am not a football aficionado, but it seemed to me that I had heard a lot about the greatness of the Cowboys that season and very little about the Rams. Furthermore, the home field advantage was with Dallas. My interest aroused, I spoke with some of the people standing around waiting for the telecast of the game. Except for one rabid Los Angeles fan, everyone thought Dallas an excellent wager at the prevailing point spread. Convinced, I bet on Los Angeles, and won. No doubt I shall not be so lucky in the future. Still, as long as the cardinal principle of the weakly efficient market guides my actions, I hope to perform better than average.

The next section of this book deals with my system of pari-mutuel wagering and the section following that with the stock market. Those readers uninterested in horse racing may skip immediately to the stock section. Both systems spring from a common basis, the exploitation of the weakly efficient market to achieve handsome profits.

PART II
WINNING IN THE PARI-MUTUEL MARKET

10
HORSE SENSE

I pass with relief from the tossing sea of Cause and Theory to the firm ground of Result and Fact.

Winston Churchill

Superior performance in the weakly efficient pari-mutuel betting market is readily achieved, we have learned, by using the last-minute information conveyed by the late odds to bet on post favorites. Superior performance, however, is not winning performance. Carving out a profitable share of the monies redistributed by the racetrack at the conclusion of each event is much more difficult for reasons of the public's demonstrated excellence in judging horseflesh and the confiscatory tax levied on the winners known as the "take." In order to turn a profit, we must discover those conditions, if such exist, under which favorable bets may arise and a means of detecting them prior to the running of the race. Referring to our expectation formula,

$$E_i = \frac{P_i}{p_i}(1 - f) - 1$$

a favorable bet crops up only when the public's probability, p_i, underestimates the true winning probability of a horse, P_i, (p_i is less than P_i) by an amount sufficient to make E_i positive. On average, E_i is negative for all horses, except possibly for very strongly bet favorites, but it is less negative for favorites than for the other horses. Consequently, any errors of judgment made by the public in isolated instances will most likely produce more opportunities for favorable bets on favorites than on the other choices. Our considerations, therefore, are limited initially to the selection of favorites.

We postulate the existence of races in which the public has erred sufficiently in determining the winning probability of the favorites to make those horses favorable bets. Counterbalancing these races must be others in which the winning probability of the favorites has been overestimated, so that overall there is an expected loss per dollar bet. The central problem is to filter out the favorable races from the noise background of all races to be run in the future. It should be clear by now that such races cannot be selected without the use of late-breaking information, which is why the closing odds are so vital. A bettor who has delayed his wager until just before the close of betting reaps the advantage of knowing the public's opinion of each of the horses in the race. Yet, the vast majority, having already committed their money, cannot make use of this information to properly adjust the odds in the minute or two before the race is run.

The theory of favorable bets, or "overlays" as they are known in racetrack parlance, is best illustrated by an actual race, the Manhattan Handicap held at Belmont Park, New York, 29 September 1976. In Figure 10-1 the first three columns are part of the usual result charts found in the daily newspapers, while the last two have been added for our purposes. Teddy's Courage, Keep the Promise, and Don Lorenzo are coupled in the wagering as a single race entry called the "field" so that a bet on the field wins if any one of these three horses wins. The probabilities add up to one, which means simply that one of the horses is certain to win. The numbers $1/(o_i + 1)$ are known as the "percentages" and would equal the public's winning probabilities p_i if the "take" were zero. This may be seen from the formula

$$p_i = \frac{1 - f}{o_i + 1}$$

derived in the appendix to Chapter 6 with $f = 0$. (o_i represents the odds on the ith horse in the race). The p_i's were calculated from another formula derived there

$$p_i = \frac{\dfrac{1}{o_i + 1}}{S}$$

where S is the sum of the percentages and equals 1.2154 in this example. Thus Caucasus' probability of winning as determined by the public was .2632/1.2154,

Figure 10-1. Result of the Manhattan Handicap, Belmont Park, New York, 29 September 1976

Horse	Finish	Dollar Odds	"Percentages" $\dfrac{1}{o_i + 1}$	Public's Probability of Winning
Caucasus	1	2.80	.2632	.2165
Trumpeter Swan	2	6.90	.1266	.1041
Kamaraan II	3	6.50	.1333	.1097
Top Crowd	4	45.00	.0217	.0179
Amata	5	60.20	.0163	.0134
Recupere	6	27.50	.0351	.0289
Improviser	7	4.50	.1818	.1496
Erwin Boy	8	3.30	.2325	.1913
Break Up The Game	9	14.60	.0641	.0527
Teddy's Courage	10	f-7.60 ⎱		
Keep The Promise	11	f-7.60 ⎰	.1163	.0957
Don Lorenzo	12	f-7.60		
Hail The Pirates	13	39.70	.0245	.0202
			1.2154	1.0000

which equals .2165 or 21.65 percent; Trumpeter Swan's winning probability was .1266/1.2154 = .1041, or 10.41 percent; and so on. The public thinks that if this race were repeated many times under the same conditions, Caucasus would win about 21 times in every 100 races, Trumpeter Swan about 10 races in every 100, and so on. Or, generalizing this statement, the public thinks that all horses off at dollar odds of $2.80 will win about 21 races in every 100, horses off at dollar odds of $6.90 will win about 10 races in every 100, and so on. If the public is correct in its thinking, the bettor's expectation is the loss of the "take." Since the public consistently underestimates the winning probabilities of favorites, however, the expectation of a wager on Caucasus is a smaller loss than the take, or something less than seventeen cents on the dollar, which prevails in New York at this writing.

Under what conditions could a bet on Caucasus be favorable? Suppose late information suggested to us, however implausible it may seem at this point of the discussion, that the next four choices in the betting, Trumpeter Swan, Kamaraan II, Improviser, and Erwin Boy each had zero probability of winning instead of the probabilities assigned to them by the public. We claim, in other words, that the public erred in judging this race and that the table should look like Figure 10-2.

The dollar odds on the four horses with zero win probabilities are no longer related either to the percentages or the probabilities of winning. The winning probability for Caucasus is calculated as before except that the reduced sum of the percentages is used—p = .2632/.5412 = .4863 or 48.63 percent, which is much larger than the 21.65 percent of the public. Our expectation from a bet on

Figure 10-2. Result Chart of the Manhattan Handicap with System Probabilities Instead of the Public's Probabilities

Horse	Finish	Dollar Odds	System Percentage	System Probability of Winning
Caucasus	1	2.80	.2632	.4863
Trumpeter Swan	2	6.90	0	0
Kamaraan II	3	6.50	0	0
Top Crowd	4	45.00	.0217	.0401
Amata	5	60.20	.0163	.0301
Recupere	6	27.50	.0351	.0649
Improviser	7	4.50	0	0
Erwin Boy	8	3.30	0	0
Break Up The Game	9	14.60	.0641	.1184
Teddy's Courage	10	f-7.60		
Keep The Promise	11	f-7.60	.1163	.2149
Don Lorenzo	12	f-7.60		
Hail The Pirates	13	39.70	.0245	.0453
			.5412	1.0000

Caucasus, using the expectation formula $E = Po + (1 - P)(-\$1)$ and assuming our probability to be the true probability, is now

$$E = .4863 \times \$2.80 + .5137(-\$1) = +0.85$$

or eighty-five cents, instead of the public's expectation of minus seventeen cents. This result is also obtained using another form for the expectation derived in the appendix to Chapter 6,

$$E = 1/S - 1 = 1/.5412 - 1 = +0.85.$$

If we are right and the public wrong, we expect to make a profit on bets like this of eighty-five cents on every dollar. Wagers on the other horses in the race with non-zero win probabilities may have positive expectations also, but our considerations for now are limited to favorites.

Who is right? Was the win probability estimated by the public or ours closest to the true and unknown win probability? The question cannot be answered until the nature of the late-breaking information that caused us to assign zero probabilities of winning to four of the horses in the race is assessed. All we have seen thus far is a strictly mathematical procedure for discovering a favorable bet which has yet to be related to reality.

The basic principle that enables us to assign zero win probabilities to certain horses (from my earlier published works, it is called the Principle of Maximum Confusion) is now proposed: The betting public is most likely to err in determining the winning probability of the favorite in those races wherein the historical record of the favorite is surprisingly similar or inferior to that of one or more other horses in the race. Why isn't one of those other horses the favorite? is the question that must be asked. And the answer is to be found, obviously, in the existence of information not generally available in the past performances of the horses. Because the favorite and the other horses appear very much alike on the surface, or the favorite even appears inferior, we assume that many bettors, unaware of hidden factors, opt for the bigger payoff available on longer odds horses, thereby making those horses overbet and the favorite underbet. In the converse case, where one horse has a record outstanding in every respect relative to its competition, it is certain that its superlative attributes will not be lost on the public. Bets on this type of favorite will surely have a negative expectation.

Our program is this: Using an adequate sample of past races, calculate the expectations of the favorites when the probabilities of winning of those horses whose records are similar or superior to the favorite are taken as zero, exactly as was done in the above example. Any number other than zero could be used, but zero makes the calculations easier. Since no horse in a race ever has a zero win probability, our expectation will not conform to the true expectation. If, however, our basic premise is correct, there will be a certain cutoff in our set of expectations from all the races considered above which the favorite will present a favorable bet and below which it will not. In the sample studied in my book *Horse Sense*, the cutoff appeared at $E = +0.32$; favorites with expectations greater than or equal to $+0.32$ were favorable bets, whereas those with less were not. In this book, the cutoff will be different, both because of different rules for evaluating the historical record and the higher "takes" characteristic of today's racing.

The fundamental problem now is to spell out the conditions in the historical record of the horses which make today's closing odds surprising. Such is defined to be the case when the favorite is "similar" to another choice, similar meaning that the past performances of the two horses satisfy certain Rules of Similarity. If these rules hold, the longer odds horse is assigned a zero winning probability.

Referring to our example, we shall see that the favorite Caucasus is "similar" to Trumpeter Swan, Kamaraan II, Improviser, and Erwin Boy by the Rules of Similarity. Therefore, Caucasus is an underbet favorite to our way of thinking with a positive expectation of $+0.85$. The fact that Caucasus happened to win this one race proves nothing. Only if the actual won and lost records of a sufficiently large sample of favorites with $E_{system} = +0.85$ shows a profit will our system receive support.

Because of their somewhat technical nature, I shall defer consideration of the Rules of Similarity and related betting strategies until the next two chapters and pass immediately to the results obtained on two samples of thoroughbred races run in the United States during the period from 1974 to 1977. The first sample comprises 649 races run in the years 1974, 1975, and 1976, the second, 593 races run in 1977 just as this book was nearing completion. Figure 10-3 gives the pertinent data for all favorites. The percentage of winning favorites is near the norm obtained for much larger samples by many people over the years, although the return on sample I (-20.5%) is greater than the take and indicates overbetting of favorites. Such sample-to-sample fluctuations in the percentage return are not uncommon for these numbers of races. The generally higher losses on these fa-

Figure 10-3. Performance Data of All Favorites in Two Race Samples

	Total Number of Races	Number of Winning Favorites	% of Winning Favorites	Return from $1 Flat Bets on All Favorites	% Return
Sample I	649	199	30.7%	-$132.90	-20.5%
Sample II	593	196	33.1%	-$ 82.60	-13.9%

Figure 10-4. Performance Data of System Favorites

	Number of System Bets on Favorites	Number of Winners	% Winners	Return on $1 Flat Bets on System Favorites	System % Return
Sample I	192	128	66.7%	+$157.20	+81.9%
Sample II	226	118	52.2%	+$ 97.00	+42.9%

vorites compared to those shown in Chapter 6 arise because of the greater take lately.

The system choices fared as shown in Figure 10-4, still considering only the post favorites. The results speak for themselves: the system's percentage winners and the rate of return appear truly remarkable, a profit over 80 percent of the amount bet in sample I and almost 43 percent in sample II. But before rushing out to the races in quest of a fortune, we had better subject the results to a proper statistical analysis in order to ascertain whether or not they were nothing more than lucky streaks not likely to recur in the future. Such will be done shortly, but first let us look at the results for the second choices. And finally, the results for third choices in the betting, which point marks the system's state of the art at the present time:

The returns on second and third choices are even higher than for the favorites, but note the long time intervals between wagers. On average, there will be one bet on a second choice in every seven races, whereas on third choices, there will be one bet in every thirteen races. For favorites, the frequency of betting averages to one wager in every three races. Altogether, a system bet will occur on average in one out of every two races.

A more detailed breakdown of the results for each value of the system expectation E_{system} is given in the table in Figure 10-7.

The magic number for the system expectation, the value that spells the difference between profit and loss, is fairly sharply defined at $E_{system} = 0.43$. Those

Figure 10-5. Performance Data of System Second Choices

	Number of System Bets on Second Choices	Number of Winners	% Winners	Return on $1 Flat Bets on System Second Choices	% Return on Second Choices
Sample I	103	60	58.3%	+$121.60	+118%
Sample II	73	38	52.1%	+$ 64.20	+ 88%

Figure 10-6. Performance Data of System Third Choices

	Number of System Bets on Third Choices	Number of Winners	% Winners	Return on $1 Flat Bets on System Third Choices	% Return on Third Choices
Sample I	59	31	52.5%	+$107.50	+182%
Sample II	34	17	50.0%	+$ 48.80	+144%

favorites with a system expectation less than 0.43 are very unfavorable bets. In the great majority of these latter races, the favorite is a standout when compared to the other horses in the race, and their excellence is not lost on the crowd, which proceeds to overbet them on the basis of the incomplete data in the past performances. Those favorites with system expectations of 0.43 and higher are

Figure 10-7. Performance Data of All Favorites According to the System Expectation E_{system}

SAMPLE I FAVORITES

E_{system}	Number of Favorites	Number of Winners	% Winners	Return on $1 Flat Bets	% Return
0 and less	249	32	12.9%	-$172.10	-69.1%
0.01 to 0.10	62	14	22.6%	-28.60	-46.1%
0.11 to 0.20	55	7	12.7%	-40.20	-73.1%
0.21 to 0.30	42	6	14.3%	-29.10	-69.3%
0.31 to 0.40	41	9	22.0%	-19.00	-46.3%
0.41 to 0.42	8	3	37.5%	-1.10	-13.8%
0.43	10	7	70.0%	+6.70	+67.0%
0.44 to 0.45	8	7	87.5%	+7.60	+95.0%
0.46 to 0.59	52	33	63.5%	+30.50	+58.7%
0.60 and up	122	81	66.4%	+112.40	+92.1%
All favorites	649	199	30.7%	-$132.90	-20.5%

SAMPLE II FAVORITES

E_{system}	Number of Favorites	Number of Winners	% Winners	Return on $1 Flat Bets	% Return
0 and less	125	23	18.4%	-$65.70	-52.6%
0.01 to 0.10	70	18	25.7%	-22.70	-32.4%
0.11 to 0.20	52	10	19.2%	-30.00	-57.7%
0.21 to 0.30	75	16	21.3%	-39.40	-52.5%
0.31 to 0.40	35	9	25.7%	-17.50	-50.0%
0.41 to 0.42	10	2	20.0%	-4.30	-43.0%
0.43	9	4	44.4%	+1.00	+11.1%
0.44 to 0.45	12	7	58.3%	+5.60	+46.7%
0.46 to 0.59	55	24	43.6%	+7.00	+12.7%
0.60 and up	150	83	55.3%	+83.40	+55.6%
All favorites	593	196	33.1%	-$82.60	-13.9%

favorable bets and are for the most part favorites with no obvious superiority over other animals in the race. They are favorites on the basis of hidden evidence not available in the published record.

Similar tables follow for the second choices, excluding races in which the favorite is a system bet, and for the third choices, excluding races in which the favorite or the second choice is a system bet.

The data is somewhat thin about the system expectation +0.43, but choosing this value for the line of demarcation between favorable and unfavorable wagers is not inconsistent with the results shown for all the first three choices. More conservative bettors may wish to limit their wagers to those races where E_{system} is +0.60 and up. It is noteworthy that the return on all second choices for those races in which the favorite is not a system bet ($E_{system\ favorites}$ is less than

Figure 10-8. Performance Data of All Second Choices According to the System Expectation E_{system}, Excluding Races in which the Favorite Is a System Bet

SAMPLE I SECOND CHOICES

E_{system}	Number of Second Choices	Number of Winners	% Winners	Return on $1 Flat Bets	% Return
0 and less	220	44	20.0%	−$39.80	−18.1%
0.01 to 0.10	36	3	8.3%	−25.00	−69.4%
0.11 to 0.20	37	7	18.9%	−5.60	−15.1%
0.21 to 0.30	31	1	3.2%	−27.40	−88.4%
0.31 to 0.40	25	5	20.0%	−3.80	−15.2%
0.41 to 0.42	5	1	20.0%	−1.40	−28.0%
0.43	4	2	50.0%	+5.00	+125%
0.44 to 0.45	6	4	66.7%	+11.00	+183%
0.46 to 0.59	25	13	52.0%	+25.10	+100%
0.60 and up	68	41	60.3%	+80.50	+118%
All second choices	457	121	26.5%	+$18.60	+4.1%

SAMPLE II SECOND CHOICES

E_{system}	Number of Second Choices	Number of Winners	% Winners	Return on $1 Flat Bets	% Return
0 and less	140	23	16.4%	−$37.00	−26.4%
0.01 to 0.10	52	7	13.5%	−26.50	−51.0%
0.11 to 0.20	31	5	16.1%	−6.90	−22.3%
0.21 to 0.30	40	6	15.0%	−10.60	−26.5%
0.31 to 0.40	27	3	11.1%	−14.90	−55.2%
0.41 to 0.42	4	0	0%	−4.00	−100%
0.43	1	0	0%	−1.00	−100%
0.44 to 0.45	4	1	25.0%	+1.20	+30.0%
0.46 to 0.59	21	9	42.9%	+15.80	+75.2%
0.60 and up	47	28	59.6%	+51.30	+109%
All second choices	367	82	22.3%	−$32.60	−8.9%

Figure 10-9. Performance Data of All Third Choices According to the System Expectation E_{system}, Excluding Races in which the Favorite or the Second Choice Is a System Bet

SAMPLE I THIRD CHOICES

E_{system}	Number of Third Choices	Number of Winners	% Winners	Return on $1 Flat Bets	% Return
0 and less	194	30	15.5%	−$5.80	−3.0%
0.01 to 0.10	23	4	17.4%	−3.00	−13.0%
0.11 to 0.20	27	5	18.5%	+.70	+2.6%
0.21 to 0.30	25	3	12.0%	−12.40	−49.6%
0.31 to 0.40	22	5	22.7%	+8.30	+37.7%
0.41 to 0.42	4	2	50.0%	+6.90	+173%
0.43	1	0	0%	−1.00	−100%
0.44 to 0.45	2	0	0%	−2.00	−100%
0.46 to 0.59	22	11	50.0%	+40.30	+183%
0.60 and up	34	20	58.8%	+70.10	+206%
All Third Choices	354	80	22.6%	+$102.10	+28.8%

SAMPLE II THIRD CHOICES

E_{system}	Number of Third Choices	Number of Winners	% Winners	Return on $1 Flat Bets	% Return
0 and less	155	22	14.2%	−$22.70	−14.6%
0.01 to 0.10	31	3	9.7%	−13.30	−42.9%
0.11 to 0.20	22	4	18.2%	+1.90	+8.6%
0.21 to 0.30	36	3	8.3%	−19.50	−54.2%
0.31 to 0.40	13	0	0%	−13.00	−100%
0.41 to 0.42	3	1	33.3%	+2.70	+90.0%
0.43	2	0	0%	−2.00	−100%
0.44 to 0.45	2	0	0%	−2.00	−100%
0.46 to 0.59	7	2	28.6%	+1.90	+27.1%
0.60 and up	23	15	65.2%	+51.30	+223%
All Third Choices	294	50	17.0%	−$14.70	−5.0%

+0.43) is near break-even, positive for sample I and negative for sample II, whereas the return for all third choices in those races for which neither the favorite nor the second choice is a system bet is a positive 28.8 percent for sample I and only a slightly negative 5.0 percent for sample II. Lastly, in those races where both the favorite and the second choice are system bets, a bet on the second choice is extremely unfavorable.

It appears as if we have successfully plucked from two random samples of races only those races offering favorable wagers on the first three choices in the betting. Now we must test the validity of the system, or, in other words, discover what the chances are that somebody picking blindly from these two samples could produce results as favorable as ours. If the chances are good, then our results probably arose from pure luck alone, and the system has demonstrated no claim to serious consideration by others. If, by contrast, it can be shown that a person selecting blindly has little chance of reproducing our results, the validity of the system receives important support.

We proceed by combining samples I and II and classifying the results according to the dollar odds, as in the table in Figure 10-10. All favorites having a system expectation of +0.43 and higher comprise the right-hand side of the table. The far right-hand column, *Expected number of winners ± 2 s.d.'s*, is the range of winners to be anticipated when a person selects blindly a sample of the size given in the column headed *Number of system bets*. Thus, from the 158 races with odds-on favorites (those off at odds less than even money), our system chose 45 for betting and 26 won. Assuming the favorite win percentage of 51.3 percent for the 158 races is close to the true probability of winning for all odds-on favorites, we should expect that a system that has no validity whatsoever would obtain 23 winning favorites in a 45-race sample ($0.513 \times 45 = 23$) with a standard deviation of 3.4 (s.d. = $\sqrt{45 \times 0.513 \times 0.487} = 3.4$). With a 95-percent probability, therefore, the number of winning favorites should fall in the range 23 ± 2 s.d.'s, or between 16 and 30 winners for any 45-race sample when the 45 races are chosen randomly. Our system, then, in picking only 26 races with winning favorites out of 45 has not demonstrated any extraordinary powers of selection for odds-on favorites. Whether or not the system works for this type of favorite is indeterminate at this juncture.

When the favorites in the longer odds categories are considered, however, the situation changes dramatically. In each of the five remaining odds categories, the number of races selected with winning favorites lies far above the expected range, so much so that the probability of doing this by blind luck alone is much less than 1 chance in 1,000, much less even than throwing ten heads in a row flip-

Figure 10-10. Performance and Expectation Data on All Favorites According to the Dollar Odds

	ALL FAVORITES			SYSTEM FAVORITES		
Dollar Odds	Number of Races	Number of Winning Favorites	% Wins	Number of System Bets	Number of Winners	Expected Number of Winners ±2 s.d.'s
Odds-on	158	81	51.3%	45	26	23 ± 7
1.0–1.5	317	121	38.2%	121	80	46 ± 11
1.6–1.9	238	78	32.8%	101	57	33 ± 9
2.0–2.4	284	63	22.2%	96	49	21 ± 8
2.5–2.9	160	35	21.9%	39	23	9 ± 5
3.0 and up	85	17	20.0%	16	11	3 ± 3
Totals	1242	395	31.8%	418	246	133 ± 19

ping a fair coin. It is almost impossible to accomplish such a feat without some sort of legerdemain, that is, a valid system.

Another, more sophisticated test is known as the "chi-square" test. Chi-square (χ^2) is a single number that sums up succinctly the goodness-of-fit between sets of results derived from two models of reality. Applied to our data, it measures the extent of agreement between the number of winning favorites obtained by random selection (the strongly efficient market model) and the number of winning favorites obtained using our system (a weakly efficient market model). If the agreement is good, our system is worthless and a person using it no better off than a person selecting blindly. If the agreement is poor, the strongly efficient market is not a good representation of reality. The numerical value of χ^2 may be found from the last two columns in Figure 10-10:

$$\chi^2 = \frac{(26-23)^2}{23} + \frac{(80-46)^2}{46} + \frac{(57-33)^2}{33} + \frac{(49-21)^2}{21} + \frac{(23-9)^2}{9} + \frac{(11-3)^2}{3}$$

$$= 123.4$$

This value, when looked up in a chi-square table using 6 degrees of freedom corresponding to our 6 categories, has an infinitesimal probability of occurrence (much less than 1 chance in 1,000) when selections are made at random. It is very unlikely, therefore, that our system's results came about through lucky stabs. The chi-square test undermines the strongly efficient market model of pari-mutuel betting and supports our system of selection based on the weakly efficient market model. The same conclusion must be drawn when chi-square is applied to the second- and third-choice results.

Further support for our system arises from its general similarity to the one I reported earlier in *Horse Sense*, which was tested on completely different samples by myself and by many of my readers who realized analogous results.

11
THE RULES OF SIMILARITY

How hard to collect
The thousand fragments
Of each and every horse!

Paraphrase on lines by Giorgos Seferiades

From our point of view, races in which the past performances of all the horses appear identical make for the most favorable wagering opportunities on favorites, since the public must then choose a favorite on the basis of hidden and late-breaking information. In contrast, all other systems of which I am aware try to pick a winner through an interpretation of the published record supposedly superior to that of the public consensus. None of them is profitable. Not even the consumption of huge amounts of computer time has availed to outdo the public's judgment in weighting the numerous factors entering into a horse race. In this chapter, we concern ourselves with these same factors, but only to discover under what conditions different horses appear alike to the public.

Some idea of the nature of the historical record may be gathered from the compressed form of the past performances of the horses that I have adopted in this book, which abstracts key elements of the more complete record published every racing day in the *Daily Racing Form*. Learning to read this newspaper is an indispensable prerequisite for applying the system to be presented.*

Sample past performance lines on a fictitious horse follow:

Power Horse: 30 Oct 77-1 Key 7f Clm 3500 114 2 (filly)
23Oct77-2Key 7f Clm 3500 7^8 1no 112 5.10 11
15Oct77-9Key $1\frac{1}{16}$ Clm 3500 4 $4^{2\frac{1}{2}}$ $8^{7\frac{1}{2}}$ 113 20.20 10
13Aug77-1Atl 7f Clm 3000 10^{12} 3^{nk} 115 17.30 12

Following along line by line, Power Horse is the name of the horse entered in today's race, which is to be run on 30 October 1977 as the first at Keystone at the seven-furlong distance and at a claiming price of $3,500 (explained below).

---

*The *Daily Racing Form* publishes in its regular editions a detailed explanation of the data in the past performances. A wealth of background information and an exposition of typical handicapping methods is contained in Tom Ainslie, *Ainslie's Complete Guide to Thoroughbred Racing* (New York: Trident Press, 1968).

Power Horse carries 114 pounds including the jockey and its closing odds as shown on the "tote" are two to one. The horse is a filly, a fact that will be noted only when a female is pitted against males. The second line shows that the horse last raced on 23 October 1977 in the second race at Keystone at a distance of seven furlongs in a $3,500 claiming race. Its position at the quarter-mile call of that race (two furlongs from the start) was seventh, eight lengths off the leader, and it finished first, a nose ahead of the second-place finisher. The weight carried in that race was 112 pounds, the closing dollar odds were $5.10, and eleven horses competed. Its previous race was on 15 October 1977 in the ninth race at Keystone at a distance of $1\frac{1}{16}$ miles in a $3,500 claiming event. It was fourth at the quarter-mile call; fourth at the half mile call ($\frac{1}{2}$ mile or four furlongs from the start), $2\frac{1}{2}$ lengths off the leader; and eighth, $7\frac{1}{2}$ lengths off the winner, at the finish. The interpretation of the rest of this line and the following line, where the finish was third, a neck behind the winner, should be clear. In races of one mile or more, the two calls shown, the quarter-mile and half-mile, are both utilized by the system.

To keep horses of comparable ability competing against one another and to ensure interesting race programs, a free-market classification of horses in the form of what is known as the claiming system serves effectively. The claiming price is the price at which a horse entered in a claiming race may be bought or claimed from the owner. Thus an owner is not likely to enter a horse in a race against animals of lesser ability (a lower claiming price) for fear of losing it at too low a price. By the same token, if the horse is entered in a race with too high a claiming price, it stands little chance of winning the purse. Higher class horses are entered in allowance and handicap races where the horses cannot be claimed. The highest class horses are those running in stakes and name handicaps, like the Kentucky Derby and the Suburban Handicap. Further details are contained under *class* in the definitions appended to this chapter.

With this brief introduction into the manner of presentation of the historical records of race horses, we are ready to consider the Rules of Similarity for post time favorites. They are divided into two sections, A and B, each with a number of subdivisions. Section A specifies certain rules under which the favorite is not to be bet. This set of rules is a consequence of recent research that has uncovered a major inefficiency in the pari-mutuel market and deals with the position of a horse during the early running of a race. Briefly, a horse that tends to lag behind in the early running may be disadvantaged to an extent unappreciated by the betting public. Although it is well known that a come-from-behind horse is more apt to suffer bad racing luck than a front-running horse (and the odds usually reflect this knowledge), I contend in addition that slow starts may be indicative of unsuspected poor physical condition or of inferior class.

Section B compares the favorite with other horses in the race, and its objective is to ascertain the extent of similarity in the historical record. Both sections are a decided improvement over previously published rules. It should be noted that there is nothing unique about these Rules of Similarity, and it is quite possible that more effective rules may be developed in the future.

A few remarks about the presentation are appropriate. Our everyday means of communication are beset with ambiguities, and every discipline has had to define and redefine its language in order to come to grips with reality. Such is the case here. To prevent the details of the system from becoming too wordy and murky, I have introduced for the sake of brevity certain words and phrases, indicated by italics when they first appear and collected in an appendix at the end of this chapter, which are to have the meanings assigned to them and no other. These definitions must be understood to apply the Rules of Similarity, although their general meaning will be clear enough on a first reading.

A full discussion of the Rules of Similarity, complete with explanations and examples, follows. The reader will also find the rules alone in the appendix to this chapter. It is intended that in the form presented there the rules will be accessible and useful to the bettor who has fully acquainted himself with the system and the part the rules play in it but who needs a quick and ready reference to the rules at the time he is betting.

RULES OF SIMILARITY

Section A—Rules under which the Favorite Is not to Be Bet

Rule 1. The favorite satisfies all the following conditions:

    a. It made a *slow start* in its last and *recent* race

    b. It did not win *easily* in its last race or in its *previous* race less than thirty-two days ago

    c. It did not show a *sharp drop in class* or, if today's race is not a stakes race, run in a stakes race in its last three starts

    d. It has started at least once at the present *meeting*

    e. It did not finish first or second in its only start at the present meeting

and one or more of the following:

    aa. The favorite's last race was lower in *class* than its previous race, or its previous race showed a slow start and was lower in class than its *pre-previous* race, but not if today's race is a *route* and its last or previous race the only *sprint* in its last four races

    bb. Today's race is a sprint and the favorite's last was a nonwinning route or its previous race was a nonwinning route with a slow start

    cc. Today's race is a route, the favorite's last race was a nonwinning route and its previous race a sprint, or its previous race was a nonwinning route with a slow start and its pre-previous race a sprint, but not if the sprint race was the only sprint in its last four starts

dd. The favorite's last race was lower in class than today's race, or its previous race showed a slow start and was lower in class than today's race, or its previous and pre-previous races showed slow starts and the pre-previous race was lower in class than today's race, but not if today's race is a route and its last a sprint

ee. Today's race is a sprint and the favorite's last was a nonwinning race, its previous race a route, and its pre-previous race a sprint with a slow start in class less than that of today's race

ff. The favorite's last race was at odds equal to or shorter than its previous race in which it made a *fast start*, or the favorite showed a slow start and a finish of third or worse in its previous race at shorter odds than its pre-previous race in which it made a fast start

Rule 2. Today's race is longer than the favorite's last and recent race or its last at the meeting in which it made a slow start, or today's race distance is longer than or equal to the favorite's last and recent race in which it made a slow start and longer than its previous and recent or at-the-meeting race, but not if today's race is a route, its last a sprint with a finish five or more lengths off the winner, and its previous race a route, or if its last race was in class more than 25 percent higher than today's race (but not if today's race is a starter or optional claiming race), or if the favorite's last race was not run at the present meeting. (In Rule 2, neglect changes in route races of less than $\frac{1}{16}$ mile. Also, the following distances are assumed to be equivalent: $5\frac{1}{2}$ furlongs on turf and 6 furlongs on dirt; 7 or $7\frac{1}{2}$ furlongs on turf and 1 mile, 1 mile 70 yards, or $1\frac{1}{16}$ miles on dirt; 1 or $1\frac{1}{16}$ on turf and $1\frac{1}{8}$ miles on dirt).

Rule 3. The favorite satisfies the following conditions:

a. Today's race is a sprint

b. The favorite's last and recent race was a nonwinning route with a fast start in class not more than 25 percent higher than today's race;

c. The favorite has started at least once at the present meeting

and either one of the following:

aa. The favorite made a slow start in its previous race in lower class than its pre-previous race

bb. The favorite made a slow start in its previous race at odds shorter than or equal to its pre-previous race in which it made a fast start

(NOTE: Rule 1c does not apply if today's race is a starter or optional claiming race. Rules 1aa, 1dd, and 3aa do not apply to past starter and optional claiming races).

Several examples will clarify the intent of the Rules of Section A. They should be carefully studied by professionally oriented readers.

Example 1:

One Horse: 22 Dec 77-1	Aqu	6f	Clm 5000		115	9/5	
12Dec77-2Aqu 6f Clm 5000			6^5		2no	114	3.50	10
5Dec77-3Aqu 6f Clm 6000			8^4		7^7	114	9.00	8
30Nov77-1Aqu 6f Clm 6000			4^3		6^8	113	8.10	9

One Horse is a favorite not to be bet according to Rule 1 of Section A: The conditions of subsections a–e are fulfilled, and it is easily seen that subsection aa applies since the last race shows a slow start in lower class than the previous race. Such a drop in class, combined with the horse's inability to get off to a fast start against supposedly inferior animals, raises a question as to where the horse belongs and suggests more uncertainty than the odds reflect.

Example 2:

Two Horse: 22 Dec 77-2	Aqu	6f	Clm 5000		115	9/5	
12Dec77-4Aqu 6f Clm 5000			7^4		3^1	115	4.00	11
5Dec77-4Aqu 6f Clm 5000			10^8		5^6	114	3.60	10
30Nov77-9Aqu 6f Clm 6000			7^6		7^5	114	9.70	8

Subsections a–e are satisfied, as is aa, since the previous race shows a slow start in lower class than the pre-previous race. Two Horse is, therefore, a favorite not to be bet.

Example 3:

Three Horse: 22 Dec 77-3	Aqu	1	Clm 5000		115	9/5		
15Dec77-4Aqu 6f Clm 5000			7^4		6^9	115	12.00	10
8Dec77-4Aqu $1\frac{1}{16}$ Clm 5500		8	8^6	2^3	115	3.00	10
1Dec77-4Aqu $1\frac{1}{8}$ Clm 6000		4	5^4	1^1	115	9.50	9
22Oct77-5Bel $1\frac{1}{8}$ Clm 6000		5	6^5	2^2	115	4.60	6

Subsection aa of Rule 1 is not satisfied since today's race is a one-mile route and the last race was the only sprint in the last four races. Three Horse is a possible bet, but it first must be checked against all the other rules of Section A. The reader should verify that none of them apply. Here, the one sprint race was likely a conditioner and gives no hint of the horse's potential.

Example 4:

Four Horse: 22 Dec 77-5 Med 6f Clm 6500 112 2

1Dec77-2Med	$1\frac{1}{16}$	Clm 7500	6	6^5	2^{nk}	112	2.50	9
22Nov77-9Med	$1\frac{1}{8}$	Clm 7500	3	3^2	2^2	115	3.10	8
7Nov77-1Med	6f	Clm 7500	7^5		6^7	118	11.50	7

Rule 1, subsections a–e and bb apply, and this favorite is not to be bet. Also, subsection ff of Rule 1 applies since the favorite shows a slow start in its last race at shorter odds than in its previous race, in which it made a fast start. A slow start in a route race is indicative of an even slower start against fast breaking sprinters, yet this disadvantage is not properly accounted for in the odds.

Example 5:

Five Horse: 22 Dec 77-8 Med 6f Clm 6500 112 5/2

12Dec77-1Med	6f	Clm 7500	6^5		3^1	112	7.60	9
3Dec77-9Med	$1\frac{1}{16}$	Clm 7500	6	4^3	$4^{4\frac{1}{2}}$	114	5.80	9
27Aug77-1Mth	6f	Clm 8000	4^3		1^{nk}	118	4.00	10

Rule 1, a–e and bb apply since the previous race was a nonwinning route with a slow start. The favorite is not to be bet. Note that aa is also satisfied because of the class drop from the pre-previous to the previous race.

Example 6:

Six Horse: 22 Dec 77-1 Lrl $1\frac{1}{16}$ Clm 4000 114 8/5

10Dec77-2Lrl	$1\frac{1}{16}$	Clm 4000	10	8^7	$2^{\frac{1}{2}}$	114	3.10	10
1Dec77-3Lrl	6f	Clm 4000	7^5		7^9	119	6.50	11
20Sep77-4Bow	7f	Clm 4000	4^4		3^1	120	5.90	8

Rule 1, a–e and cc are satisfied, and this favorite is not to be bet. A horse which cannot show a fast start against routers after running in sprints is likely to be out of condition.

Example 7:

Seven Horse: 22 Dec 77-1 Key 6f Clm 4000 117 6/5

16Dec77-1Key	6f	Clm 3500	7^5	1^1	114	3.50	9
9Dec77-2Key	6f	Clm 3500	6^4	3^1	114	5.20	7
2Dec77-3Key	6f	Clm 3500	5^5	2^2	114	6.10	8

Rule 1, a–e and dd apply, and the favorite is not to be bet. Races in which horses may be entered for a range of claiming prices are frequently run. For purposes of this rule, always compare the highest claiming price of today's race with the claiming price of the horse in its last race as shown in the past performance line.

Example 8 :

Eight Horse: 22 Dec 77-2	Key	6f	Clm 4000	117	6/5				
16Dec77-2Key	6f	Clm 4500		7^5		1^1	114	3.80	9
9Dec77-1Key	6f	Clm 3500		6^4		3^1	114	3.50	7
2Dec77-1Key	6f	Clm 3000		3^2		1^1	112	1.40	8

Rule 1, a–e and dd apply since the previous race shows a slow start in lower class than today's race. The favorite is no bet. Horses showing slow starts in lower class races are likely to be outclassed in higher company.

Example 9:

Nine Horse: 22 Dec 77-9	Key	6f	Clm 10000	118	2				
10Dec77-6Key	6f	Clm 10000		7^5		2no	118	5.00	8
1Nov77-7Key	$1\frac{1}{16}$	Clm 10000		3	3^2	4^4	118	6.70	9
21Oct77-7Key	6f	Clm 8000		8^5		$4^{2\frac{1}{2}}$	118	5.90	8

Rule 1, a–e and ee apply, and the favorite is not to be bet.

Example 10:

Ten Horse: 22 Dec 77-8	Aqu	6f	Allowance	118	2				
15Dec77-8Aqu	6f	Allowance		5^4		2^1	118	4.00	7
4Dec77-8Aqu	6f	Allowance		7^3		3^1	118	4.10	8
22Nov77-8Aqu	6f	Allowance		2^1		4^2	118	6.90	8

Rule 1, a–e and ff apply, and the favorite is not to be bet. A slow start after a fast start accompanied by dropping odds, which indicated that the public expected the horse to do better, is a disappointing performance not adequately factored into the betting.

Example 11:

Eleven Horse: 22 Dec 77-9	Aqu	7f	Allowance	120	2				
15Dec77-7Aqu	6f	Allowance		7^5		2^{nk}	120	3.20	7
1Dec77-7Aqu	6f	Allowance		6^4		3^1	122	6.40	7
2Jly77-7Bel	6f	Allowance		5^3		4^5	122	7.10	8

Rule 2 applies since today's race is longer than the last in which the favorite showed a slow start, and it is not to be bet. There is too much betting in obvious situations like this by people figuring the slow starter needs just a little more distance to win.

Example 12:

Twelve Horse:	22 Dec 77-8	Med	1^{70}		Allowance	119	5/2	
15Dec77-8Med	7f	Allowance	8^4		8^7	120	11.10	9
1Dec77-8Med	7f	Allowance	10^5		$3\frac{1}{2}$	122	21.10	12
10Nov77-7Med	6f	Allowance	7^8		7^{10}	120	30.50	7

Today's race at a distance of 1 mile 70 yards is longer than the last and longer than the previous and recent race in which the favorite finished third. Therefore, Rule 2 applies and the favorite is not to be bet.

Example 13:

Thirteen Horse:	22 Dec 77-1	Med	$1\frac{1}{16}$		Clm 3500	116	2	
15Dec77-1Med	6f	Clm 4500	10^9		8^9	116	6.40	10
1Dec77-9Med	$1\frac{1}{16}$	Clm 3500	4	4^3	2^2	116	4.90	9
30Oct77-2Med	$1\frac{1}{8}$	Clm 3500	5	4^5	4^3	116	3.20	10

Rule 2 does not apply here because today's race is a route, the last a sprint with a finish five or more lengths off the winner, and the previous race a route. Rule 2 also does not apply because the last race was in class more than 25 percent higher than today's race (4,500 is 28 percent higher than 3,500). The favorite is a possible bet since Rule 1 does not apply either.

Example 14:

Fourteen Horse:	4 Nov 77-1	Aqu	$1\frac{1}{16}$		Clm 15000	115	2	
25Oct77-1Aqu	$1\frac{1}{16}$	Clm 14000	8	8^{15}	$1^{3\frac{1}{2}}$	112	5.20	9
17Oct77-7Aqu	7f	Clm 15000	9^{13}		$3^{5\frac{1}{4}}$	114	6.10	10
3Oct77-6Bel	6f	Clm 14000	7^{10}		$4^{4\frac{1}{2}}$	114	3.60	7

Rule 1 does not apply since the favorite won its last race easily. However, Rule 2 does: Today's race is at the same distance as the last and longer than the previous and recent race. The favorite is not to be bet.

Example 15:

Fifteen Horse: 22 Dec 77-9   Lrl   6f   Clm 3500   114   3
16Dec77-1Lrl	$1\frac{1}{16}$	Clm 4000	3	2^2	5^6	114	4.00	8
10Dec77-2Lrl	6f	Clm 3500	6^6		3^3	114	5.60	8
2Dec77-3Lrl	6f	Clm 4000	5^4		3^4	116	8.90	12

The conditions of Rule 3, a and b are fulfilled, as are 3, aa and bb. Since it is
only necessary for either 3aa or 3bb to apply, the favorite is not to be bet.

These rules will be covered again in the next chapter's analyses of actual races.
Now we turn our attention to Section B of the Rules of Similarity. If a favorite
is not to be bet by Section A, Section B need not be considered. Those favorites
eligible for wagers by Section A are to be compared for similarity with other
choices in the race using the rules of Section B. The presentation of each rule
of Section B will be followed by several fictitious examples designed to illustrate
each rule as concisely as possible.

SECTION B—Rules under which the Favorite Is Similar to Another Horse

Rule 1. Last race finishes the same

> The favorite ran a *poor last race*, is *equivalent in class* to the other horse,
> finished in the same position as the other horse in its last race, and is
> not a *router-in-sprint*, but a *normal or soft betting pattern* must exist if
> the other horse did not run its last race in *class Z* and one or more of
> the following conditions hold:
> a. The other horse ran more than twenty-one days ago
> b. The favorite has run at the present *meeting* and the other has not
> c. Today's race is a *route* race and the favorite is a *sprouter* or *router*
>   and the other horse a *sprinter*
> d. There is a nine-pound or more *relative weight shift* in favor of the
>   favorite
> e. The favorite is a male and the other horse a female

Example 1: 22 Aug 77-1   Sar   6f   Clm 5000

Favorite: 117   5/2
15Aug77-1Sar	6f	Clm 5000	4^3	5^5	113	4.80	9
9Aug77-2Sar	6f	Clm 5000	3^1	$5^{2\frac{1}{4}}$	113	6.50	10
2Aug77-1Sar	6f	Clm 5000	2^{nk}	3^3	114	9.40	8

Second choice: 122 5/2

16Aug77-2Sar 6f Clm 5000	1^1	$5^{4\frac{1}{2}}$	114	3.70	9
6Aug77-9Sar 6f Clm 5000	2^1	4^4	118	4.20	10
21Jun77-1Bel 6f Clm 5000	$2^{\frac{1}{2}}$	3^1	119	2.70	10

Third choice: 117 4 (filly)

15Aug77-2Sar 6f Clm 5000	3^3	$5^{7\frac{1}{4}}$	112	5.10	8
9Aug77-2Sar 6f Clm 5000	$5^{3\frac{1}{2}}$	13^{11}	113	7.60	14
27Jly77-3Aqu 6f Clm 5000	4^2	1^1	115	3.70	11

Fourth choice: 117 9/2

23Jly77-1Del 6f Clm 5000	1^1	$5^{2\frac{1}{2}}$	116	2.40	10
11Jly77-2Del 6f Clm 5000	2^{nk}	7^6	115	4.00	10
3Jly77-3Del 6f Clm 5000	1^2	1^{nk}	114	2.00	10

The notation has been changed slightly by putting the specifications of today's race on the line above the favorite. In this hypothetical race at Saratoga, a few hundred dollars more is bet on the favorite than the second choice even though the "tote" odds on both horses are 5/2. Totalizator boards display only approximate odds, and 5/2 denotes a dollar odds range from $2.50 to $2.90. A bettor wishing to know the favorite must look at the money bet on the two horses in the win pool, also shown.

When deciding whether or not the favorite is to be bet in a race, one must first check its record against Section A. In a race like this, where the favorite shows a fast start in its last and recent race, Rules 1 and 2 of Section A do not apply, and Rule 3 may apply only if its last and recent race was a route. It should be clear that Section A need not be considered in this race, and the favorite may now be compared with the other choices by means of the rules of Section B.

Example 1 serves to introduce the procedure of comparing the favorite for similarity with another choice in the race using Rule 1 of Section B, which applies when the favorite ran a poor last race and finished in the same position behind the winner as the other choice in its last race. Here again, certain definitions are employed which may be found at the end of this chapter. In Example 1, the favorite, in finishing fifth five lengths off the winner in its last race seven days ago, ran a poor last race. It is equivalent in class to the other choices since all past races shown were for the $5,000 claiming price, and it is not a router-in-sprint. Looking now at the last race finish of the second choice, we find it is also a fifth. Before similarity is confirmed, however, subsections a-e must be checked to see if a normal or soft betting pattern is required. It is easily seen not to be the case, and the favorite is similar to the second choice by this rule.

The third choice also finished fifth in its last race; but in checking subsections a-e, we notice that the favorite is a male and the third choice a filly, which by subsection e requires a normal or soft betting pattern. With the favorite's closing odds at five to two, the closing odds on the third choice must be nine to two or longer for similarity. Since this is not the case, the favorite is not similar to the third choice.

The fourth choice also finished fifth in its last race, but at another track, Delaware Park, and more than twenty-one days ago. According to subsections a and b, a normal or soft betting pattern must exist at the close of betting. It does and the favorite is similar to the fourth choice.

The use of betting patterns allows for obvious differences in the records of the two horses that handicappers try to take into account. It is well known, for example, that fillies do not run as well against males as against other females. Thus all other factors being the same, a filly's probability of winning against a male should be lower (its odds longer) by a certain amount. If the betting is even weaker than this, as evidenced by a normal or soft betting pattern, there are underlying reasons for this smaller win probability not appreciated by the public which proceeds to overbet the horse on the basis of its similarity to the favorite.

Rule 2. Good last race finish of the favorite not as good as the other's last race finish when the favorite did not race the other horse in the other's last race

The favorite ran a *good last race*, is equivalent in class to the other horse, did not race the other in the other's last race, is not a router-in sprint, and the other horse shows a better finish in its last race, but a normal or soft betting pattern must exist if one or more of the following conditions hold:

a. The other horse last ran more than twenty-one days ago, but not if today's race is a sprint and the other finished first or second
b. Today's race is a route race and the favorite is a sprouter or router while the other horse is a sprinter which did not win its last race or run in class Z
c. The other horse finished first or second less than one length off the winner in its only start at the meeting

Example 2: 22 Aug 77-4   Sar $1\frac{1}{8}$ Clm 15000

Favorite: 117   9/5

15Aug77-5Sar	$1\frac{1}{16}$	Clm 15000	3	4^3	3^4	117	3.60	9
2May77-6Aqu	$1\frac{1}{16}$	Clm 20000	4	4^2	$3^{2\frac{1}{2}}$	116	2.90	8
23Apr77-5Aqu	$1\frac{1}{16}$	Clm 20000	3	2^1	2^2	116	3.40	8

Second choice: 120 7/2

30Jly77-7Sar	$1\frac{1}{8}$	Clm 18000	2	2^1	$2^{\frac{1}{2}}$	118	2.20	9
16Jly77-6Del	$1\frac{1}{8}$	Clm 15000	2	$1^{\frac{1}{2}}$	1^3	118	2.10	10
9Jly77-5Del	1	Clm 20000	1	1^1	2^{nk}	118	3.10	8

The favorite clearly satisfies the conditions of Rule 2: its last race was a good last race, it is equivalent in class to the second choice, it did not race the second choice in its last race, it is not a router-in-sprint, and the other horse showed a better finish in its last race. Now, subsections a, b, and c must be checked to see if a normal or soft betting pattern is required for similarity. Since the second choice ran more than twenty-one days ago, a normal or soft betting pattern is required by subsection a. Also, since the second choice finished second in its only start at the Saratoga meeting, subsection c requires a normal or soft betting pattern. Such a pattern does exist (closing odds 9/5 and 7/2), and the horses are similar.

Rule 3. Good last race finish of the favorite the same or better than the other's good last race or fourth place finish when the favorite did not race the other in the other's last race

The favorite ran a good last race, is equivalent in class to the other horse, did not race the other horse in the other's last race, is not a router-in-sprint, and the other horse finished second, third, fourth, or less than three lengths off the winner in its last race if a normal or soft betting pattern exists for a one-place better finish by the favorite, a soft betting pattern for a two-place better finish by the favorite, a very weak betting pattern for a three-place better finish by the favorite, and any betting pattern for the same finish by both, but apply a *plus-one relative finish change* if one or more of the following conditions hold:

a. The other horse last ran more than twenty-one days ago
b. The favorite has run at the present meeting and the other horse has not
c. Today's race is a route race and the favorite is a sprouter or a router while the other horse is a sprinter which did not win its last race or run in class Z
d. The favorite showed *early speed* in its last race and the other horse a slow start
e. There is a nine-pound or more relative weight shift in favor of the favorite
f. The favorite won its last race or finished less than three lengths off the winner and the other horse finished five or more lengths off the winner

and apply a *minus-one relative finish change* if one or more of the following conditions hold:

  g. The other horse last raced in class Z
  h. There is a nine-pound or more relative weight shift against the favorite
  i. The favorite finished five or more lengths off the winner in its last race and the other horse less than three lengths off the winner
  j. The favorite made a slow start in its last race and the other horse showed early speed

(In this rule, a last race finish by either horse of fifth or worse less than three lengths off the winner is to be considered a fourth-place finish).

Example 3: 14 Oct 77-3   Bel   7f   Clm 10000

Favorite: 118   5/2

7Oct77-4Bel 6f Clm 9000	4^2	1^1	115	3.50	9
19Sep77-5Bel 6f Clm 8000	3^1	2no	115	3.10	9
12Sep77-5Bel 7f Clm 8000	5^2	$3^{1\frac{1}{2}}$	114	6.70	10

Second choice: 112   3

3Oct77-2Bel 6f Clm 12000	2^2	2^4	120	4.00	7
20Sep77-4Bel 6f Clm 12500	1^1	3^3	119	4.50	6
1Sep77-5Bel 6f Clm 12500	2^2	4^4	119	5.10	7

Third choice: 118   5

1Oct77-6Med 6f Clm 10000	3^1	2^5	118	3.00	10
22Sep77-6Med 6f Clm 10000	4^2	2^2	118	4.10	9
10Sep77-6Med 6f Clm 11000	2^1	3^2	118	4.20	9

Fourth choice: 118   7

6Oct77-5Bel 6f Clm 10000	1^1	$5^{2\frac{1}{2}}$	120	5.30	10
29Sep77-5Bel 6f Clm 10000	2^{nk}	3^{nk}	112	3.70	8
13Sep77-4Bel 6f Clm 10000	1^1	1^2	112	1.60	9

The favorite satisfies all the conditions of Rule 3: it shows a better last race finish than the other choices, is equivalent in class, did not race any of the others in their last races, is not a router-in-sprint. And the other horses finished second, third, fourth, or less than three lengths off the winner in their last races. Now we must see if the proper betting patterns exist by checking the last race finishes and subsections a–j.

The favorite shows a one-place better finish than the second choice, which requires the existence of a normal or soft betting pattern. However, checking each subsection in turn, we find that subsections g and h apply. The second choice ast raced in Class Z (in class 20 percent or more higher than the favorite's last ace and higher than the class of the favorite's last three races) and there is an 11-pound relative weight shift against the favorite (the favorite picks up three pounds off its last race while the second choice drops eight pounds). Therefore, a minus-one relative finish change must be effected making the last race finishes the same. Now the favorite is similar to the second choice regardless of the odds pattern.

Subsections b and f apply when comparing the favorite to the third choice: the favorite has run at the present Belmont Park meeting whereas the third choice is coming in from Meadowlands, the favorite won its last race and the third choice finished five lengths off the winner. Each subsection calls for a plus-one relative finish change, but since a maximum change of only one place is permitted in the definition, the favorite shows now a two-place better finish. A glance at the odds reveals a soft betting pattern (5/2 for the favorite against 5/1 for the third choice), and the horses are similar.

The finish of the fourth choice is to be considered a fourth, making the favorite's finish three places better. None of the subsections apply and a very weak betting pattern is needed. Such a one does exist (5/2 and 7/1), and the favorite is similar to the fourth choice.

Rule 4. Good last race finish by the favorite and a poor last race by the other horse with early speed or in class Z

    a. The favorite ran a good last race and the other horse ran a poor last race in class Z or showed early speed less than thirty-two days ago if either Rule 2 or Rule 3 can be applied to the other's previous race

    b. The favorite finished third, fourth less than three lengths off the winner, fourth three or more lengths off the winner with a slow start or fifth or worse less than three lengths off the winner in its last and recent race and the other horse's last race was 25 percent or more higher in class than today's race if a normal or soft betting pattern exists, or any betting pattern if the other finished first, second, third, or fourth in its previous race

Example 4: 22 Nov 77-6   Aqu $1\frac{1}{8}$ Clm 25000

Favorite: 118   6/5

15Nov77-6Aqu $1\frac{1}{8}$ Clm 22500	2	2^3	3^5	118	3.10	7
8Nov77-6Aqu $1\frac{1}{8}$ Clm 25000	1	1^{nk}	2^3	118	3.70	8
31Oct77-5Aqu 7f Clm 25000	4^3		3^2	118	5.60	10

Second choice: 115   2
14Nov77-8Aqu	$1\frac{1}{8}$	Allowance	8	8^7	8^{15}	114	21.40	8
3Nov77-7Aqu	$1\frac{1}{8}$	Clm 25000	5	$4^{2\frac{1}{2}}$	1^2	118	4.90	9
24Oct77-6Aqu	$1\frac{1}{8}$	Clm 35000	6	6^5	3^1	118	6.10	

Third choice 118   3
16Nov77-6Aqu	$1\frac{1}{8}$	Clm 25000	1	1^3	8^7	118	2.90	8
10Nov77-6Aqu	$1\frac{1}{8}$	Clm 20000	1	1^3	1^5	117	1.20	8
1Nov77-5Aqu	7f	Clm 20000	2^2		1^1	117	1.40	

Fourth choice: 118   4
7Nov77-5Aqu	$1\frac{1}{8}$	Allowance	6	6^4	5^7	118	11.70	10
31Oct77-6Aqu	$1\frac{1}{8}$	Clm 35000	6	5^5	5^8	116	10.20	
2Sep77-5Bel	$1\frac{1}{4}$	Clm 25000	5	4^3	5^9	114	9.70	

The favorite ran a good last race and the second choice ran last in Class Z (fo
purposes of the system, an allowance race is equivalent in class to the highes
price claiming races being run at the meeting, which is at least $35,000). Rule 4
specifies that Rule 2 may be applied to the previous race of the second choic
and the horses are similar. The third choice showed early speed in its poor las
race, so that its previous race may be considered. Rule 4a applies again, and the
horses are similar by Rule 2. In establishing equivalence in class, follow the pro
cedure in the definition. Since the favorite's last race class was less than that o
the third choice, the horses are class equivalent.

The favorite is similar to the fourth choice by Rule 4b.

Rule 5. Good last race finish at the meeting by a favorite not equivalent in clas to the other horse

The favorite ran a good last race at the meeting, is not a router-in
sprint, and is not equivalent in class to the other horse and one or more
of the following conditions hold:

a. The other horse scored an easy win in its last and recent race and
normal or soft betting pattern exists
b. The favorite made slow starts in its last three or all its past races and
either Rule 2 or Rule 3 applies neglecting the "equivalent in class"
requirement
c. The favorite did not finish first or second less than five lengths of
the winner or made slow starts in its last three or all its past race
and the other horse is a first-time starter or showed early speed in it
last and recent race if a normal or soft betting pattern exists

Example 5: 22 Nov 77-3   Aqu   6f   Clm 10000

Favorite: 122   7/5

15Nov77-3Aqu 6f Clm 10000	10^8	3^1	122	4.00	11
2Nov77-2Aqu 6f Md 10000	9^7	$1^{\frac{1}{2}}$	122	5.80	12
16Oct77-1Aqu 6f Md 10000	8^4	6^3	122	19.20	10

Second choice: 122   3

9Nov77-1Aqu 6f Clm 8000	2^2	1^4	118	2.00	8
1Nov77-2Aqu 6f Clm 7500	1^2	1^1	118	3.20	9
30Sep77-3Aqu 6f Clm 7500	2^{nk}	3^2	118	3.50	10

Third choice: 115   3

11Nov77-2Aqu 6f Clm 7500	3^2	2^{nk}	118	2.40	7
3Nov77-9Aqu 6f Clm 7500	2^1	1^{nk}	118	5.60	8
27Oct77-1Aqu 6f Clm 7500	1^1	2^1	118	6.20	9

Fourth choice: 115   7/2

Despite the slow start by the favorite in its good last race at Aqueduct Race Track, Section A rules do not apply. Although the favorite is not equivalent in class to the second choice, the latter scored an easy win in its last and recent race and a normal betting pattern exists. Therefore, the favorite is similar to the second choice by Rule 5a.

The favorite is not equivalent in class to the third choice, but Rule 5b applies. Since the favorite made slow starts in its last three races, Rule 2 may be applied without the "equivalence in class" requirement and the two horses are similar.

Rule 5c makes the favorite similar to the first-time starter fourth choice.

Rule 6. Last and recent race finish by the favorite of first or second in its only start at the meeting

>   The favorite finished first or second in its last and recent race and all the other starts if any at the meeting after a race elsewhere or its only start at the meeting within the last thirty-one days if Rule 14 applies considering the race as an easy win.

Example 6:

Examples of the use of this rule will be given below under Rule 14.

Rule 7. Last race together

>   a. The favorite finished behind the other horse in the other's last race, but a normal or soft betting pattern must exist if one or more of the

following conditions hold:

   i. A relative weight shift moves the favorite $\frac{1}{2}$ length or more ahead of the other

   ii. The race was either horse's only start at the meeting after a race elsewhere, but not if a relative weight shift moves the other from less than one length to one or more lengths ahead of the favorite or the favorite finished two or more places behind the other horse

   iii. The favorite was off at shorter odds in the last race and a very weak betting pattern existed between the two horses

   iv. The favorite shows a better finish in a subsequent race

   v. The favorite showed early speed in the last race

b. The favorite beat the other horse in the other's last race and a normal or soft betting pattern exists for a one-place better finish, a soft betting pattern for a two-place better finish, and a very weak betting pattern for a three-or-more place better finish, but apply a plus-one relative finish change if one or more of the following conditions hold:

   i. The favorite beat the other horse by three or more lengths, but not if the race was either's only start at the meeting after a race elsewhere

   ii. The favorite ran in a more recent race than the race together

   iii. There is a relative weight shift of seven pounds or more in favor of the favorite

and apply a minus-one relative finish change if one or more of the following conditions hold:

   iv. The favorite finished less than $\frac{1}{2}$ length ahead of the other horse after adjusting for any relative weight shift

   v. The favorite made a slow start, the other a fast start, and today's race is not longer than the last race

   vi. There is a relative weight shift of seven pounds or more against the favorite

   vii. A relative weight shift makes the other horse one length or less better than the favorite

   viii. The race was either's only start at the meeting after a race elsewhere if the favorite was off at longer odds than the other in the last race

c. The favorite beat the other horse in its last race and a relative weight shift makes the other more than one length better than the favorite, but a normal or soft betting pattern must exist if the favorite ran in a subsequent race

d. The favorite beat the other horse in the last race of each if the other was off at shorter odds in the last race and a soft betting pattern exists in today's race

Example 7a: 15 Dec 77-5   Aqu   6f   Clm 20000

Favorite: 118   3

9Dec77-6Aqu	6f Clm 20000	1^2	3^3	120	2.50	8
28Nov77-6Aqu	6f Clm 20000	1^1	4^2	118	1.20	7
7Nov77-5Aqu	6f Clm 20000	$1^{\frac{1}{2}}$	2no	118	1.00	6

Second choice: 120   7/2

9Dec77-6Aqu	6f Clm 20000	7^5	$1^{\frac{1}{2}}$	110	9.00	8
17Aug77-6Sar	6f Clm 25000	8^8	8^{15}	115	21.70	8
9Aug77-7Sar	6f Clm 15000	6^5	2^2	115	8.60	9

Third choice: 114   7/2

28Nov77-6Aqu	6f Clm 20000	3^3	3^2	120	3.50	7
30Sep77-6Bel	6f Clm 20000	2^2	1^1	118	1.10	8
16Sep77-7Mth	6f Clm 20000	1^1	1^2	118	1.40	9

The favorite finished behind the second choice in the last race of each. According to Rule 7a, we must now check the subsections i–v to determine if a normal or soft betting pattern is required for similarity. With the favorite at 3/1 and the second choice at 7/2 in today's race, such is not the case. There is a relative weight shift of twelve pounds off the last race in favor of the favorite, which improves its performance (at three pounds equaling one length) by four lengths relative to the second choice, thereby making the favorite better than the second choice by one length. Subsection i demands a normal or soft betting pattern in this event, and the horses are not similar. For instructive purposes, let us see what the other subsections say. The last race was the only start at the meeting by the second choice, and subsection ii would require a normal or soft betting pattern except for the fact that the favorite finished two places behind the second choice. Subsection iii also demands a normal or soft betting pattern since the favorite was off at shorter odds in the last race and a very weak betting pattern existed. And lastly, subsection v demands a normal or soft betting pattern since the favorite showed early speed in the last race.

The favorite raced the third choice in the latter's last race and shows a subsequent race with a better finish. Consequently, subsection iv requires a normal or soft betting pattern. Note that subsection v does also. Subsection ii does not require a normal or soft betting pattern even though the last race by the third choice was its only start at the meeting because the relative weight shift off that race makes the third choice more than one length better than the favorite.

Example 7b: 3Nov 77-4   Lrl   6f   Allowance

Favorite: 118   8/5

27Oct77-8Lrl	6f	Allowance	6^4	1^{nk}	118	4.20	8
21Oct77-7Lrl	6f	Allowance	7^5	3^1	118	6.40	10
2Oct77-6Bow	6f	Allowance	8^8	4^5	120	9.70	9

Second choice: 118   5/2

27Oct77-8Lrl	6f	Allowance	3^2	2^{nk}	118	3.30	8
9Oct77-6Bow	6f	Allowance	$4^{1\frac{1}{2}}$	1^2	118	1.90	8
30Sep77-7Bow	6f	Allowance	2^1	3^2	115	4.20	9

Third choice: 108   7/2

27Oct77-8Lrl	6f	Allowance	1^1	4^3	122	1.40	8
21Oct77-7Lrl	6f	Allowance	1^2	1^3	118	1.00	10
29Sep77-8Bow	6f	Allowance	1^1	1^{nk}	118	1.50	6

Section A must be checked for all favorites showing a slow start in the last and recent race. The favorite here is a permissible bet and Rule 7b will now be used to establish similarity. The favorite finished one place ahead of the second choice in their last race at Laurel, which requires a nonexistent normal or soft betting pattern for similarity. Now, however, we must check all the subsections for both plus-one and minus-one relative finish changes. Subsection iv applies since the favorite finished less than $\frac{1}{2}$ length ahead of the second choice after any weight adjustments (none in today's race) and allows a minus-one relative finish change. Hence, the two horses are regarded as having the same finish in the last race and any betting pattern will do for similarity. The favorite is similar to the second choice. Subsection v also allows a minus-one relative finish change since the favorite made a slow start and the second choice a fast start in the last race at the same distance as today's race. Under the system rules, only one minus-one relative finish change is permitted, however. Finally, subsection viii allows a minus-one relative finish change since the last race was the second choice's only start at the meeting and it was off at odds shorter than today's favorite.

The favorite finished three places and three lengths ahead of the third choice in their last race. Rule 7b demands a very weak betting pattern in this case with a plus-one relative finish change from subsection i and a minus-one relative finish change from subsection vi. Therefore, there is no net relative finish change and a very weak betting pattern is still required for similarity. Since it does not exist, the favorite is not similar to the third choice by Rule 7b. However, Rule 7c applies since the fourteen-pound relative weight shift makes the third choice more than one length better than the favorite, and the horses are similar. Also, the favorite is similar to the third choice by Rule 7d since the third choice was off at shorter odds than today's favorite in their last race and a weak betting pattern exists in today's race.

Rule 8. Good previous race
    The favorite ran a *good previous race* and Rules 2, 3, 5, or 7 can be applied using this race as if it were a good last race.

NOTE: Apply Section A and establish equivalence in class using the favorite's last three races in the usual manner.

Example 8: 19 Oct 77-5   Bel   6f   Clm 7500

Favorite: 114   5/2
    12Oct77-3Bel 6f Clm 7500 3^1 10^{11} 112   3.20   9
    3Oct77-2Bel 6f Clm 8000 2^{nk} 2^1 112   2.70   10
    21Aug77-4Sar 6f Clm 7500 1^1 1^3 112   1.10   9

Second choice: 114   4
    9Oct77-5Bel 6f Clm 6500 1^2 1^2 114   1.80   7
    2Oct77-4Bel 6f Clm 8000 1^1 4^3 114   4.40   8
    19Sep77-4Bel 6f Clm 7500 1^1 2^1 114   3.10   9

The favorite ran a poor last race and a good previous race. Equivalence in class exists since the favorite's lowest class race ($7,500) is less than the second choice's highest class race ($8,000). The favorite is similar to the second choice by Rule 2 since its previous race finish is not as good as the last race finish of the second choice.

Rule 9. Favorite away
    a. The favorite and the other horse have been *away* and are equivalent in class, but, unless the other horse raced in class Z or showed early speed in its last race, a normal or soft betting pattern must exist if
        i. The favorite has started at the present meeting and the other has not, or
        ii. The favorite finished first or second in its last race and the other did not
    b. The favorite and the other horse have been away, are not equivalent in class, and either a very weak betting pattern exists or the favorite made slow starts in its last three races or in all its starts
    c. The favorite is a first-time starter, the other horse is a one-time starter that ran a poor last race without showing early speed, and a normal or soft betting pattern exists
    d. The favorite has been away, did not win or finish second less than

five lengths off the winner in its last race, and the other horse either won (not easily), finished second, third, or fourth less than three lengths off the winner in its last and recent race, or fourth three or more lengths off the winner and a normal or soft betting pattern exists, or less than three lengths off the winner and a normal or soft betting pattern exists, or won easily or showed early speed and a normal or soft betting pattern exists, but with the following conditions:

    i. If the favorite's last race was higher in class than today's race and the other horse finished first or second or showed early speed in its only start at the meeting after a race elsewhere in class equal to or less than today's race, the horses are not similar by this rule

    ii. In sprints, if the favorite is not equivalent in class to the other horse, a normal or soft betting pattern must exist or any betting pattern if the favorite finished fifth or worse in its last race

e. The favorite has been away, finished first or second less than five lengths off the winner in its last race, and the other horse finished first or second in its last and recent race, or third, fourth, or less than three lengths off the winner and a normal or soft betting pattern exists, but with the following conditions:

    i. If the other horse finished first or second or showed early speed in its only race at the meeting after a race elsewhere in class equal to or less than today's race, the horses are not similar by this rule

    ii. In sprints, if the favorite is not equivalent in class to the other, the horses are not similar

f. The favorite has been away, the other's last race was a poor last race and Rule 9d or Rule 9e may be applied to the other's previous race less than thirty-two days ago considering the other's previous race as its last and recent race.

g. The favorite has been away, did not win its last race in class higher than or equal to today's race, and the other horse ran a poor last race in class 25 percent or more higher than today's race or showed early speed in class higher than or equal to today's race if a normal or soft betting pattern exists or any betting pattern if the other ran first, second, third, or fourth in its previous race in class equal to or higher than today's race.

NOTE: Use Rule 7 if the favorite raced the other horse in the other's last race.

Example 9a: 8 Nov 77-4   Aqu   6f   Allowance

Favorite: 122   9/5

20Sep77-6Bel	6f	Allowance	$2^{1\frac{1}{4}}$		1^2	118	2.20	8
17Aug77-7Sar	6f	Allowance	3^3		3^2	118	4.40	9
15Jly77-6Aqu	6f	Allowance	4^2		$2^{\frac{1}{2}}$	118	5.10	10

Second choice: 122   3

3Sep77-7Bel 6f Allowance	1^1		5^3	118	3.10	8
20Aug77-8Mth 6f Allowance	1^2		1^5	116	0.60	7
13Aug77-8Mth 6f Allowance	1^1		$1^{\frac{1}{2}}$	116	1.60	8

Third Choice: 122   7/2

25Oct77-6Bel 6f Allowance	5^6		3^3	116	4.90	10
17Oct77-5Bel 6f Allowance	6^4		4^5	118	7.80	7
9Oct77-2Bel 6f MdSpWt	$2^{\frac{1}{2}}$		1^1	122	2.20	10

Fourth choice: 113   9/2

3Oct77-4Bel 6f Clm 22500	1^2		1^2	116	1.00	9
27Sep77-5Bel 6f Clm 25000	1^1		2^2	118	1.80	8
14Sep77-5Bel 6f Clm 25000	1^2		3^1	118	2.30	9

Fifth choice: 122   9/2

2Nov77-7Aqu 6f Allowance	3^3		2^2	113	5.10	8
27Oct77-6Bel 6f Clm 35000	4^2		1^1	114	6.20	9
12Oct77-5Bel 6f Clm 30000	2^1		1^2	113	4.50	8

It should first be noted that Section A need not be considered for favorites that have been away. The favorite is similar to the second choice by Rule 9a, since both horses have been away, are equivalent in class, and a normal betting pattern exists to allow for the first place finish by the favorite in its last race.

The favorite is similar to the third choice by Rule 9e. A normal or soft betting pattern is required for the third place finish of the third choice in its last race and such exists.

The fourth choice has been away, but the favorite is not equivalent in class to it. Rule 9b requires a very weak betting pattern to exist for similarity, and, since it does not exist in today's race, the horses are not similar.

The favorite is not similar to the fifth choice because, according to Rule 9e, the favorite is not similar to a horse which finished first or second in its only start at the present meeting in class equal to or less than today's race.

Example 9b: 10 Nov 77-2   Aqu   6f   Md 10000

Favorite: 120   2
  First-time starter

Second choice: 120   4
  First-time starter

Third choice: 120   4

3Nov77-1Aqu 6f Md 10000	7^7		9^8	118	5.10	9

Fourth choice: 120   9/2

30Oct77-2Bel 6f Md 8000	2^2	3^3	118	3.60	10
23Oct77-1Bel 6f Md 12500	5^4	6^7	118	7.30	10

Fifth choice: 120   7

22Oct77-9Bel 6f Md 10000	8^9	8^{15}	115	21.10	8
12Oct77-1Bel 6f Md 8000	4^5	3^3	112	28.40	9

Sixth choice: 120   7

4Nov77-2Aqu 6f Md 15000	6^4	7^7	116	8.20	10
21Oct77-3Bel 7f Md 20000	8^6	10^{19}	115	32.60	11

The favorite is similar to the second choice in this maiden claiming race by Rule 9a since both horses have been away (both are first-time starters). The favorite is similar to the third choice by Rule 9c, to the fourth choice by Rule 9d, to the fifth choice by Rule 9f, and to the sixth choice by Rule 9g.

Rule 10. The only race in the last twenty-one days a poor last race

The favorite ran a poor last race that was its only race in the last twenty-one days, is equivalent in class to the other horse, did not race the other horse in the other's last race, and any one of the following conditions apply:

a. The other horse ran a last and recent race that was neither a good last race nor a fourth place finish and was its only start in the last twenty-one days, but a normal or soft betting pattern must exist if
  i. The favorite raced at the present meeting and the other did not, or
  ii. The favorite showed a better finish in its previous race than the other in its previous race, but not if the other's previous race was in class Z, or
  iii. The other horse is a one-time starter
b. The other horse has been away if a normal or soft betting pattern exists, or any betting pattern if the favorite did not finish fourth in in its last race and the class of the other's last race was 25 percent or more higher than today's race
c. Rules 9d, e, f, or g can be applied assuming the favorite to have been away and using its previous race finish as its last race finish

Example 10: 15 Dec 77-5   Aqu   7f   Clm 15000

Favorite: 116   5/2

28Nov77-6Aqu 7f Clm 15000	9^4	10^8	116	7.10	11
1Oct77-5Key 6f Clm 20000	4^3	3^3	117	3.90	7
15Sep77-6Key 6f Clm 20000	$5^{2\frac{1}{2}}$	1no	117	6.50	7

Second choice: 116   3

2Dec77-4Aqu 6f Clm 17500	6^5	8^9	116	6.20	9
15Nov77-3Aqu 7f Clm 15000	4^3	2^2	116	4.30	10
1Nov77-5Aqu 6f Clm 20000	6^8	5^3	118	7.20	6

Third choice: 116   4

23Sep77-4Bel 6f Clm 16000	1^2	4^5	120	4.30	9
9Sep77-3Bel 7f Clm 15000	1^3	$1^{\frac{1}{2}}$	120	2.70	10
2Sep77-6Bel 6f Clm 25000	2no	5^3	122	2.50	7

Fourth choice: 116   9/2

10Dec77-4Aqu 6f Clm 10000	3^3	2^{hd}	112	1.70	9
3Dec77-3Aqu 7f Clm 10000	4^3	$2^{\frac{1}{2}}$	118	2.40	8
16Nov77-2Aqu 6f Clm 9000	2^1	$1^{2\frac{1}{2}}$	120	0.70	7

The favorite's poor last race was its only start in the last twenty-one days, as is the case for the second choice. Since the favorite is equivalent in class to the other and its previous race shows a worse finish, any betting pattern is permissible by Rule 10a and the favorite is similar to the second choice.

Since the third choice has been away, Rule 10b demands a normal or soft betting pattern. It does not exist in this race and the favorite is not similar to the third choice.

Although the fourth ran a good last race, the favorite is not equivalent in class to it, and the horses are not similar.

Rule 11. Sharp drop in class

The favorite showed a sharp drop in class and no early speed in a last and recent race and one of the following conditions apply:

a. The other horse has been away if a normal or soft betting pattern exists or any betting pattern if the other won its last race

b. The other horse is making its first start at the meeting if the favorite has raced at the meeting and a normal or soft betting pattern exists, or any betting pattern if the favorite has raced only once at the meeting

c. The favorite is equivalent in class to the other horse

d. The other horse ran in a last and recent race and won or finished second, or finished third or fourth if a normal or soft betting pattern exists, or finished less than three lengths off the winner if a normal or soft betting pattern exists

e. The other horse showed early speed in a last and recent race (only in a sprint if today's race is a sprint) and did not win easily

f. The other horse ran a last and recent race that was neither a good last race nor a fourth-place finish three or more lengths off the winner if Rule 11d can be applied to a previous and recent race of the other and a normal or soft betting pattern exists

NOTE: Use Rule 7 if the favorite raced the other horse in the other's last race.

Example 11: 16 Dec 77-2   Med   6f   Clm 5000

Favorite: 109   2

7Dec77-3Med 6f Clm 8000	5^4	7^{11} 114	5.00	12
22Nov77-9Med 6f Clm 9000	$2^{\frac{1}{2}}$	4^4 114	1.70	9
27Sep77-1Med 6f Clm 9000	$2^{\frac{1}{2}}$	$4^{\frac{1}{2}}$ 114	2.40	10

Second choice: 117   5/2

9Dec77-4Pen 5½f Clm 3500	1^2	$1^{4\frac{1}{2}}$ 116	2.90	9
22Nov77-5Pen 6f Clm 5000	$2^{2\frac{1}{2}}$	9^{29} 114	27.70	9
21Oct77-5Pen 6f Clm 5000	5^4	7^{15} 112	10.00	7

Third choice: 114   7/2

9Dec77-3Med 6f Clm 10000	2^1	5^7 114	8.80	7
30Nov77-4Med 6f Clm 10000	3^2	6^{10} 116	12.20	9
14Nov77-3Med 6f Clm 12000	4^4	9^{11} 118	11.90	10

Fourth choice: 114   5

9Aug77-5Atl 6f Clm 5000	$7^{2\frac{1}{4}}$	11^{14} 114	7.80	12
26Jly77-3Atl 6f Clm 6000	$4^{2\frac{1}{2}}$	6^{10} 118	2.30	6
19Jly77-7Atl 6f Clm 7500	2^4	$4^{4\frac{1}{2}}$ 116	5.80	8

Fifth choice: 117   6

9Dec77-1Key 6f Clm 5000	6^5	10^{18} 118	5.00	10
28Nov77-3Key 6f Clm 6000	10^8	$4^{3\frac{1}{2}}$ 114	3.30	11
8Nov77-9Med 6f Clm 5000	$9^{7\frac{1}{4}}$	$2^{\frac{1}{2}}$ 114	11.90	12

Section A need not be considered since the favorite shows a sharp drop in class off its last and recent race at Meadowlands. The favorite is similar to the second choice by Rule 11d.

The favorite is equivalent in class to the third choice and therefore similar to the latter by Rule 11c. Also, similarity exists by Rule 11e since the third choice showed early speed in its last and recent race.

The favorite is similar to the fourth choice by Rule 11a or Rule 11b, and to the fifth choice by Rule 11f. Rule 11f allows Rule 11d to be applied to the previous and recent race of the fifth choice.

Rule 12. Early speed

a. The favorite showed early speed in a good last race, or a fast start in its last race and early speed in a good previous race, or a slow start in its last race in class higher than today's race and early speed in a good previous race, or early speed in a poor last race and a good previous race, and the other horse did not show early speed or win with a fast start in its only race at the meeting, and one of the following conditions holds:

  i. The other horse is a first-time starter and a normal or soft betting pattern exists, or any betting pattern if the favorite started only once at the present meeting

  ii. The other horse has been away and finished first, second, third, or less than three lengths off the winner in its last race and a normal or soft betting pattern exists, or any betting pattern if the other raced last in class 25 percent or more higher than today's race or if the favorite started only once at the present meeting

  iii. The other horse has been away and finished fourth or worse three or more lengths off the winner in its last race and a very weak betting pattern exists, or a soft betting pattern if the other raced last in class 25 percent or more higher than today's race or if the favorite started only once at the present meeting

  iv. The other horse ran in its last and recent race and its previous race in class Z, both 20 percent or more higher than today's race, and finished fifth or worse three or more lengths off the winner in its last race if a normal or soft betting pattern exists, or any betting pattern if the finish of the other's previous race was first, second, third, or less than three lengths off the winner or the favorite started only once at the present meeting.

b. The favorite did not finish first or second in the last 31 days and

  i. showed early speed in a last and recent race in class 20 percent or more higher than today's race and the other horse's last race and higher than the other's last three races, or

  ii. showed a fast start in its last and recent race and early speed in a recent previous race both of which were 20 percent or more higher in class than today's race and the other horse's last race and higher than the other's last three races,

and one of the following conditions holds:

  i. The other horse ran first or second in a recent race

  ii. The other horse ran third, fourth, or less than three lengths off the winner in a recent race and a normal or soft betting pattern exists

  iii. The other horse has been away.

Example 12a: 24 Oct 77-5   Aqu   6f   Clm 20000

Favorite: 119   6/5

10Oct77-4Bel 6f Clm 20000	$1\frac{1}{2}$		2^{hd}	119	2.70	7
29Sep77-3Bel 6f Clm 25000	$1\frac{1}{2}$		2^{hd}	117	5.50	9
20Sep77-3Bel 6f Clm 30000	$6^{2\frac{1}{2}}$		11^{11}	119	5.10	12

Second choice: 116   2

24Feb77-7GP 6f Allowance	$2\frac{1}{2}$	$2\frac{1}{2}$	120	3.00	9
30Oct76-8Mth 6f Allowance	2^1	1^6	122	1.40	7
19Oct76-7Mth 6f Allowance	3^2	1^{nk}	122	1.90	8

Third choice: 119   5/2

9Oct77-5Med 6f Clm 35000	1^{hd}	6^8	116	3.50	8
15Sep77-6Med 6f Allowance	3^{nk}	11^{12}	115	33.30	11
26Jly77-6Atl 6f Allowance	1^3	1^{hd}	119	2.40	7

Fourth choice: 116   6

12Sep77-1Bel 6f Clm 20000	4^5	5^5	116	4.80	9
5Sep77-5Bel 6f Clm 22500	3^5	$4^{8\frac{1}{2}}$	116	5.60	9
6Aug77-3Sar 6f Clm 25000	1^1	2^{hd}	116	1.40	9

The favorite showed early speed in a good last race. If Rules 2 through 6 (Section B) do not suffice to establish similarity, Rule 12a may be used. The favorite is similar to the second choice by Rule 12a(ii) since the latter finished second in its last race over twenty-one days ago in class more than 25 percent higher than today's race.

The favorite is similar to the third choice by Rule 12a(iv.) and to the fourth choice by Rule 12a(iii.).

Example 12b: 1 Dec 77-4Aqu $1\frac{1}{8}$ Clm 5000

Favorite: 117   2

22Nov77-1Aqu $1\frac{1}{8}$ Clm 7500	1	1^2	9^{12}	116	5.60	9
31Oct77-2Aqu 7f Clm 7500	$4^{2\frac{1}{2}}$		3^4	118	6.10	8
1Sep77-2Bel $1\frac{1}{16}$ Clm 7500	1	1^1	2^2	119	3.70	8

Second choice: 117   5/2

20Nov77-1Aqu $1\frac{1}{8}$ Clm 6000	4	4^4	1^2	115	2.70	8
28Oct77-1Bel 1 Clm 6500	3	3^5	$2^{2\frac{1}{2}}$	113	3.30	9
1Oct77-9Bel $1\frac{1}{8}$ Clm 6500	5	6^7	4^5	113	9.70	10

Third choice: 117   7/2

6Aug77-4AP	$1\tfrac{1}{16}$ Clm 6000	4	4^9	5^{16}	112	13.20	8
22Jly77-4AP	6f Clm 7000	4^6		3^6	116	5.20	9
14Jly77-6AP	$1\tfrac{1}{16}$ Clm 6500	9	$9^{8\tfrac{1}{2}}$	$5^{5\tfrac{1}{4}}$	120	4.00	10

The favorite is similar to the second choice by Rule 12b(i.) and to the third choice by Rule 12b(iii.).

Rule 13. Router in sprint

The favorite is a sprinter or sprouter in a sprint race, shows a sharp drop in class, or has been away, and the other horse is a router which ran a last and recent race in class less than 10 percent higher than the highest class of the favorite's last three races, did not win easily, and did not show early speed unless a very weak betting pattern exists.

NOTE: In this rule, a 7- or $7\tfrac{1}{2}$-furlong turf race is to be considered a route race.

Example 13: 2 Dec 77-5   Key   6f   Clm 10000

Favorite: 116   7/5

23Nov77-4Key	6f Clm 10000	2^2		3^3	116	2.20	9
16Nov77-3Key	6f Clm 10000	3^1		1no	117	2.00	8
14Oct77-6Bow	6f Clm 10000	1^2		1^{nk}	118	1.80	7

Second choice: 116   3

25Nov77-5Key	1 Clm 10000	4	3^3	2^1	116	3.00	8
18Nov77-6Key	1 Clm 10000	3	4^5	3^2	116	2.50	9
31Oct77-7Med	1 Clm 10000	4	4^3	1^1	116	4.90	10

Third choice: 116   3

20Nov77-5Aqu	1 Clm 10000	1	1^2	6^7	118	4.70	7
12Nov77-4Aqu	1 Clm 10000	2	3^{nk}	5^{10}	118	3.10	6
4Nov77-5Aqu	1 Clm 10000	3	3^2	3^2	118	3.00	6

The favorite is similar to the second choice, which is a router in a sprint race and which did not win easily or show early speed in its last race, by Rule 13. It is not similar to the third choice. Although the latter is a router, it showed early speed in its last and recent race and a very weak betting pattern does not exist.

Rule 14. Easy win last race or previous race

a. The favorite won its last and recent race easily, is equivalent in class to the other horse, did not race against the other horse in the last race of each, and one of the following conditions holds:

    i. The other horse finished first or second less than five lengths off the winner in a last and recent race

    ii. The other horse finished second five or more lengths off the winner, third, fourth, or less than three lengths off the winner in a last and recent race, and a normal or soft betting pattern exists

    iii. The other horse is making its first start at the meeting after a race elsewhere if the favorite has started at the meeting, and a normal or soft betting pattern exists

    iv. The other horse has been away and a normal or soft betting pattern exists, or any betting pattern if the other won its last race or raced last in class Z

    v. The other horse ran a last and recent race in class Z with a fifth or worse finish three or more lengths off the winner, but a normal or soft betting pattern must exist if the other horse showed early speed or if the favorite has started at the meeting and the other has not

    vi. The other horse ran a poor last race and a previous race in class Z if a soft betting pattern exists

    vii. The other horse finished fifth or worse three or more lengths off the winner in its last race and one of the Rules 2, 3, 4, 5, or 6 can be applied to the other's previous and recent race

  b. The favorite's last race was not an easy win and Rule 14a can be applied using its previous and recent race as its last race

NOTE: If today's race is a sprint, the favorite's easy win must have been in a sprint, and if today's race is a route, the favorite's easy win must have been in either a 7- or $7\frac{1}{2}$-furlong race or a route race.

Example 14a: 4 Nov 77-1   Aqu $1\frac{1}{16}$ Clm 15000

Favorite: 118   2

25Oct77-1Aqu $1\frac{1}{16}$ Clm 14000	4	4^5	$1^{3\frac{1}{2}}$	112	5.20	9
17Oct77-7Aqu 7f Clm 15000	9^{13}		$3^{5\frac{1}{4}}$	114	6.10	10
3Oct77-6Bel 6f Clm 14000	7^9		4^4	114	3.60	7

Second choice: 118   7/2

24Oct77-7Key $1\frac{1}{16}$ Clm 15000	3	3^4	3^2	122	2.50	8
11Oct77-6Key 6f Clm 15000	7^1		4^5	120	8.70	10
1Sep77-6Mth $1\frac{1}{16}$ Clm 15000	4	5^4	1^1	118	3.20	9

Third choice: 118 4
27Oct77-8Aqu 7f Allowance 5^5 6^7 118 11.20 9
21Oct77-8Aqu $1\frac{1}{16}$ Allowance 2 2^2 4^3 120 6.60 8
19Sep77-8Bel $1\frac{1}{16}$ Allowance 3 3^1 2^2 116 4.40 7

Fourth choice: 118 5
13Aug77-8Atl $1\frac{1}{8}$ Clm 20000 6 6^5 4^3 118 3.20 12
6Aug77-8Mth $1\frac{1}{16}$ Clm 15000 4 4^2 1^1 117 2.60 8
31Jly77-8Mth $1\frac{1}{16}$ Clm 15000 3 3^1 2no 117 3.60 9

Fifth choice: 118 6
26Oct77-3Aqu $1\frac{1}{8}$ Clm 15000 3 3^3 5^3 115 6.30 8
21Oct77-8Aqu $1\frac{1}{8}$ Allowance 6 7^5 4^5 116 8.20 8
24Sep77-7Bel 7f Allowance 10^{10} 10^{22} 113 25.40 10

Sixth choice: 118 7
31Oct77-4Aqu $1\frac{1}{8}$ Clm 15000 5 5^3 5^3 115 6.30 8
15Oct77-4Aqu $1\frac{1}{8}$ Clm 15000 4 4^4 2^1 116 5.20 8
10Sep77-3Bel 7f Clm 15000 8^9 8^{13} 118 19.10 8

The favorite is similar to the second choice by Rules 14a(ii.) and (iii.), to the third choice by Rule 14a(v.), to the fourth choice by Rules 14a(iii.) and (iv.), to the fifth choice by Rule 14a(vi.), and to the sixth choice by Rule 14a(vii).

Example 14b: 20 Dec 77-3 Aqu 6f Clm 7500

Favorite: 116 5/2
13Dec77-3Aqu 6f Clm 7500 8^4 8^6 116 4.90 8
7Dec77-4Aqu 6f Clm 7500 1^1 1^5 116 2.80 9
30Nov77-1Aqu 6f Clm 7500 2^2 $2^{\frac{1}{2}}$ 118 3.40 10

Second choice: 116 3
13Dec77-4Aqu 6f Clm 8500 1^2 $1^{\frac{1}{2}}$ 116 2.30 9
2Dec77-5Aqu 6f Clm 8000 1^2 1^{nk} 119 1.50 10
27Nov77-5Aqu 6f Clm 8000 1^3 2^1 119 1.90 9

Rule 14b allows the favorite's easy win in its previous and recent race to be used in Rule 14a. The favorite is similar to the second choice by Rule 14a(i.).

Rule 15. Slow start by the other horse

The favorite ran a good last race, or a good previous race, or shows a sharp drop in class, or has been away, or showed early speed, and the other horse made a slow start in a last and recent race in class no more than 25 percent higher than today's race, did not run in a stakes race in its last three races if today's race is not a stakes race, did not win easily in its last race or its previous race less than thirty-two days ago, has started at least once at the present meeting, did not finish first or second in its only start at the meeting, and one of the following conditions is satisfied:

a. The other horse's last race was a nonwinning race (or a win if in class less than today's race) in lower class than its previous race, or its previous race shows a slow start and was lower in class than its pre-previous race, but with the following qualifications:

   i. If today's race is a route race,

     aa. do not consider past sprint races

     bb. and if the last and pre-previous races are routes and the previous race a sprint, apply this subsection ignoring the sprint race

   ii. If today's race is a sprint, do not consider a drop in class from a route race to a sprint race, but

     aa. if the last race was a route with a fast start, apply this subsection to previous and pre-previous sprint races, and

     bb. if the previous race was a route, apply this subsection to pre-previous and last sprint races

b. Today's race is a route and the other horse's last race was a route and its previous race a sprint, or the other horse's previous race was a route with a slow start and its pre-previous race a sprint, but not if the sprint is the only one in its last four starts and shows a slow start

c. Today's race is a sprint and the other horse's last race was a route, or its previous race was a route with a slow start, or its pre-previous race was a route with a slow start and its previous race showed a slow start

d. The last race of the other horse was at shorter odds than its previous race in which it made a fast start, or its previous race showed a slow start and a third-or-worse finish at shorter odds than its pre-previous race in which it made a fast start, but with the following qualifications:

   i. If today's race is a sprint and the other horse's last race was a route with a fast start, apply this rule to previous and pre-previous sprint races

   ii. If today's race is a route, do not consider past sprint races

Example 15: 22 Dec 77-4   Aqu $1\frac{1}{8}$ Clm 12500

Favorite: 118   5/2

12Dec77-4Aqu $1\frac{1}{8}$ Clm 10000	3	3^3	$1^{\frac{1}{2}}$	115	3.40	8
6Dec77-3Aqu 7f Clm 10000	$5^{2\frac{1}{2}}$		3^3	118	2.90	9
1Sep77-5Bel 1 Clm 10000	1	1^1	4^3	118	3.00	10

Second choice: 118   3

11Dec77-2Aqu $1\frac{1}{16}$ Clm 8500	9	8^6	$1^{\frac{1}{2}}$	114	2.00	9
3Dec77-1Aqu 6f Clm 8500	10^7		9^{14}	115	9.60	10
28Nov77-2Aqu $1\frac{1}{8}$ Clm 10000	7	7^5	$4^{2\frac{1}{2}}$	116	7.40	8
22Nov77-4Aqu $1\frac{1}{8}$ Clm 9000	8	8^9	3^2	113	4.10	8

Third choice: 110   7/2

16Dec77-9Aqu 6f Clm 12500	10^{10}		9^8	114	14.60	12
9Dec77-6Aqu $1\frac{1}{8}$ Clm 12500	6	6^9	4^3	116	4.10	9
1Dec77-5Aqu 1 Clm 15000	6	$6^{2\frac{1}{2}}$	3^2	116	6.50	8

Note that the favorite is not equivalent in class to the second choice and, therefore, is not similar by Rule 3 or any other rule up to this point. The favorite is similar to the second choice by Rule 15a(i,bb): Ignoring the sprint race, the second choice dropped in class from a $10,000 claiming pre-previous race to an $8,500 claiming last race and showed a slow start in its last race. The winning last race was in class less than today's race and this rule still applies. On the other hand, Rule 15b does not apply here because the previous race of the second choice was the only sprint in its last four races.

The favorite is similar to the third choice by Rule 15d. A fast start in its previous route race is followed by a slow start at shorter odds in its previous race, and the last sprint is not to be considered in today's route race (it must show a slow start, however). Rule 15a also applies since there is a drop in class from the pre-previous race to the previous race which shows a slow start.

Rule 16. Slow start by other horse in race shorter than today's race
> Today's race is longer than the other horse's last and recent race in which it showed a slow start, or today's race is at the same distance as the other's last race and longer than the previous race with slow starts shown in both races, but not if one of the following conditions holds:
> a. Today's race is a route, its last a sprint with a finish five or more lengths off the winner, and its previous race a route
> b. Its last race was in class more than 25 percent higher than today's race

    c. Its previous race occurred less than thirty-two days ago in class higher than or equal to today's race and shows a fast start at odds shorter than or equal to the last race (consider only sprints in sprint races)

    d. It did not win its last race easily

    e. It has started only once before unless a normal or weak betting pattern exists

NOTE: In Rule 16, neglect changes in route races of less that $\frac{1}{16}$ mile. Also, the following distances are assumed to be equivalent: $5\frac{1}{2}$ furlongs on turf and 6 furlongs on dirt; 7 or $7\frac{1}{2}$ furlongs on turf and 1 mile, 1 mile 70 yards, or $1\frac{1}{16}$ miles on dirt; 1 or $1\frac{1}{16}$ miles on turf and $1\frac{1}{8}$ miles on dirt.

Do not apply Rules 15 and 16 if the other's last race was a starter or optional claiming race. Do not apply Rule 15a if the other's previous race was a starter or optional claiming race.

In Section B, if the other horse is part of an entry or the field, the favorite is similar to the entry or field whenever the favorite is similar to one of the horses in the entry or field.

If a disqualification in the record changes the finish of a horse, use the better of the two finishes shown.

Example 16: Same as Example 15.

The second choice shows a slow start in its last race at a distance $\frac{1}{16}$ mile shorter than today's distance. All the conditions of Rule 16 hold and the favorite is similar to the second choice by this rule.

The presentation of the Rules of Similarity is now complete. All of them, together with the definitions of terms used, are collected in the appendix that follows in order to expedite their application both to the actual past races analyzed in the next chapter and to future races at the track.

Many readers will be astonished at the omission from the system of a number of factors usually considered to be of importance in predicting the outcome of a horse race, the times of past races, for example. However, the system works extremely well as now constituted, so that the effects of other factors are either implied or averaged out. Further refinement is undoubtedly possible.

APPENDICES TO CHAPTER 11
I: DEFINITION OF TERMS USED IN THE SYSTEM

AWAY—A horse has been away if it has not raced in the last twenty-one days. It includes first-time starters.

BETTING PATTERN—A relation between the odds on the favorite in a race and the odds on another choice, as shown in the accompanying table. A normal betting pattern occurs when the public's win probability for a horse is approximately 60 percent or less of the favorite's win probability, a weak betting pattern is approximately 50 percent or less of the favorite's win probability, and a very weak betting pattern is approximately 40 percent or less of the favorite's win probability. A normal betting pattern includes all odds longer than those shown in the table's normal betting pattern column, and similarly for weak and very weak betting patterns. A soft betting pattern includes the weak and very weak betting patterns.

Favorite Odds	Normal Betting Pattern	Weak Betting Pattern	Very Weak Betting Pattern
2/5, 1/2	7/5	9/5	5/2
3/5	8/5	2	3
4/5	9/5	5/2	7/2
1	2	3	4
6/5	5/2	3	9/2
7/5, 3/2, 8/5	3	7/2	9/2
9/5	3	4	5
2	7/2	9/2	6
5/2	9/2	5	7
3	5	6	8
7/2	6	7	9
4	7	8	10
9/2	8	9	11
5	9	10	12
6	10	11	13
7	11	12	14

CLASS—An ordering of races according to the capabilities of the horses. The following types of races are considered equivalent: stakes and name handicaps; allowance, handicap, and maiden special weight; claiming and maiden claiming labeled with the same claiming price; allowance and the highest price claiming race run at a meeting. This last equivalency may be used to establish the class of a horse moving from one track to another when there is a class change from allowance to claiming or *vice versa*. (If uncertainty exists on this point, pass the race). Optional claiming and starter races are restricted to horses having previously run for a stated claiming price. In the optional claimer, the owner has the option of entering his horse to be claimed or not to be claimed.

Stakes and name handicaps are considered to be 33 percent higher in class than allowance races, while the percentage differences in class for other type races (excluding optional claiming and starter races) depends on the claiming price. The accompanying table shows percentage increases in claiming prices used in the system for typical races:

Claiming Price	20 Percent Higher	25 Percent Higher
$3000	3600	3750
3500	4200	4375
4000	4800	5000
5000	6000	6250
6000	7200	7500
7500	9000	9375
8000	9600	10000
10000	12000	12500
12500	15000	15625
15000	18000	18750
20000	24000	25000
25000	30000	31250
30000	36000	37500
35000	42000	43750
40000	48000	50000

CLASS Z—The class of a horse which last raced in a class 20 percent or more higher than the favorite's last race and higher than or equal to the favorite's last three races or all the favorite's past races. Starter and optional claiming races are not to be considered; when these occur in the favorite's record, use the last three other type races.

EQUIVALENT IN CLASS—The favorite is equivalent in class to another horse if any of the following conditions hold:
a. The class of the favorite's last race was the same or lower than the other's last race; if the favorite's previous and pre-previous races both were higher in class than the other's three last races, a normal or soft betting pattern must exist
b. The classes of any two of the favorite's last three races were the same as two of the other's last three races, or the lowest class of the favorite's last three races was lower than the highest class of the other's last three races, but if the favorite's last was 25 percent or more higher in class than the other's last and higher than or equal to the other's previous race, a normal or soft betting pattern must exist

c. The favorite is a first-time starter, or has started only once before, or twice before if it did not finish first or second

d. The favorite ran one race of its last three in class lower than or equal to the last race of a one-time starter or the higher class of the two races of a two-time starter. (Note: Do not consider starter or optional claiming races, but use the most recent other type races in this definition.)

Example a:

Favorite:	Clm 5000	Second choice:	Clm 5000
	Clm 7500		Clm 5000
	Clm 7500		Clm 5000

The last race classes are the same, but a normal or soft betting pattern is required for equivalence in class because the favorite's previous and pre-previous races were both higher in class than all the other's last three races.

Example b:

Favorite:	Clm 5000	Second choice:	Clm 4000	Third choice:	Clm 4000
	Clm 4000		Clm 4000		Clm 4500
	Clm 4000		Clm 4000		Clm 4000

Two of the favorite's last three races are of the same class as two of the second choice, and the horses are equivalent in class if a normal or soft betting pattern exists since the favorite's last was 25 percent higher in class than the other's last. The favorite is equivalent in class to the third choice if a normal or soft betting pattern exists since the lowest class of the favorite's last three races ($4,000) is lower than the highest class of the other's ($4,500). The favorite's last, being 25 percent higher in class than the other's last, requires a normal or soft betting pattern.

EARLY SPEED—A horse showing early speed in a race was first or second at the ¼-mile call in a race of the same or higher class than today's race, or first in a race of lower class providing today's race is less than 25 percent higher in class.

EASILY—A horse won easily if it finished two or more lengths in front of the second place finisher, or if the comment *handily* or *easily* appears in the past performance line.

FAST START—A ¼-mile call in the first half of the field, also including a fourth in a seven-horse race, a third in a five-horse race, a ¼-mile call less than three lengths off the leader in sprints, and a ½-mile call less than three lengths off the leader in routes.

GOOD LAST RACE—A last and recent race in which a horse finished first, second, third, or fourth or worse less than three lengths off the winner, or fourth with a slow start.

GOOD PREVIOUS RACE—A recent race in which the horse finished first, second, third, or fourth or worse less than three lengths off the winner, or fourth with a slow start and which occurred preceding a poor last race.

MEETING—A sequence of consecutive racing days at the same track.

POOR LAST RACE—A last and recent race in which a horse finished fourth three or more lengths off the winner with a fast start, or fifth or worse three or more lengths off the winner.

PREVIOUS RACE—The race preceding the last race.

PRE-PREVIOUS RACE—The race preceding the previous race.

RECENT—Occurred in the last twenty-one days.

RELATIVE FINISH CHANGE—A change in the last race finish of the favorite as compared to another horse, which may be specified by the system. A plus-one change improves the last race finish of the favorite from a one-place better finish to a two-place better finish and from a two-place better finish to a three-place better finish; a minus-one change sets back the last race finish of the favorite from a one-place better finish to an even finish, from a two-place better finish to a one-place better finish, and from a three-or-more-place better finish to a two-place better finish. There is never to be a change of more than one place, and any number of plus-one changes are canceled by a single minus-one change and *vice versa*.

RELATIVE WEIGHT SHIFT—The difference in weights carried by the favorite and another horse in their last race or races less the difference in weight carried in today's race. For use in Rule 7, every three pounds of relative weight shift translates into 1 length of separation at the finish. A neck separation is $\frac{1}{4}$ length, a head $\frac{1}{8}$ length, a nose $\frac{1}{16}$ length.

ROUTE—A race at a distance of one mile or longer.

ROUTER—A horse which ran its last three races in routes, or four out of its last five races, or five out of its last nine, and did not run first or second in a recent sprint.

ROUTER-IN-SPRINT—A router which did not (1) finish first, or second with a fast start, or show early speed in a recent and last or previous sprint race, or (2) show a sharp drop in class, or (3) run in a last and recent race 25 percent or more higher in class than today's race.

SHARP DROP IN CLASS—A pattern of a horse's three last races one of which was run in class more than 25 percent higher than today's race and with finishes specified as follows: (1) a last race finish of third with a slow start, fourth less than three lengths off the winner with a slow start, fourth three or more lengths off the winner, or fifth or worse three or more lengths off the winner; (2) a previous race finish of second with a slow start, third or worse less than three lengths off the winner with a slow start, or third or worse three or more lengths off the winner; (3) a pre-previous race finish of first or second with a slow start, or third or worse. (Note: This definition does not apply if today's race is a starter or optional claiming race, and it does not apply if the horse ran in a starter or optional claiming race in any of its last three races.)

SLOW START—A ¼-mile call that is not a fast start.

SPRINT—A race at a distance of less than one mile.

SPRINTER—A horse which does not show a route race in its past performances.

SPROUTER—A horse which has shown a route race in its past performances and is not a router.

II. RULES OF SIMILARITY

Section A—Rules Under which the Favorite Is not to Be Bet

Rule 1. The favorite satisfies all the following conditions:
    a. It made a *slow start* in its last and *recent* race
    b. It did not win *easily* in its last race or in its *previous* race less than thirty-two days ago
    c. It did not show a *sharp drop in class* or, if today's race is not a stakes race, run in a stakes race in its last three starts
    d. It has started at least once at the present *meeting*
    e. It did not finish first or second in its only start at the present meeting
and one or more of the following:
    aa. The favorite's last race was lower in *class* than its previous race, or its previous race showed a slow start and was lower in class than its *pre-previous* race, but not if today's race is a *route* and its last or previous race the only *sprint* in its last four races
    bb. Today's race is a sprint and the favorite's last was a nonwinning route or its previous race was a nonwinning route with a slow start
    cc. Today's race is a route, the favorite's last race was a nonwinning route and its previous race a sprint, or its previous race was a non-winning route with a slow start and its pre-previous race a sprint, but not if the sprint race was the only sprint in its last four starts

dd. The favorite's last race was lower in class than today's race, or its previous race showed a slow start and was lower in class than today's race, or its previous and pre-previous races showed slow starts and the pre-previous race was lower in class than today's race, but not if today's race is a route and its last a sprint

ee. Today's race is a sprint and the favorite's last was a nonwinning race, its previous race a route, and its pre-previous race a sprint with a slow start in class less than that of today's race

ff. The favorite's last race was at odds equal to or shorter than its previous race in which it made a *fast start*, or the favorite showed a slow start and a finish of third or worse in its previous race at shorter odds than its pre-previous race in which it made a fast start

Rule 2. Today's race is longer than the favorite's last and recent race or its last at the meeting in which it made a slow start, or today's race distance is longer than or equal to the favorite's last and recent race in which it made a slow start and longer than its previous and recent or at-the-meeting race, but not if today's race is a route, its last a sprint with a finish five or more lengths off the winner, and its previous race a route, or if its last race was in class more than 25 percent higher than today's race (but not if today's race is a starter or optional claiming race), or if the favorite's last race was not run at the present meeting. (In Rule 2, neglect changes in route races of less than $\frac{1}{16}$ mile. Also, the following distances are assumed to be equivalent: $5\frac{1}{2}$ furlongs on turf and 6 furlongs on dirt; 7 or $7\frac{1}{2}$ furlongs on turf and 1 mile, 1 mile 70 yards, or $1\frac{1}{16}$ miles on dirt; 1 or $1\frac{1}{16}$ miles on turf and $1\frac{1}{8}$ miles on dirt).

Rule 3. The favorite satisfies the following conditions:
a. Today's race is a sprint
b. The favorite's last and recent race was a nonwinning route with a fast start in class not more than 25 percent higher than today's race
c. The favorite has started at least once at the present meeting
and either one of the following:
aa. The favorite made a slow start in its previous race in lower class than its pre-previous race
bb. The favorite made a slow start in its previous race at odds shorter than or equal to its pre-previous race in which it made a fast start

(NOTE: Rule 1c does not apply if today's race is a starter or optional claiming race. Rules 1aa, 1dd, and 3aa do not apply to past starter and optional claiming races.)

III. RULES OF SIMILARITY

Section B—Rules under which the Favorite Is Similar to Another Horse

Rule 1. Last race finishes the same

The favorite ran a *poor last race*, is *equivalent in class* to the other horse, finished in the same position as the other horse in its last race, and is not a *router-in-sprint*, but a *normal or soft betting pattern* must exist if the other horse did not run its last race in *class Z* and one or more of the following conditions hold:

a. The other horse ran more than twenty-one days ago
b. The favorite has run at the present *meeting* and the other has not
c. Today's race is a *route* race and the favorite is a *sprouter* or *router* and the other horse a *sprinter*
d. There is a nine-pound or more *relative weight shift* in favor of the favorite
e. The favorite is a male and the other horse a female

Rule 2. Good last race finish of the favorite not as good as the other's last race finish when the favorite did not race the other horse in the other's last race

The favorite ran a *poor last race*, is *equivalent in class* to the other horse, finished in the same position as the other horse in its last race, and is not a *router-in-sprint*, but a *normal or soft betting pattern* must exist if the other horse did not run its last race in *class Z* and one or more of the following conditions hold:

a. The other horse last ran more than twenty-one days ago, but not if today's race is a sprint and the other finished first or second
b. Today's race is a route race and the favorite is a sprouter or router while the other horse is a sprinter which did not win its last race or run in class Z
c. The other horse finished first or second less than one length off the winner in its only start at the meeting

Rule 3. Good last race finish of the favorite the same or better than the other's good last race or fourth place finish when the favorite did not race the other in the other's last race

The favorite ran a good last race, is equivalent in class to the other horse, did not race the other horse in the other's last race, is not a router-in-sprint, and the other horse finished second, third, fourth, or less than three lengths off the winner in its last race if a normal or soft betting pattern exists for a one-place better finish by the favorite, a soft betting pattern for a two-place better finish by the favorite, a very weak betting pattern for a three-place better finish by the favorite, and any betting pattern for the same finish by both, but apply a *plus-one relative finish change* if one or more of the following conditions hold:

a. The other horse last ran more than twenty-one days ago
b. The favorite has run at the present meeting and the other horse has not
c. Today's race is a route race and the favorite is a sprouter or a router while the other horse is a sprinter which did not win its last race or run in class Z
d. The favorite showed *early speed* in its last race and the other horse a slow start
e. There is a nine-pound or more relative weight shift in favor of the favorite
f. The favorite won its last race or finished less than three lengths off the winner and the other horse finished five or more lengths off the winner

and apply a *minus-one relative finish change* if one or more of the following conditions hold:

g. The other horse last raced in class Z
h. There is a nine-pound or more relative weight shift against the favorite
i. The favorite finished five or more lengths off the winner in its last race and the other horse less than three lengths off the winner
j. The favorite made a slow start in its last race and the other horse showed early speed

(In this rule, a last race finish by either horse of fifth or worse less than three lengths off the winner is to be considered a fourth-place finish)

Rule 4. Good last race finish by the favorite and a poor last race by the other horse with early speed or in class Z

a. The favorite ran a good last race and the other horse ran a poor last race in class Z or showed early speed less than thirty-two days ago if either Rule 2 or Rule 3 can be applied to the other's previous race
b. The favorite finished third, fourth less than three lengths off the winner, fourth three or more lengths off the winner with a slow start, or fifth or worse less than three lengths off the winner in its last and recent race and the other horse's last race was 25 percent or more higher in class than today's race if a normal or soft betting pattern exists, or any betting pattern if the other finished first, second, third or fourth in its previous race

Rule 5. Good last race finish at the meeting by a favorite not equivalent in class to the other horse

The favorite ran a good last race at the meeting, is not a router-in-sprint, and is not equivalent in class to the other horse and one or more of the following conditions hold:

a. The other horse scored an easy win in its last and recent race and a normal or soft betting pattern exists

b. The favorite made slow starts in its last three or all its past races and either Rule 2 or Rule 3 applies neglecting the "equivalent in class" requirement

c. The favorite did not finish first or second less than five lengths off the winner or made slow starts in its last three or all its past races and the other horse is a first-time starter or showed early speed in its last and recent race if a normal or soft betting pattern exists

Rule 6. Last and recent race finish by the favorite of first or second in its only start at the meeting

The favorite finished first or second in its last and recent race and all other starts if any at the meeting after a race elsewhere or its only start at the meeting within the last thirty-one days if Rule 14 applies considering the race as an easy win.

Rule 7. Last race together

a. The favorite finished behind the other horse in the other's last race, but a normal or soft betting pattern must exist if one or more of the following conditions hold:

    i. A relative weight shift moves the favorite $\frac{1}{2}$ length or more ahead of the other

    ii. The race was either horse's only start at the meeting after a race elsewhere, but not if a relative weight shift moves the other from less than one length to one or more lengths ahead of the favorite or the favorite finished two or more places behind the other horse

    iii. The favorite was off at shorter odds in the last race and a very weak betting pattern existed between the two horses

    iv. The favorite shows a better finish in a subsequent race

    v. The favorite showed early speed in the last race.

b. The favorite beat the other horse in the other's last race and a normal or soft betting pattern exists for a one-place better finish, a soft betting pattern for a two-place better finish, and a very weak betting pattern for a three-or-more place better finish, but apply a plus-one relative finish change if one or more of the following conditions hold:

      i. The favorite beat the other horse by three or more lengths; but not if the race was either's only start at the meeting after a race elsewhere

     ii. The favorite ran in a more recent race than the race together

    iii. There is a relative weight shift of seven pounds or more in favor of the favorite

and apply a minus-one relative finish change if one or more of the following conditions hold:

     iv. The favorite finished less than $\frac{1}{2}$ length ahead of the other horse after adjusting for any relative weight shift

      v. The favorite made a slow start, the other a fast start, and today's race is not longer than the last race

     vi. There is a relative weight shift of seven pounds or more against the favorite

    vii. A relative weight shift makes the other horse one length or less better than the favorite

   viii. The race was either's only start at the meeting after a race elsewhere if the favorite was off at longer odds than the other in the last race

  c. The favorite beat the other horse in its last race and a relative weight shift makes the other more than one length better than the favorite, but a normal or soft betting pattern must exist if the favorite ran in a subsequent race

  d. The favorite beat the other horse in the last race of each if the other was off at shorter odds in the last race and a soft betting pattern exists in today's race

Rule 8. Good previous race

The favorite ran a *good previous race* and Rules 2, 3, 5, or 7 can be applied using this race as if it were a good last race.

NOTE: Apply Section A and establish equivalence in class using the favorite's last three races in the usual manner.

Rule 9. Favorite away

  a. The favorite and the other horse have been *away* and are equivalent in class, but, unless the other horse raced in class Z or showed early speed in its last race, a normal or soft betting pattern must exist if

    i. the favorite has started at the present meeting and the other has not, or

    ii. the favorite finished first or second in its last race and the other did not.

b. The favorite and the other horse have been away, are not equivalent in class, and either a very weak betting pattern exists or the favorite made slow starts in its last three races or in all its starts

c. The favorite is a first-time starter, the other horse is a one-time starter that ran a poor last race without showing early speed, and a normal or soft betting pattern exists

d. The favorite has been away, did not win or finish second less than five lengths off the winner in its last race, and the other horse either won (not easily), finished second, third, or fourth less than three lengths off the winner in its last and recent race, or fourth three or more lengths off the winner and a normal or soft betting pattern exists, or less than three lengths off the winner and a normal or soft betting pattern exists, or won easily or showed early speed and a normal or soft betting pattern exists, but with the following conditions:

   i. If the favorite's last race was higher in class than today's race and the other horse finished first or second or showed early speed in its only start at the meeting after a race elsewhere in class equal to or less than today's race, the horses are not similar by this rule

   ii. In sprints, if the favorite is not equivalent in class to the other horse, a normal or soft betting pattern must exist or any betting pattern if the favorite finished fifth or worse in its last race

e. The favorite has been away, finished first or second less than five lengths off the winner in its last race, and the other horse finished first or second in its last and recent race, or third, fourth, or less than three lengths off the winner and a normal or soft betting pattern exists, but with the following conditions:

   i. If the other horse finished first or second or showed early speed in its only race at the meeting after a race elsewhere in class equal to or less than today's race, the horses are not similar by this rule

   ii. In sprints, if the favorite is not equivalent in class to the other, the horses are not similar

f. The favorite has been away, the other's last race was a poor last race and Rule 9d or Rule 9e may be applied to the other's previous race less than thirty-two days ago considering the other's previous race as its last and recent race

g. The favorite has been away, did not win its last race in class higher than or equal to today's race, and the other horse ran a poor last race in class 25 percent or more higher than today's race or showed early speed in class higher than or equal to today's race if a normal or soft betting pattern exists or any betting pattern if the other ran first, second, third, or fourth in its previous race in class equal to or higher than today's race

NOTE: Use Rule 7 if the favorite raced the other horse in the other's last race.

Rule 10. The only race in the last twenty-one days a poor last race

The favorite ran a poor last race that was its only race in the last twenty-one days, is equivalent in class to the other horse, did not race the other horse in the other's last race, and any one of the following conditions apply:

a. The other horse ran a last and recent race that was neither a good last race nor a fourth place finish and was its only start in the last twenty-one days, but a normal or soft betting pattern must exist if
   i. the favorite raced at the present meeting and the other did not, or
   ii. the favorite showed a better finish in its previous race than the other in its previous race, but not if the other's previous race was in class Z, or
   iii. the other horse is a one-time starter
b. The other horse has been away if a normal or soft betting pattern exists, or any betting pattern if the favorite did not finish fourth in its last race and the class of the other's last race was 25 percent or more higher than today's race
c. Rules 9d, e, f, or g can be applied assuming the favorite to have been away and using its previous race finish as its last race finish

Rule 11. Sharp drop in class

The favorite showed a sharp drop in class and no early speed in a last and recent race and one of the following conditions apply:

a. The other horse has been away if a normal or soft betting pattern exists or any betting pattern if the other won its last race
b. The other horse is making its first start at the meeting if the favorite has raced at the meeting and a normal or soft betting pattern exists, or any betting pattern if the favorite has raced only once at the meeting
c. The favorite is equivalent in class to the other horse
d. The other horse ran in a last and recent race and won or finished second, or finished third or fourth if a normal or soft betting pattern exists, or finished less than three lengths off the winner if a normal or soft betting pattern exists
e. The other horse showed early speed in a last and recent race (only in a sprint if today's race is a sprint) and did not win easily
f. The other horse ran a last and recent race that was neither a good last race nor a fourth place finish three or more lengths off the win-

ner if Rule 11d can be applied to a previous and recent race of the other and a normal or soft betting pattern exists

NOTE: Use Rule 7 if the favorite raced the other horse in the other's last race.

Rule 12. Early speed

    a. The favorite showed early speed in a good last race, or a fast start in its last race and early speed in a good previous race, or a slow start in its last race in class higher than today's race and early speed in a good previous race, or early speed in a poor last race and a good previous race, and the other horse did not show early speed or win with a fast start in its only race at the meeting, and one of the following conditions holds:

       i. The other horse is a first-time starter and a normal or soft betting pattern exists, or any betting pattern if the favorite started only once at the present meeting

      ii. The other horse has been away and finished first, second, third, or less than three lengths off the winner in its last race and a normal or soft betting pattern exists, or any betting pattern if the other raced last in class 25 percent or more higher than today's race or if the favorite started only once at the present meeting

     iii. The other horse has been away and finished fourth or worse three or more lengths off the winner in its last race and a very weak betting pattern exists, or a soft betting pattern if the other raced last in class 25 percent or more higher than today's race or if the favorite started only once at the present meeting

     iv. The other horse ran in its last and recent race and its previous race in class Z, both 20 percent or more higher than today's race, and finished fifth or worse three or more lengths off the winner in its last race if a normal or soft betting pattern exists, or any betting pattern if the finish of the other's previous race was first, second, third, or less than three lengths off the winner or the favorite started only once at the present meeting

    b. The favorite did not finish first or second in the last thirty-one days and

       i. showed early speed in a last and recent race in class 20 percent or more higher than today's race and the other horse's last race and higher than the other's last three races, or

      ii. showed a fast start in its last and recent race and early speed in a recent previous race both of which were 20 percent or more

higher in class than today's race and the other horse's last race
and higher than the other's last three races,
and one of the following conditions holds:

   i. The other horse ran first or second in a recent race

  ii. The other horse ran third, fourth, or less than three lengths off
the winner in a recent race and a normal or soft betting pattern
exists

 iii. The other horse has been away

Rule 13. Router in sprint

The favorite is a sprinter or sprouter in a sprint race, shows a sharp
drop in class, or has been away, and the other horse is a router which
ran a last and recent race in class less than 10 percent higher than the
highest class of the favorite's last three races, did not win easily, and
did not show early speed unless a very weak betting pattern exists.

NOTE: In this rule, a 7- or $7\frac{1}{2}$-furlong turf race is to be considered a route race.

Rule 14. Easy win last race or previous race

  a. The favorite won its last and recent race easily, is equivalent in class
to the other horse, did not race against the other horse in the last
race of each, and one of the following conditions holds:

    i. The other horse finished first or second less than five lengths
off the winner in a last and recent race

   ii. The other horse finished second five or more lengths off the
winner, third, fourth, or less than three lengths off the winner
in a last and recent race and a normal or soft betting pattern
exists

  iii. The other horse is making its first start at the meeting after a
race elsewhere if the favorite has started at the meeting, and a
normal or soft betting pattern exists

  iv. The other horse has been away and a normal or soft betting
pattern exists, or any betting pattern if the other won its last
race or raced last in class Z

   v. The other horse ran a last and recent race in class Z with a fifth
or worse finish three or more lengths off the winner, but a normal or soft betting pattern must exist if the other horse showed
early speed or if the favorite has started at the meeting and the
other has not

  vi. The other horse ran a poor last race and a previous race in class
Z if a soft betting pattern exists

vii. The other horse finished fifth or worse three or more lengths off the winner in its last race and one of the Rules 2, 3, 4, 5, or 6 can be applied to the other's previous and recent race

b. The favorite's last race was not an easy win and Rule 14a can be applied using its previous and recent race as its last race

NOTE: If today's race is a sprint, the favorite's easy win must have been in a sprint, and if today's race is a route, the favorite's easy win must have been in either a 7- or 7½-furlong race or a route race.

Rule 15.. Slow start by the other horse

The favorite ran a good last race, or a good previous race, or shows a sharp drop in class, or has been away, or showed early speed, and the other horse made a slow start in a last and recent race in class no more than 25 percent higher than today's race, did not run in a stakes race in its last three races if today's race is not a stakes race, did not win easily in its last race or its previous race less than thirty-two days ago, has started at least once at the present meeting, did not finish first or second in its only start at the meeting, and one of the following conditions is satisfied:

a. The other horse's last race was a nonwinning race (or a win if in class less than today's race) in lower class than its previous race, or its previous race shows a slow start and was lower in class than its pre-previous race, but with the following qualifications:

  i. If today's race is a route race,
     aa. do not consider past sprint races
     bb. and if the last and pre-previous races are routes and the previous race a sprint, apply this subsection ignoring the sprint race

  ii. If today's race is a sprint, do not consider a drop in class from a route race to a sprint race, but
     aa. if the last race was a route with a fast start, apply this subsection to previous and pre-previous sprint races, and
     bb. if the previous race was a route, apply this subsection to pre-previous and last sprint races

b. Today's race is a route and the other horse's last race was a route and its previous race a sprint, or the other horse's previous race was a route with a slow start and its pre-previous race a sprint, but not if the sprint is the only one in its last four starts and shows a slow start

c. Today's race is a sprint and the other horse's last race was a route, or its previous race was a route with a slow start, or its pre-previous race was a route with a slow start and its previous race showed a slow start

d. The last race of the other horse was at shorter odds than its previous race in which it made a fast start, or its previous race showed a slow start and a third-or-worse finish at shorter odds than its pre-previous race in which it made a fast start, but with the following qualifications:

   i. If today's race is a sprint and the other horse's last race was a route with a fast start, apply this rule to previous and pre-previous sprint races

   ii. If today's race is a route, do not consider past sprint races

Rule 16. Slow start by other horse in race shorter than today's race

Today's race is longer than the other horse's last and recent race in which it showed a slow start, or today's race is at the same distance as the other's last race and longer than the previous race with slow starts shown in both races, but not if one of the following conditions holds:

a. Today's race is a route, its last a sprint with a finish five or more lengths off the winner, and its previous race a route

b. Its last race was in class more than 25 percent higher than today's race

c. Its previous race occurred less than thirty-two days ago in class higher than or equal to today's race and shows a fast start at odds shorter than or equal to the last race (consider only sprints in sprint races)

d. It did not win its last race easily

e. It has started only once before unless a normal or weak betting pattern exists

NOTE: In Rule 16, neglect changes in route races of less that $\frac{1}{16}$ mile. Also, the following distances are assumed to be equivalent: $5\frac{1}{2}$ furlongs on turf and 6 furlongs on dirt; 7 or $7\frac{1}{2}$ furlongs on turf and 1 mile, 1 mile 70 yards, or $1\frac{1}{16}$ miles on dirt: 1 or $1\frac{1}{16}$ miles on turf and $1\frac{1}{8}$ miles on dirt.

Do not apply Rules 15 and 16 if the other's last race was a starter or optional claiming race. Do not apply Rule 15a if the other's previous race was a starter or optional claiming race.

In Section B, if the other horse is part of an entry or the field, the favorite is similar to the entry or field whenever the favorite is similar to one of the horses in the entry or the field.

If a disqualification in the record changes the finish of a horse, use the better of the two finishes shown.

12
THE SYSTEM IN PRACTICE

To do good is noble. But to teach others to do good is more noble—and much easier.

Mark Twain

Before confronting the system with the harsh reality of the racetrack, let us summarize briefly the main aspects of the theory's development. First, the pari-mutuel betting market was shown to be weakly efficient as regards favorites. Second, the existence of races in which late-breaking information could be utilized for profitable wagering was hypothesized. This information was then assumed detectable through the application of the Rules of Similarity in which those horses "similar" to the favorite had zero winning probability. An expectation E_{system} was then calculated from the formula

$$E_{system} = \frac{1}{S} - 1$$

where S is the sum of the "percentages" $1/(o_i + 1)$ for the horses in the race without any contributions from horses similar to the favorite. Those favorites with E_{system} equal to or greater than +0.43 were then seen to be profitable bets.

In employing the system at the track, certain simplifications are necessary. It is not possible to use the odds at the close of betting in calculating the percentages, so the last or next-to-last odds flash on the "tote" before the close must be used. Changes infrequently occur on this last change of odds which affect the decision to bet or not to bet; sometimes a horse becomes a bet and sometimes a horse that was bet should not have been, but this state of affairs cannot be helped and will average out over the long run. Furthermore, it is impractical to reach a decision on similarity, calculate the percentages and corresponding system expectation, and bet all in the short—approximately one-minute—time interval available. To render the system operable, therefore, the following procedure should be practiced.

Betting Procedure

1. Check Section A of the *Rules of Similarity* to ascertain whether or not the favorite is a suitable bet. If it is, determine whether or not the favorite is similar

to each of the next three choices in the race, and any other horse at odds of 7/1 or less using Section B of the *Rules of Similarity*.

Well before post time, determine which horses are similar to one another irrespective of the odds and which horses would be similar depending on the betting patterns at the close. This part of the procedure can be done using the *Daily Racing Form* at home or, after a sufficient amount of expertise in handling the Rules of Similarity and the definitions has been acquired, at the track. Weight changes and scratches must be noted upon arrival at the track since these factors may affect the similarities. The number of horses considered for similarity is limited to the first four choices or horses at odds of 7/1 or less to save time.

2. When another horse is similar to the favorite, use the following table to obtain a certain number of points corresponding to the odds on that horse at the last flash of the "tote" before post time.

Odds	Points	Odds	Points	Odds	Points
6/5	45	3	25	8	11
7/5	42	7/2	22	9	10
3/2	40	4	20	10	9
8/5	38	9/2	18	11	8
9/5	36	5	16	12	8
2	33	6	14	13	7
5/2	28	7	12	14	7

The odds in the table are the approximate odds flashed on the tote. They are not the undisplayed exact odds which are calculable from the monies bet in the win pool. Not enough time exists to use exact odds. The point values are the percentages multiplied by 100.

3. Add the points on all the horses similar to the favorite. No calculation of the percentages or the system expectation is necessary.

4. When the point sum equals or exceeds the amount given in the next table for a given "take," the favorite is to be bet.

Take	Point sum
14%	45
15%	47
16%	49
17%	51

The take varies from state to state and like all other taxes increases steadily over the years. Obviously, a bettor should play in a state where this tax on winning is least. The *Daily Racing Form* carries the legal take in the headings above the past result charts. It may also be calculated from a formula derived in the appendix to Chapter 6, $1 - f = 1/S$, where f is the legal take plus a little extra for breakage.

Each point sum in the table represents the contributions to the sum of percentages from horses similar to the favorite. When divided by 100, subtracted from the sum of the percentages for all horses in the race, and substituted in the formula for the system expectation $E_{system} = (1/S) - 1$, they lead to $E_{system} = +0.43$, just the dividing line between favorable and unfavorable bets.

I have only limited data for takes over 17 percent. It appears that an increased system expectation is necessary for higher takes because there tend to be more horses in a race at odds of 7/1 and shorter. The higher the take, the shorter the odds in general tend to be. My best estimate of point sums for higher takes are as follows:

Take	Point sum
18%	54
19%	58
20%	61

5. If the favorite is not to be bet, the above procedure is to be repeated for the second choice. Determine which horses are similar to the second choice just as was done for the favorite. Add up the points corresponding to the odds on the similar horses, but when the favorite is similar to the second choice, use the points corresponding to the odds on the second choice. The proper number of points for a bet on the second choice is the same as for the favorites. Note that the favorite cannot be similar to the second choice when a normal or soft betting pattern is required since the odds on the favorite are shorter than those on the second choice.

6. If neither the favorite nor the second choice turns out to be a bet, repeat the procedure of Section 5 for the third choice. Note that neither the favorite nor the second choice can be similar to the third choice when a normal or soft betting pattern is required.

7. Make only flat bets on all selections to avoid last minute complications arising from the amount to be bet. A good idea is to start with a pool of capital and risk one-twentieth of it on each bet. The loss of starting capital is unlikely with this procedure (see Chapter 16).

Let us now follow the actions of an experienced bettor as he applies the system at the racetrack. Upon arriving at the track, he locates a vantage point from which he will be able to observe the "tote" board and place a bet in the last few seconds before the close of betting. A stopwatch is helpful to time the flashes of the tote, not the horses, so that the last flash before post time can be accurately judged. If lines form in front of the betting windows, a certain amount of jockeying will prevent being shut out. The advent of exotic wagering—exactas, quinellas, doubles, triples—has made last-minute betting easier because of the reduced crowds at the regular betting windows. Needless to say, exotic wagers are not to be considered: They are blind bets made without a knowledge of the closing odds and the takes are usually much higher than for regular betting.

Five minutes before post time, our bettor takes up his vantage point, ready to make a bet if called for. By this time, the general betting picture in most races has clarified—the favorite and the next three choices have been determined along with their approximate odds. Knowing he may have as many as three split-second decisions to make, he keeps his eye alerted to all the betting patterns that may develop as the tote flashes its continuing stream of information. Simultaneously, he watches the lines at the betting windows, ready to bet his predetermined amount, if called for. Excluded from his mind are all the imponderables, rumors, tips, and emotional biases that concern and bemuse the average fan, because he knows all such matters are accurately reflected in the odds. Finally, at the last flash before post time, the decision is made: to bet or not to bet.

To illustrate how a day may go, we shall follow through in their entirety two racing cards, analyzing each of the races and noting any unusual betting circumstances. The first day was a very good one for the system: 24 October 1977 at Aqueduct Racetrack, New York. The "take" in New York in 1977 was 17 percent, so that a sum of 51 points was needed for a bet.

Race 1: 24 Oct 77-1   Aqu   7f   Clm 25000 to Clm 20000

Favorite: Comical Passtime   116   2

13Oct77-7Bel 6f Clm 25000	6^3	$3^{1\frac{1}{2}}$	116	19.30	8
3Oct77-6Bel 7f Clm 27500	4^3	9^{15}	114	21.10	9
29Aug77-5Bel 6f Clm 35000	4^4	8^{22}	116	20.90	8

Second choice: Reflection Pool   121   9/2

13Oct77-7Bel 6f Clm 22500	$5^{2\frac{1}{2}}$	1^{nk}	114	3.80	8
3Oct77-6Bel 7f Clm 27500	8^6	5^4	115	5.60	9
24Sep77-2Bel 6f Clm 25000	7^8	3^{10}	116	3.80	8

Third choice: Oars Up 114 5

13Oct77-7Bel	6f	Clm 25000	7^4		7^3	116	7.80	8
7Sep77-8Med	1^{70}	TAllowance	7	8^{16}	8^9	112	7.00	9
18Aug77-8AP	$1\frac{1}{8}$	Allowance	2	$2^{2\frac{1}{2}}$	$7^{9\frac{1}{2}}$	112	9.90	7
11Aug77-8AP	1	Allowance	3	7^7	$6^{6\frac{1}{4}}$	112	2.40	8
2Aug77-7AP	1	Allowance	9	9^{11}	2^{hd}	116	3.10	9

Fourth choice: Utterly 114 5

12Oct77-7Bel	$1\frac{1}{16}$	TAllowance	2	2^1	$3^{4\frac{1}{2}}$	115	9.90	7
26Sep77-4Bel	$1\frac{1}{16}$	Clm 17500	2	$2^{1\frac{1}{2}}$	1^8	114	4.20	6
14Sep77-5Bel	6f	Clm 19000	6^6		4^7	114	7.10	8

Fifth choice: Jenni's Whistle 116 6

13Oct77-7Bel	6f	Clm 25000	$3\frac{1}{2}$		5^2	116	7.00	8
20Sep77-8Med	$1\frac{1}{16}$	Clm 30000	4	5^4	7^{20}	114	5.50	7
29Jly77-6Atl	1	TAllowance	6	$5^{3\frac{1}{2}}$	1^{hd}	115	0.70	7

Sixth choice: Wanton Woman 116 6

29Aug77-5Mth	6f	Allowance	$2\frac{1}{2}$		1^4	117	1.00	6
16Aug77-4Sar	6f	Clm 20000	$2^{1\frac{1}{2}}$		$2^{2\frac{1}{2}}$	116	2.50	7
6Aug77-3Sar	6f	Clm 22500	9^{11}		9^{18}	114	8.50	9

This race was for horses entered to be claimed for prices in the range $20,000–$25,000. According to the race conditions, for each $2,500 reduction in the claiming price from $25,000, a horse was allowed a two-pound weight reduction. Although the favorite, Comical Passtime, shows a slow start in its last and recent race, Section A of the *Rules of Similarity* need not be considered since the horse has not started at the Aqueduct meeting. Comparing the favorite with the second choice, Reflection Pool, we see they faced each other in their last race and Reflection Pool won. Rule 7 (*Last race together*) and subsection a (*the favorite finished behind the other horse*) apply. Since a relative weight shift of seven pounds moves the favorite more than 1/2 length ahead of the second choice here, a normal or soft betting pattern must exist and does. Therefore, the favorite is similar to the second choice and collects 18 points corresponding to the 9/2 odds on the latter. Note that no other Rule of Similarity applies.

The third choice also raced in the 13 Oct 77 race and finished behind the favorite. Rule 7b requires a very weak betting pattern for a three-or-more-place better finish, and no changes are indicated by subsections (i.) through (viii.). Since only a weak betting pattern exists, the favorite is not similar to the third choice by Rule 7. However, Rule 13 applies because Oars Up is a router in a sprint race (four of its last five races are routes), and the horses are similar. Add

16 points more to the favorite's sum of points. (The symbol T in the previous race line denotes a turf race.)

The fourth choice, Utterly, did not race the favorite in its last race. Now we note that the favorite ran a good last race with the same finish as Utterly, so Rule 3 is to be checked. All its conditions are fulfilled and the horses are similar. In a case like this with an equal last race finish and a weak betting pattern, none of the subsections of Rule 3 need to be checked since they can require at worst a normal betting pattern. Add 16 points to the favorite's sum.

The fifth choice, Jenni's Whistle, was beaten by the favorite in the last race. Rule 7 applies immediately since a very weak betting pattern exists and no subsection need be checked. Add 14 more points.

The favorite is similar to the sixth choice, Wanton Woman, by Rule 2. No subsections need be checked since a very weak betting pattern exists. Add 14 points.

There were no other horses at odds of 7/1 or less. Adding up all the points, we obtain a total of 78 points against the 51 required for a bet. The favorite is, therefore, a bet in this race, and it won. It was clear long before post time which horse would be the favorite and that the favorite would be bet. The first race being the first half of the daily double, there were no lines at the betting windows to contend with. That Comical Passtime was made such a strong favorite in this race was surprising.

Race 2: 24 Oct 77-2   Aqu $1\frac{1}{8}$ Starter Handicap 10000

Favorite: Rare Joel   122   4/5

6Oct77-6Bel $1\frac{1}{4}$	TAllowance	3	3^6	4^1	117	7.70	7
24Sep77-5Bel $1\frac{1}{16}$	Allowance	1	$1^{\frac{1}{2}}$	1^6	117	1.40	8
9Sep77-7Bel $1\frac{1}{16}$	TAllowance	6	$5^{7\frac{1}{2}}$	5^3	117	3.30	6

Second choice: Franglais   113   4

8Oct77-5Bel $1\frac{1}{4}$	TAllowance	5	5^3	5^2	117	14.30	6
30Aug77-7Mth 6f	Clm 10000	5^2		$1^{4\frac{1}{2}}$	116	2.40	9
20Apr77-7Aqu $1\frac{1}{16}$	Clm 25000	1	1^{hd}	$5^{3\frac{1}{2}}$	117	3.60	9

Third choice: Quillon Dagger   124   4

17Oct77-8Med $1\frac{1}{16}$	Allowance	5	$5^{2\frac{1}{2}}$	$1^{2\frac{1}{2}}$	116	1.10	6
27Sep77-8Med $1\frac{1}{16}$	Allowance	5	$5^{5\frac{1}{2}}$	$2^{\frac{3}{4}}$	119	1.90	6
19Sep77-8Med 1^{70}	Allowance	8	$6^{3\frac{1}{2}}$	$2^{\frac{1}{2}}$	119	6.40	10

Fourth choice: Good Shot II   108   6

12Oct77-3Bel 1⅛	Hcp 7500s	6	5^4	$3^{6\frac{1}{4}}$	111	5.60	8
5Oct77-1Bel 1¼	TClm 14000	7	9^{12}	9^{14}	113	8.70	12
19Sep77-5Bel 1 1/16	Clm 10000	4	$3^{2\frac{1}{2}}$	5^{11}	117	3.60	8
2Sep77-5Bel 1⅛	Clm 10000	6	5^6	$4^{4\frac{1}{4}}$	117	2.50	8

This race is a starter handicap, a race for horses which have started for a claiming price of $10,000 or less since 1 December 1976. The weights in the race are assigned by the racing secretary so as to make the outcome as close as possible. In making Rare Joel such a pronounced favorite, the public obviously did not think too highly of his opinion.

The favorite shows a fast start in a good last race and did not race any of the other horses in their last races. Section A may be neglected. Rule 2 applies to the third choice, Rule 3 to the second choice, and the favorite is similar to both. However, the favorite is not equivalent in class to the fourth choice, Good Shot II, so Rule 3 cannot be applied. No other rule is applicable, and the favorite is not similar to the fourth choice. Adding the points on the second and third choices, we get 20 + 20 = 40, not enough for a bet on the favorite.

We turn our attention to the second choice, Franglais. Section A may be neglected since this is its first start at the meeting. It also ran a good last race and is similar to the favorite and the third choice by Rule 2. Rule 2 does not apply to the fourth choice, however, because Franglais is not equivalent in class to Good Shot II. Neglecting the latter's last race (a starter handicap), Franglais' last race is more than 25 percent higher in class than Good Shot's previous race and a normal or soft betting pattern is demanded, or odds on Good Shot of 7/1 or longer for odds on Franglais of 4/1. No other rule is applicable, and the second choice is not similar to the fourth choice. Adding up points for the second choice, we obtain 20 + 20 = 40 points; again, not enough for a second choice bet.

The third choice, Quillon Dagger, may now be considered for a bet. Since it shows an easy win in a good last race and a better finish than the other horses, Rule 3 and Rule 14 must be checked. Looking at Rule 3 first, Quillon Dagger shows a three-place better finish than the favorite, which requires a very weak betting pattern to exist (none of the subsections affect this requirement). Such a pattern obviously does not exist since the favorite is at shorter odds than 4/1, so that the third choice is not similar to the favorite. Also, for the same reason, it is not similar to the second choice. Rule 14a (ii.) requires a normal or soft betting pattern for similarity with the favorite and second choice, and this pattern does not exist. And finally, Quillon Dagger is not equivalent in class to

Good Shot II, so that neither Rule 3 nor Rule 14 can be applied. Its sum of points is 0, and it is no bet.

There is no bet to be made in this race although the favorite won. Toward the close of betting, it was necessary to watch closely the odds on the second and fourth choices. If they had fallen into a normal or soft betting pattern, Franglais would have been a bet. As it was, the conclusion here is that this is a properly bet race. Over the long run, losses would be incurred betting on races like this.

Race 3: 24 Oct 77-3   Aqu   6f   MdSpWt

Favorite: Drake's Dream   119   4/5

10Sep77-1Bel	6f	MdSpWt	1^{hd}		$2^{2\frac{3}{4}}$	118	2.60	9
31Aug77-9Mth	6f	MdSpWt	$2^{1\frac{1}{2}}$		$3^{1\frac{1}{4}}$	119	10.60	11

Second choice: Topfable   119   5/2

6Oct77-1Bel	6f	MdSpWt	$5^{1\frac{3}{4}}$		$4^{6\frac{1}{4}}$	119	7.60	10
7Jun77-4Bel	5½f	MdSpWt	10^{14}		8^{19}	122	3.20	10

Third choice: Pursuer   109   6

12Apr77-6Hia	6f	MdSpWt	$3^{3\frac{1}{2}}$		4^8	113	1.40	12
29Mar77-6Hia	6f	MdSpWt	2^{hd}		2^{hd}	112	1.10	10
4Feb77-3GP	6f	MdSpWt	2^{hd}		$7^{7\frac{1}{2}}$	120	1.60	10

Fourth choice: Bajapa   119   10

20Jun77-3Bel	6f	MdSpWt	$6^{5\frac{1}{4}}$		10^{20}	114	68.50	12
6Jun77-5Bel	6f	MdSpWt	$2^{\frac{1}{2}}$		7^{18}	114	6.20	9
15May77-2Hol	6f	MdSpWt	6^4		$5^{8\frac{1}{2}}$	109	4.80	10

This is a race for maidens, horses which have never won a race. The favorite's last race occurred more than twenty-one days ago and Rule 9 should first be checked. The favorite is similar to the second choice by Rule 9e, to the third choice by Rule 9a, and to the fourth choice by Rule 9a. Adding up the points, 28 + 14 + 9 = 51 and the favorite is a bet. In a marginal odds pattern where the points add up to a bare 51, a decision on a bet may alternate between yes and no with every flash of the tote. Pursuer went from odds of 5/1 to odds of 6/1 in the last two minutes. A further drop and there would have been no bet. As mentioned earlier, the profitability of betting on odds-on favorites like this one has not been established and some readers may prefer to skip bets on these favorites.

Race 4: 24 Oct 77-4   Aqu   6f   Clm 30000 to Clm 25000

Favorite: Joyous Pleasure   115   9/5

8Sep77-9Bel	1 1/16	Clm 20000	6	3^4	2^2	117	3.60	10
30Aug77-5Bel	1 1/16	TClm 25000	1	1^1	$4^{7\frac{1}{4}}$	117	4.20	
4Jly77-3Bel	7f	Clm 30000	3^2		9^{13}	117	2.90	1

Second choice: Arcoba   117   9/5

1Oct77-5Med	6f	Clm 35000	1^{hd}		6^8	116	3.50	8
15Sep77-6Med	6f	Allowance	3^{nk}		11^{12}	115	33.30	11
26Jly77-6Atl	6f	Allowance	1^3		1^{hd}	119	2.40	7

Third choice: Porcelain Flower   110   7/2

6Oct77-7Key	6f	Allowance	$3^{2\frac{1}{2}}$		2no	113	1.40	10
25Sep77-1Key	6f	Clm 7500	5^3		1^4	116	2.30	9
8Jun77-9Bel	7f	Md 13000	3^2		4^{14}	110	4.90	12

Fourth choice: Annie Active   117   5

11Oct77-8Bel	7f	Allowance	$4^{3\frac{1}{2}}$		6^{16}	117	34.40	6
3Oct77-7Bel	$1\frac{1}{16}$	TAllowance	2	$2^{1\frac{1}{2}}$	7^{24}	117	21.50	7
18Sep77-8Rkm	6f	Barb'aAnnH	$8^{7\frac{1}{4}}$		$5^{1\frac{3}{4}}$	112	23.00	8

Here again, the favorite has been away and Rule 9 is the first to be considered. (Section A does not apply to away horses.) Since the second choice has also been away, Rule 9a applies and the favorite is similar to the second choice. A normal or soft betting pattern is not needed when the other raced last in Class Z. Rule 9e applies to the third choice and the favorite is also similar to Porcelain Flower. Rule 9g applies to the fourth choice and the favorite is similar to Annie Active. For the New York 1977 fall meetings at Belmont and Aqueduct, an allowance race was taken equivalent to a $50,000 claimer, so Annie Active's last race was more than 25 percent higher in class than today's race. Adding up the points, 36 + 22 + 16 = 74 points. The favorite is a bet, and it won. It should be noted that although Arcoba vied for favoritism with Joyous Pleasure, it is not equivalent in class to the latter and could not be similar under Rule 9a or any other rule. Joyous Pleasure would have been bet whether it were the second choice or the favorite.

Race 5: 24 Oct 77-5   Aqu   6f   MdSpWt

Favorite: Honors Up   119   6/5

10Oct77-4Bel	6f	MdSpWt	$1^{1\frac{1}{2}}$		2^{hd}	119	2.70	7
29Sep77-3Bel	6f	Clm 40000	$1^{\frac{1}{2}}$		2^{hd}	119	5.50	9
19Sep77-3Bel	6f	MdSpWt	$6^{2\frac{3}{4}}$		11^{11}	119	5.10	12

Second choice: Ask Why   119   3

17Oct77-4Aqu	6f	MdSpWt	$6^{8\frac{1}{2}}$		2^{nk}	119	5.30	11
26Sep77-5Bel	6f	MdSpWt	$6^{9\frac{1}{2}}$		$2^{4\frac{3}{4}}$	119	6.30	7
10Sep77-5Bel	6f	MdSpWt	$7^{5\frac{1}{4}}$		$5^{3\frac{3}{4}}$	119	7.70	7

Third choice: Idmon   119   5

10Oct77-4Bel	6f	MdSpWt	3^2		3^5	119	1.90	7
21Jun77-4Bel	$5\frac{1}{2}$f	MdSpWt	$4^{5\frac{1}{2}}$		4^2	109	12.90	10

Fourth choice: Miss Ivor   119   6

23Sep77-4Bel 6f MdSpWt		$6^{6\frac{1}{2}}$		5^{16}	119	28.50	8

Section A does not apply when a favorite shows a fast start in a last sprint race.
Rule 3 applies to the second choice and the third choice, and the favorite is
similar to both these horses. Rule 3 does not apply to the fourth choice, which
has been away and finished fifth in its last race. Note, however, that the favorite
showed early speed in its last and recent race, so that the early speed rule, Rule
12, must be checked. Rule 12a(iii.) applies and the favorite is similar to the
fourth choice. 25 + 16 + 14 = 55 points, and the favorite is to be bet. It won. Well
before post time, it was obvious that this would be the case.

Race 6: 24 Oct 77-6   Aqu $1\frac{1}{16}$ (Turf)   Allowance

Favorite: Naples   117   7/5

29Sep77-7Bel	$1\frac{1}{16}$	Allowance	3	$2^{\frac{1}{2}}$	$2^{\frac{1}{2}}$	117	6.20	7
13Sep77-7Bel	$1\frac{1}{16}$	TAllowance	1	1^2	4^5	117	4.60	10
29Aug77-7Bel	$1\frac{1}{16}$	TAllowance	5	5^7	$4^{1\frac{3}{4}}$	117	3.30	12

Second choice: Equal Honor   114   7/2

15Oct77-2Bel	$1\frac{1}{16}$	Allowance	4	$4^{3\frac{1}{2}}$	3^8	114	7.80	7
28Sep77-7Bel	6f	Allowance	8^{19}		$7^{5\frac{1}{2}}$	113	48.40	8
13May77-7Aqu	$1\frac{1}{16}$	TAllowance	3	2^1	$7^{8\frac{1}{2}}$	109	17.60	8

Third choice: Lady Parida   114   4

13Jun77-6Mth	$1\frac{1}{16}$	TAllowance	4	3^2	2^3	113	3.30	8
6Jun77-7Atl	$1\frac{1}{16}$	Allowance	7	7^{13}	3^{13}	112	0.70	7
26May77-7Mth	1^{70}	Allowance	5	4^{10}	3^2	113	0.90	8

Fourth choice: Native Fruit   119   5

15Oct77-8Key	1^{70}	BrynMawr	12	11^{17}	9^{11}	118	33.90	12
26Sep77-7Bel	$1\frac{1}{16}$	Allowance	3	2^3	1^{nk}	113	0.80	5
16Sep77-7Bel	$1\frac{1}{16}$	Allowance	2	2^7	$2^{3\frac{1}{2}}$	113	7.50	6

Fifth choice: Drawing Room   114   5

15Oct77-2Bel	$1\frac{1}{16}$	Allowance	6	$5^{4\frac{1}{2}}$	$4^{8\frac{1}{2}}$	114	3.50	7
7Oct77-8Bel	$1\frac{1}{16}$	TAllowance	7	$7^{4\frac{1}{2}}$	$2^{\frac{3}{4}}$	114	2.30	8
21Sep77-7Bel	$1\frac{1}{16}$	Allowance	7	$7^{9\frac{1}{2}}$	$2^{7\frac{1}{4}}$	113	0.90	7

The favorite has been away, indicating Rule 9 should first be checked. Rule
9e applies to the second choice and the fifth choice, and the favorite is similar
to both. The third choice has also been away, and the favorite is similar to it by
Rule 9a. Both Rule 9f and 9g apply to the fourth choice, whose last race was a
stakes race. 22 + 20 + 16 + 16 = 74, and the favorite is to be bet. It won.

Race 7: 24 Oct 77-7   Aqu   1   Clm 50000 to Clm 45000

Favorite: Port Authority   113   8/5

24Sep77-7Bel	6f	Allowance	$5^{6\frac{1}{4}}$		$3^{3\frac{3}{4}}$	114	1.50	7
10Sep77-7Bel	6f	Allowance	4^2		7^4	122	2.20	8
23Aug77-8Sar	7f	Allowance	$4^{1\frac{1}{4}}$		5^{nk}	117	3.20	7

Second choice: Federation   113   5/2

7Oct77-6Bel	$1\frac{1}{16}$	Clm 40000	5	$5^{4\frac{1}{2}}$	$2^{1\frac{1}{4}}$	117	7.70	9
20Aug77-2Sar	$1\frac{1}{16}$	TClm 45000	8	8^8	8^{13}	113	26.00	10
27Jly77-5Bel	$1\frac{1}{16}$	TClm 50000	6	$8^{4\frac{1}{2}}$	$7^{9\frac{1}{4}}$	112	11.40	8

Third choice: Jump Over the Moon   114   3

4Oct77-6Bel	7f	Allowance	$6^{8\frac{1}{2}}$		5^4	117	4.70	7
26Sep77-6Bel	1	Allowance	7	6^{15}	$2^{2\frac{1}{2}}$	117	5.50	8
30Aug77-6Bel	7f	Clm 40000	5^3		$4^{1\frac{1}{4}}$	113	2.30	6

Fourth choice: Ragamuffin   113   6

15Oct77-7Bel	7f	Handicap	$2^{\frac{1}{2}}$		6^{17}	107	14.00	6
7Oct77-6Bel	$1\frac{1}{16}$	Clm 35000	1	1^2	$3^{1\frac{1}{4}}$	113	13.50	9
1Oct77-7Bel	$1\frac{1}{16}$	Allowance	5	5^3	7^{22}	117	11.40	7

Fifth choice: Kanawha River   110   7

30Sep77-7Bel	$1\frac{1}{16}$	TClm 35000	7	7^{12}	$5^{3\frac{1}{4}}$	117	1.70	7
21Sep77-5Bel	$1\frac{1}{16}$	Clm 30000	7	7^{11}	3no	117	1.10	7
5Sep77-5Bel	$1\frac{1}{16}$	TAllowance	7	$7^{4\frac{1}{4}}$	$6^{5\frac{1}{2}}$	113	20.70	8

The favorite has been away so Rule 9 should be first checked. Rule 9d applies to the second choice, and the favorite is similar to Federation. Rule 9f applies to the third and fourth choices, and the favorite is similar to both. The favorite also is similar to the third choice by Rule 16. Rule 9b applies to the fifth choice, and the favorite is similar to Kanawha River. $28 + 25 + 14 + 12 = 79$, and the favorite is to be bet. It won.

Race 8: 24 Oct 77-8   Aqu $1\frac{1}{16}$ (Turf)   Long Island Handicap

Favorite (entry): Javamine   121   4/5

15Oct77-6Med	$1\frac{1}{4}$	Q. Charl'eH	5	5^{19}	2^3	120	1.00	7
28Sep77-6Bel	$1\frac{1}{2}$	ManhattanH	3	3^8	6^5	113	2.70	6
13Sep77-8Bel	1	MasketteH	7	8^{13}	$5^{5\frac{1}{4}}$	115	5.80	8

Favorite (entry): Nijana   119   4/5

15Oct77-5Bel	1	Handicap	5	5^5	$2^{2\frac{3}{4}}$	122	4.10	6
11Oct77-8Del	$1\frac{1}{16}$	TParloH	8	$7^{6\frac{1}{2}}$	1^1	119	1.00	8
25Aug77-8Sar	$1\frac{1}{16}$	THandicap	6	6^{10}	2^{hd}	116	3.50	7

Second choice: Pearl Necklace   123   2

15Oct77-5Bel	1	Handicap	1	$1^{1\frac{1}{2}}$	$1^{2\frac{3}{4}}$	121	2.40	6
6Oct77-8Bel	$1\frac{1}{16}$	THandicap	2	$1^{1\frac{1}{2}}$	$1^{\frac{3}{4}}$	117	2.00	6
22Sep77-8Bel	1	THandicap	2	1^{hd}	1^5	116	3.00	6

Third choice: Harvest Girl   110   7

24Sep77-8Bel	$1\frac{1}{8}$	RuffianH	7	12^{19}	11^{21}	110	5.10	12
13Sep77-8Bel	1	MasketteH	2	2^1	3^{nk}	111	6.10	8
26Aug77-6Sar	7f	Allowance	2^2		$1^{2\frac{1}{4}}$	114	3.80	6

Fourth choice: Flying Above   113   8

15Oct77-5Bel	1	Handicap	2	$3^{2\frac{1}{2}}$	6^{29}	115	3.70	6
23Sep77-7Bel	$1\frac{1}{16}$	TAllowance	2	2^5	1^{hd}	113	2.20	7
12Sep77-8Bel	6f	Allowance	2^{hd}		1no	115	1.00	5

Fifth choice: Sensational   113   8

15Oct77-5Bel	1	Handicap	3	$2^{1\frac{1}{2}}$	3^4	118	5.80	6
7Oct77-6Med	$1\frac{1}{16}$	TAllowance	5	$5^{2\frac{1}{4}}$	$5^{3\frac{1}{2}}$	111	1.20	9
24Sep77-8Bel	$1\frac{1}{8}$	RuffianH	6	5^7	9^{15}	115	12.00	12

In this rich handicap race, there is a two-horse entry as the favorite. Javamine and Nijana are coupled in the wagering as one, so that only the pair can be bet. If either one wins, the holder of a ticket on the entry wins. For system purposes, only one horse in the entry is considered the favorite, that one being the horse that is picked by most of the professional selectors (the consensus) in the *Daily Racing Form*. Here, Javamine was the overwhelming choice and will be our favorite.

Also, two horses are shown at odds of 8/1, and one is the fifth choice, a circumstance not usually permitted by the system procedure. The reason for this lies in the very close betting on the two horses. If the favorite is similar to both, there is no problem: just use the points of one of them in the favorite's point sum. If the favorite is similar to only one of them, use its points in the point sum whether or not it is the fourth or fifth choice. We do not wish to take the chance of missing a wager because of a few dollars difference in the betting on these two horses.

Javamine ran a good last race, so Rules 2 and 3 should be checked first. (Section A does not apply since this is the favorite's first start at the meeting.) Because Javamine is not equivalent in class to the second choice, neither rule applies. Nor does any other rule apply, and the favorite is not similar to the second choice. Rule 5 does not apply because the favorite has not run at the meeting. It is now clear that there are not enough points on the two remaining choices for a bet on the favorite to be realized. For practice, we note that the favorite is not similar to the other choices under any rule.

Turning now to the second choice, we see that Pearl Necklace won its last and recent race easily and is similar to Javamine by Rule 14a(i.), the easy win rule. Rule 3 does not apply because a normal or soft betting pattern is demanded by the one-place better finish of Pearl Necklace, and the minus-one relative finish change of Rule 3g is canceled out by the plus-one relative finish change of Rule 3d.

Pearl Necklace is also similar to the third choice by Rule 14a(iv.) and to Sensational by Rule 14a(ii.). 33 + 12 + 11 = 56 points, and the second choice is to be bet. It won.

Race 9: 24 Oct 77-9   Aqu   7f   Md Clm 10000 to Clm 9000

Favorite: Our Jim   122   6/5

12Oct77-1Bel 6f Clm 14000	6^2		$6^{6\frac{1}{4}}$	115	14.60	10
24Aug77-5Sar 6f Md 25000	$5^{2\frac{1}{2}}$		$2^{4\frac{1}{2}}$	122	5.20	9
5Aug77-9Sar 6f Md 32500	$5^{2\frac{1}{2}}$		$5^{6\frac{1}{2}}$	120	8.60	10

Second choice: What a Greek   115   5

13Oct77-5Bel $1\frac{1}{16}$ TMdSpWt	9	$7^{7\frac{1}{4}}$	11^{23}	119	16.30	12
7Oct77-1Bel $1\frac{1}{16}$ Md 9000	5	5^5	3^4	115	1.20	11
22Sep77-9Bel 7f Md 9000	$8^{9\frac{1}{4}}$		$2^{1\frac{1}{4}}$	109	6.90	12

Third choice: Crimson Bayou   117   6

3Oct77-9Bel 6f Md 10000	$6^{5\frac{1}{4}}$		$2^{\frac{3}{4}}$	119	4.30	12
16Sep77-9Bel 6f Md 9000	$4^{\frac{3}{4}}$		2^2	114	6.90	11
30Aug77-1Bel 7f Md 9000	3^1		$3^{8\frac{1}{2}}$	113	21.80	14

Fourth choice: Sperduto   109   6

13Oct77-5Bel $1\frac{1}{16}$ TMdSpWt	1	$1^{1\frac{1}{2}}$	$6^{8\frac{1}{2}}$	112	16.10	12
5Oct77-3Bel $1\frac{1}{16}$ TMdSpWt	1	$1^{1\frac{1}{2}}$	$4^{7\frac{1}{2}}$	112	10.10	8
19Sep77-9Bel 6f Md 18000	4^3		$8^{5\frac{1}{2}}$ ·	105	12.30	10

Fifth choice: Fort Mackinaw   119   7

14Oct77-9Bel 6f Md 12500	4^3		$4^{9\frac{1}{2}}$	119	2.60	12
5Oct77-3Med 6f Md 15000	$9^{5\frac{1}{2}}$		$6^{7\frac{1}{4}}$	119	2.60	11
20Jly77-9Bel 6f Md 18000	3^1		$6^{4\frac{1}{4}}$	111	4.20	9

Section A need not be checked since none of the horses has started at the Aqueduct meeting. The favorite shows a poor last race as its only start in the last twenty-one days, so that Rule 10 must be checked as well as Rule 1. Rule 10c coupled with Rule 9f applies to the second and fourth choices, and the favorite is similar to both. Rule 1 also applies to the fourth choice, and the favorite is similar to the latter by this rule.

The favorite is not similar to the third choice by Rule 10 because it is not equivalent in class to Crimson Bayou. It is similar to the fifth choice by Rule 10c coupled to Rule 9e. $16 + 14 + 12 = 42$ points, not enough for a bet on the favorite.

Considering now the second choice, it is not a router-in-sprint (as can be seen from its previous past performance lines not shown here) and it shows a good previous race, so that Rule 8 is to be checked. But Rule 8 coupled to Rule 2, 3, 5, or 7 does not apply to the favorite, and What a Greek is not similar to Our Jim. Nor does Rule 16 apply since Our Jim showed a fast start in its last and recent race. What a Greek does show a sharp drop in class, but it is not similar to Our Jim by Rule 11c (the only subsection that could apply) because it is not equivalent in class to the favorite, a normal or soft betting pattern being required.

What a Greek is similar to the fourth choice by Rule 7a and also by Rule 11c, and to the third choice by Rule 11d, but it is not similar to Fort Mackinaw under any rule. A normal or soft betting pattern is required by Rule 11d, which does not exist. Adding up, $14 + 14 = 28$ points, not enough for a bet.

With the favorite and second choice not to be bet, we look at the third choice, Crimson Bayou. It shows a good last race and Rules 2, 3, and 4 must be checked. Rule 4 coupled to Rule 3 make Crimson Bayou similar to Our Jim. But not to What a Greek, since a normal or soft betting pattern is needed for the one-place better finish of Crimson Bayou's last race compared to What a Greek's previous race. Nor is Crimson Bayou similar to the fourth or fifth choices since normal or soft betting patterns are needed under Rule 3. There is no bet on the third choice and no bet in this race. Fort Mackinaw won.

This day's results were seven bets and seven wins, six favorites and one second choice, for a net gain of $11.40 on $1.00 flat bets. Needless to say, most days are more mundane than this.

The next racing card we consider was run at the Meadowlands in New Jersey on 13 October 1977. The take was 17 percent so that a point sum of 51 points was needed for a bet.

Race 10: 13 Oct 77-1   Med   6f   MdSpWt

Favorite: A Symphony   119   5/2

Second choice: Game Bid   119   3

Third choice: Fence Stretcher   119   3

3Oct77-5Med 6f MdSpWt	$3^{1\frac{1}{2}}$	$3^{3\frac{1}{2}}$	119	3.90	9
24Sep77-1Med 6f MdSpWt	$4^{5\frac{1}{2}}$	5^{12}	119	2.90	8
16Sep77-4Med 6f MdSpWt	$3^{1\frac{1}{2}}$	2^{6}	119	3.10	8

Fourth choice: Miss Ocala   112   5

5Oct77-1Med 6f Md 25000	3^3		$2^{\frac{3}{4}}$	112	1.40	9
15Sep77-1Med 6f Md 22500	$2^{\frac{1}{2}}$		$2^{2\frac{1}{4}}$	112	5.30	9
8Sep77-1Med 6f Md 20000	$3^{\frac{1}{2}}$		3^2	112	7.70	12

Fifth choice: Pretty Sunny   119   6

The favorite is a first time starter and Rule 9 should be checked first. The favorite is similar to the other first-time starters in the race, Game Bid and Pretty Sunny, by Rule 9a, and it is similar to Fence Stretcher and Miss Ocala by Rule 9d. Adding, $25 + 25 + 16 + 14 = 80$ points, and the favorite is a bet. However, Fence Stretcher won the race.

Race 11: 13 Oct 77-2   Med   6f   Clm 5000

Favorite: Manchester Lass   116   3

21Sep77-1Med 6f Clm 4000	2^4		$1^{3\frac{1}{4}}$	116	3.30	7
13Sep77-4Med 6f Clm 5000	$7^{5\frac{1}{2}}$		$3^{4\frac{3}{4}}$	115	11.10	10
16Aug77-4Mth 6f Clm 3500	$4^{3\frac{1}{2}}$		4^2	114	1.40	7

Second choice: Rare Voice   116   4

23Sep77-7Det 6f Clm 3500	$5^{1\frac{1}{4}}$		$1^{\frac{3}{4}}$	122	2.00	8
18Aug77-4Det 6f Clm 3000	$3^{2\frac{1}{2}}$		1^4	120	0.70	10
3Aug77-5Det 6f Clm 3500	1^{hd}		1^4	115	0.90	10

Third choice: Lightning's Prize   116   4

29Sep77-1Med 6f Clm 4000	3^1		$2^{1\frac{1}{2}}$	116	2.90	9
17May77-4CD 6f Clm 5000	5^3		9^{14}	117	12.20	9
5May77-5CD 6f Clm 7500	$3^{4\frac{1}{2}}$		11^{16}	117	22.20	12

Fourth choice: Needletrade   116   4

7Oct77-2Med 6f Clm 4000	4^3		2^9	111	2.60	12
26Sep77-3Med 6f Clm 5000	$9^{7\frac{1}{2}}$		$9^{9\frac{1}{2}}$	119	3.80	9
13Sep77-4Med 6f Clm 5000	2^{hd}		2^1	119	2.10	10

Fifth choice: Miss Captain   116   5

26Sep77-6Key 6f Clm 6500	$5^{\frac{3}{4}}$		8^{10}	116	3.40	10
22Sep77-7Key 1^{70} Clm 7500	1	$1^{1\frac{1}{2}}$	$5^{7\frac{1}{2}}$	116	5.00	10
8Sep77-7Key 6f Clm 8250	4^{nk}		$5^{4\frac{1}{2}}$	114	9.10	8

Sixth choice: Fledgling   116   7

26Sep77-3Med 6f Clm 5000	2^{hd}		$4^{1\frac{1}{4}}$	116	10.60	9
13Sep77-4Med 6f Clm 5000	1^{hd}		$5^{5\frac{1}{4}}$	115	13.00	10
3Sep77-2Mth 6f Clm 5000	2^{hd}		6^{11}	114	3.20	7

The favorite has been away, its last race having occurred twenty-two days ago. Rule 9 is first to be checked, and the favorite is similar to Needletrade by Rule 9e, to Miss Captain by Rule 9g, and to Fledgling by Rule 9e. It is not similar to Rare Voice by Rule 9e because of nonequivalence in class, or to Lightning's Prize which finished second in its only start at the meeting. Other rules that might establish similarity with an away favorite are Rules 7, 13, 15, and 16, but none apply. 20 + 16 + 12 = 48 points, and the favorite is not to be bet.

Considering the second choice, Section A does not apply. Rare Voice is not similar to Manchester Lass by Rule 3 since Rule 3a requires a normal or soft betting pattern which is not offset by other subsections. No other rule applies. Rule 3 also requires a normal or soft betting pattern for similarity with the third and fourth choices, which does not exist. No other rule applies and Rare Voice is not similar either to Lightning's Prize or Needletrade. In the case of Needletrade, a soft betting pattern is needed because there is an eleven-pound relative weight shift in favor of Rare Voice. Nor is Rare Voice similar to Fledgling, since Rule 3g requires a weak betting pattern, nor Miss Captain. With a zero point sum, the second choice is not to be bet.

The third choice is not similar to Needletrade by Rule 3 because Rule 3 requires a normal or soft betting pattern, nor to the other horses by any of the rules, so it too is no bet. There was no bet on this race, which was won by Miss Captain.

Race 12: 13 Oct 77-3   Med   6f   Md Clm 16000 to Clm 14000

Favorite: You Go First   120   2

19Jly77-2Bow 5½f MdSpWt	$5^{1\frac{3}{4}}$	4^4	120	5.70	7

Second choice: Iron Luck   109   7/2

4Oct77-3Bel 6f Md 20000	6^5	6^9	122	4.30	10
21Sep77-4Med 6f Md 20000	$2^{\frac{1}{2}}$	$6^{5\frac{1}{4}}$	116	1.20	9
25Aug77-3Sar 6f Md 35000	$5^{5\frac{1}{4}}$	$4^{6\frac{1}{2}}$	122	7.20	12

Third choice: Shottish   120   4

3Oct77-4Med 6f Md 20000	1^2	$6^{8\frac{1}{2}}$	120	7.70	11
14Sep77-1Med 6f Md 18000	$1^{1\frac{1}{2}}$	$3^{5\frac{1}{4}}$	120	3.70	12
24Aug77-1Mth 6f Md 18000	2^2	3^{10}	115	9.90	9

Fourth choice: Ancient Port   118   5

4Oct77-9Bel 6f Md 20000	3^2	10^{15}	122	4.60	10
27Sep77-3Bel 6f Md 22500	1^{hd}	$4^{3\frac{1}{2}}$	120	16.80	10
6Sep77-4Bel 6f Md 20000	1^{hd}	7^9	122	3.50	12

The favorite has been away and Rule 9 must be checked. The favorite is similar to the second choice by Rule 9g since Iron Luck's last race was 25 percent higher in class than today's race (20,000 is 25 percent greater than 16,000) and a normal betting pattern exists. The favorite is similar to the third choice and the fourth choice by both Rule 9f coupled to Rule 9d and Rule 9g. 22 + 20 + 16 = 58 points, and the favorite is a bet. It won.

Race 13: 13 Oct 77-4   Med   6f   Clm 10000 to Clm 8000

Favorite: Mostest   116   2

8Sep77-2Med	6f	Clm 12500	12^{12}		$5^{4\frac{1}{4}}$	117	15.40	12
10May77-7Atl	6f	Clm 16000	5^3		$5^{8\frac{1}{2}}$	116	4.20	7
13Apr77-7GS	$1\frac{1}{16}$	Clm 25000	3	$5^{2\frac{1}{2}}$	8^{19}	116	8.10	9

Second choice: Distinctive Wind   116   4

6Oct77-5Med	1^{70}	Clm 10000	4	$5^{3\frac{1}{2}}$	4^{14}	116	5.00	9
30Sep77-9Med	6f	Clm 12500	8^4		$5^{8\frac{1}{2}}$	119	18.30	12
2Sep77-6Mth	6f	Clm 12500	2^1		$3^{\frac{3}{4}}$	117	3.90	7

Third choice: Miss Fran's Tip   119   4

22Sep77-2Med	$1\frac{1}{16}$	Clm 11500	10	$10^{9\frac{1}{2}}$	$7^{9\frac{1}{2}}$	115	13.10	11
2Sep77-6Mth	6f	Clm 12500	$7^{6\frac{1}{2}}$		1^{hd}	115	5.70	7
25Aug77-7Mth	6f	Clm 14000	$6^{6\frac{1}{2}}$		$5^{3\frac{3}{4}}$	113	8.90	7

Fourth choice: Tootie Sue   119   5

27Sep77-2Med	6f	Clm 8000	$3^{1\frac{1}{2}}$		1no	116	3.00	11
19Sep77-1Med	6f	Clm 8000	1^{hd}		$2^{4\frac{1}{4}}$	116	6.20	8
9Sep77-9Med	6f	Clm 8500	1^{hd}		$4^{2\frac{3}{4}}$	119	3.30	10

Fifth choice: Sail on Lisa   116   5

27Sep77-2Med	6f	Clm 7500	4^4		2no	115	5.00	11
17Sep77-5Rkm	6f	Clm 5500	$1^{2\frac{1}{2}}$		$4^{\frac{3}{4}}$	114	3.00	10
7Jly77-7Rkm	6f	Clm 5000	2^1		$1^{2\frac{1}{2}}$	117	2.50	8

Sixth choice: Paddock Paula   119   6

6Oct77-4Med	6f	Clm 8500	1^{hd}		$1^{\frac{3}{4}}$	116	2.50	8
15Sep77-3Med	$1\frac{1}{16}$	Clm 10000	3	1^{hd}	$5^{8\frac{1}{2}}$	117	35.10	10
1Sep77-8Rkm	1^{40}	Allowance	6	$6^{5\frac{3}{4}}$	8^{18}	114	12.70	8

The favorite has been away and is similar to the second, fourth, and sixth choices by Rule 9d. It is similar to the third choice by Rule 15c. Rules 15 and 16 must be checked whenever the other horse shows a slow start in a recent race. Finally, the favorite is not similar to the fifth choice by Rule 9d or any other rule. 20 + 20 + 16 + 14 = 70 points; the favorite is a bet and it won.

Race 14: 13 Oct 77-5   Med   1^{70} Clm 12500 to Clm 10500

Favorite: Dewit Again   120   9/5

6Oct77-5Med	1^{70}	Clm 10000	1	1^2	1^5	122	4.00	9
22Sep77-2Med	1$\frac{1}{16}$	Clm 10500	3	2^1	1$^{\frac{3}{4}}$	115	4.10	11
15Sep77-3Med	1$\frac{1}{16}$	Clm 10000	5	4$^{2\frac{1}{4}}$	2$^{2\frac{1}{2}}$	122	10.50	10

Second choice: Powder Puff Derby   107   3

8Sep77-4Med	1$\frac{1}{16}$	Clm 8500	1	1$^{\frac{1}{2}}$	2$^{2\frac{1}{4}}$	114	1.60	7
20Aug77-3Del	1$\frac{1}{16}$	TClm 11500	1	1^1	4$^{8\frac{1}{4}}$	112	8.60	7
3Aug77-5Del	1$\frac{1}{16}$	Clm 8500	1	1$^{1\frac{1}{2}}$	1$^{1\frac{1}{2}}$	112	3.00	5

Third choice: Cape Diamond   111   7/2

22Sep77-2Med	1$\frac{1}{16}$	Clm 12500	2	3$^{1\frac{1}{2}}$	4$^{1\frac{1}{2}}$	112	15.70	11
2Sep77-6Mth	6f	Clm 10500	3^1		2^{hd}	106	3.60	7
26Aug77-5Mth	6f	Clm 10000	5$^{6\frac{1}{2}}$		3$^{2\frac{3}{4}}$	111	1.60	7

Fourth choice: Speak of the Devil   116   4

3Oct77-8Med	1^{70}	Clm 16000	9	9^{16}	5^5	116	11.10	9
21Sep77-9Med	6f	Clm 16000	11^{15}		8$^{9\frac{1}{2}}$	117	17.60	11
1Sep77-7Del	1^{70}	Allowance	6	6$^{\frac{1}{2}}$	3$^{5\frac{1}{2}}$	117	3.60	6

The favorite scored an easy win in its last race. Checking Rule 14, we see the favorite is similar to the second choice by Rule 14a(iv.), to the third choice by Rule 14a(ii.), and to the fourth choice by Rule 14a(v.). 25 + 22 + 20 = 67 points, and the favorite is a bet. It won.

Race 15: 13 Oct 77-6   Med   6f   Handicap

Favorite: Miami Sun   116   1/2

6Oct77-6Med	6f	Allowance	6$^{1\frac{1}{4}}$	1$^{1\frac{1}{4}}$	117	0.60	7
3Sep77-7Bel	6f	Allowance	1$^{\frac{1}{2}}$	3^{nk}	115	1.70	7
23Aug77-6Sar	6f	Allowance	4$^{2\frac{1}{4}}$	2$^{\frac{3}{4}}$	112	1.60	6

Second choice: Godolphin   116   5

4Oct77-6Med	6f	Allowance	3^1	2^2	122	4.30	7
8Sep77-6Med	6f	Allowance	4$^{\frac{3}{4}}$	1$^{\frac{1}{2}}$	115	4.50	7
1Sep77-8Mth	6f	Handicap	5$^{4\frac{1}{4}}$	2$^{2\frac{1}{2}}$	108	7.80	6

Third choice: Third World   113   6

4Oct77-6Med	6f	Allowance	7$^{4\frac{1}{4}}$	3^2	115	3.80	7
27Sep77-6Med	6f	Allowance	2$^{1\frac{1}{2}}$	1$^{1\frac{1}{2}}$	119	1.80	8
19Sep77-5Med	6f	Allowance	4$^{2\frac{1}{2}}$	2$^{2\frac{1}{4}}$	119	2.00	6

Fourth choice: Kohoutek   118   6

4Oct77-6Med 6f	Allowance	1^{hd}		1^2	117	8.80	7
23Sep77-6Med 6f	Allowance	8^{10}		$5^{5\frac{1}{4}}$	119	13.20	10
4Sep77-9Del 5f	THandicap	$6^{4\frac{1}{4}}$		1^{hd}	117	3.90	9

Miami Sun, a strong odds-on favorite, is similar to all the other choices by Rule 3 or Rule 6. 16 + 14 + 14 = 44 points, not enough for a bet. In this race, it is clear that there cannot be a point sum large enough for a bet on any of the choices. Miami Sun won.

Race 16: 13 Oct 77-7   Med $1\frac{1}{16}$ (Turf)   Clm 20000 to Clm 18000

Favorite: Roy Roy   116   5/2

8Oct77-2Med 6f	Clm 20000	10^{10}		$4^{2\frac{1}{2}}$	116	8.80	10
29Sep77-4Bel $1\frac{1}{16}$	Clm 20000	3	2^{hd}	5^{14}	117	2.60	7
1Sep77-4Bel $1\frac{1}{16}$	Clm 30000	8	$7^{3\frac{1}{4}}$	$3^{1\frac{1}{4}}$	117	17.80	8

Second choice: Emerald Pit   116   3

29Sep77-4Bel $1\frac{1}{16}$	Clm 20000	5	$7^{5\frac{3}{4}}$	$3^{8\frac{1}{2}}$	117	6.60	7
22Sep77-7Med 6f	Clm 20000	9^{13}		$5^{6\frac{1}{2}}$	116	17.70	10
25Jly77-7Mth 1	Allowance	6	$5^{5\frac{1}{2}}$	6^{18}	114	7.00	9

Third choice: Pratique   112   5

26Sep77-7Med $1\frac{1}{16}$	Clm 17000	4	3^5	$2^{\frac{1}{2}}$	117	3.50	6
15Sep77-5Med $1\frac{1}{16}$	Clm 15000	7	$7^{6\frac{1}{2}}$	$1^{2\frac{1}{2}}$	116	11.70	8
9Sep77-7Key 1^{70}	Clm 15000	5	$4^{3\frac{1}{2}}$	$2^{\frac{1}{2}}$	116	7.60	7

Fourth choice: Populist   116   9

28Sep77-6Med 6f	Allowance	5^3		$10^{8\frac{1}{2}}$	113	8.90	12
3Sep77-1Bel 7f	Clm 30000	$8^{6\frac{1}{2}}$		8^{19}	117	35.90	9
20Aug77-9Sar $1\frac{1}{8}$	TAllowance	10	$10^{8\frac{1}{4}}$	11^{35}	112	26.00	12

The favorite shows a slow start in its last and recent race, and Section A must be checked. Rule 2 of that section applies, and the favorite is not to be bet. Note that the favorite shows a sharp drop in class which excludes Rule 1, Section A from consideration.

The second choice also shows a sharp drop in class, but Rule 2, Section A does not apply because its last race was not at Meadowlands. Looking at Section B now, Emerald Pit is similar to Roy Roy by either Rule 3i or Rule 11c, and to the fourth choice by Rule 11c. It is similar to the third choice by Rule 11d. 25 + 16 + 10 = 51 points, and Emerald Pit is the bet. It won.

Race 17: 13 Oct 77-8   Med $1\frac{1}{16}$ Allowance

Favorite: Hot Chili   105   5/2

29Sep77-7Med	6f	Allowance	$2^{\frac{1}{2}}$		1^6	107	1.40	9
21Sep77-8Med	6f	Allowance	$2^{1\frac{1}{2}}$		2^1	112	2.10	7
5Sep77-1Bel	6f	Clm 25000	1^3		$4^{2\frac{3}{4}}$	114	20.90	8

Second choice: Gaite   112   5/2

7Sep77-8Med	1^{70}	TAllowance	4	$3^{6\frac{1}{2}}$	$4^{1\frac{1}{2}}$	117	3.10	9
24Aug77-8Mth	$1\frac{1}{16}$	LSilverH	8	$6^{2\frac{1}{4}}$	$5^{6\frac{1}{4}}$	111	18.30	11
15Aug77-7Mth	$1\frac{1}{16}$	Allowance	2	$2^{\frac{1}{2}}$	$3^{\frac{3}{4}}$	115	0.70	6

Third choice: Sahada   115   3

20Sep77-4Med	$1\frac{1}{16}$	Allowance	4	$2^{2\frac{1}{2}}$	$1^{2\frac{1}{2}}$	114	7.60	7
13Sep77-8Med	1	TAllowance	4	$4^{3\frac{1}{2}}$	2no	114	17.70	9
8Aug77-6Mth	6f	Allowance	6^3		$6^{6\frac{1}{2}}$	115	17.70	7

Fourth choice: Trader's Destiny   116   5

23Sep77-8Med	1^{70}	Allowance	9	9^{13}	9^{13}	117	3.50	10
2Sep77-7Mth	1	TAllowance	5	4^4	1^2	120	1.50	8
8Aug77-7Mth	1	Clm 25000	6	$6^{3\frac{1}{2}}$	1^{hd}	119	5.80	10

Fifth choice: Peerless Charger   112   7

3Oct77-6Med	$1\frac{1}{16}$	THandicap	6	6^8	6^{14}	110	23.60	6
20Sep77-8Med	$1\frac{1}{16}$	Clm 30000	5	6^6	$2^{2\frac{3}{4}}$	112	5.50	7
7Sep77-8Med	1^{70}	TAllowance	3	4^7	7^7	112	16.20	9

The favorite shows a good last race but not an easy win according to the note attached to Rule 14. Section A need not be considered. Rules 3, 4, and 5 of Section B must be checked but do not apply to any of the other choices. The fourth and fifth choices show slow starts in their last and recent races, and Rules 15 and 16 must be checked. The favorite is similar to the fourth choice by Rule 16. To apply this rule, we must consider the 1^{70} distance equivalent to the $1\frac{1}{16}$-mile distance of today's race since the difference is less than $\frac{1}{16}$ mile. Trader's Destiny's previous race shows a slow start at a shorter distance than today's race. The favorite is not similar to the fifth choice. There is no drop in class from Peerless Charger's pre-previous race to its previous race since $30,000 claimers are taken equivalent to allowance races at Meadowlands, so that Rule 15 does not apply. We have a point sum of 16 points, and Hot Chili is not to be bet.

The second choice has been away and is similar to the third choice by Rule 9a, to the 4th choice by Rule 16, and to the fifth choice by Rule 9f. It is not similar to the favorite (Rule 9d requires a normal or soft betting pattern when the other won its last race easily). 25 + 16 + 12 = 53 points, and Gaite is to be bet. The third choice, Sahada, won the race.

Race 18: 13 Oct 77-9   Med   6f   Md Clm 8500 to Clm 7500

Favorite: Dr. Duck   122   5/2

31Aug77-9Mth	6f	MdSpWt	3^3		5^4	122	4.20	11
30Dec76-2Lrl	6f	MdSpWt	3^1		$2^{\frac{3}{4}}$	120	1.00	12
16Dec76-3Lrl	7f	MdSpWt	1^{hd}		2^4	120	0.70	7

Second choice: Legrand   119   5/2

3Oct77-1Med	6f	Md 9000	$7^{7\frac{1}{2}}$		$3^{\frac{3}{4}}$	117	9.70	9
12Aug77-3Atl	$1\frac{1}{16}$	Md 13000	7	6^6	7^7	114	3.10	8
1Aug77-1Mth	6f	Md 12500	$7^{7\frac{1}{2}}$		$4^{5\frac{1}{2}}$	119	6.50	8

Third choice: Asperity   119   4

3Oct77-1Med	6f	Md 10000	3^3	$6^{5\frac{3}{4}}$	119	5.50	9
26Jly77-9Bel	6f	Md 10000	2^{hd}	$6^{4\frac{3}{4}}$	110	12.80	12
7Jly77-9Bel	6f	Md 12500	$6^{2\frac{3}{4}}$	9^9	115	13.30	11

Fourth choice: Barrote   119   5   (first-time starter)

The favorite has been away and is similar to the second choice by either Rule 9d or Rule 15a(ii.). It is not similar to the other choices. Therefore, its point sum is 28 and it is not to be bet.

The second choice shows a sharp drop in class, and Rule 1 of Section A does not apply. Legrand is similar to Dr. Duck by Rule 11c and to Barrote by Rule 11a or Rule 11b or Rule 5c. Since Legrand raced Asperity in their last race together, Rule 7 rather than Rule 11 must be used and Legrand is not similar to the third choice by this rule. Adding, 28 + 16 = 44 points, not enough for a bet on the second choice.

The third choice also shows a sharp drop in class and one poor race in the last twenty-one days in which it raced against Legrand. Rules 7, 10, and 11 must be checked. Asperity is similar to Dr. Duck by Rule 11b, Rule 11c, or Rule 10b, to Legrand by Rule 7a, and to Barrote by Rule 11b. 28 + 20 + 16 = 64 points, and the third choice is to be bet. It won.

This was another successful day, four favorite bets with three winners, one winner out of two second choice bets, and a third-choice winner. For the two example days, there were a total of 10 bets on favorites compared to an expected number of 6 (one out of every three races), 3 bets on second choices as compared to an expected 2.6 (one out of seven races), and 1 bet on a third choice compared to an expected 1.4 (one out of thirteen races).

This chapter was designed to give the reader some insight into the workings of the system. Anyone wishing to pursue this path to riches should practice on several hundred more races until he can handle all the rules and the betting procedure with expertise. At the same time, the confidence gained in the effectiveness of the system will prove of inestimable psychological benefit during those unavoidable dry spells when nothing seems to go right. The most sobering experience in the over 120 racing cards covered by the data was a day on which five bets produced five losers. Many other days proved very dull; there were one, two, or three wagers, sometimes none, and maybe at most one winner. The kind of day it will turn out to be is more unpredictable than the weather. Further considerations on amassing wealth at the races are reserved to the last chapter.

PART III
WINNING IN THE STOCK MARKET

13

A NEW AND RIGOROUS DEMONSTRATION OF WEAK EFFICIENCY IN THE STOCK MARKET

It is always hard to realize that the numbers and equations we play with at our desks have something to do with the real world.

Steven Weinberg

The random walk character of the changes in stock market prices has been well substantiated by research extending over seventy-five years. Only the time constant, the length of the interval during which prices adjust to new information, remains the subject of serious argument. Is the adjustment instantaneous, or do non-Brownian price movements occur on the release of news and can these be profitably exploited by Mr. Average to perform better than average? This is the problem addressed in this chapter.

I shall present a stock market model based on the comparison of published estimates of corporate quarterly earnings with the earnings actually reported each quarter in the news media. Selections based on this model have significantly outperformed the stock market averages for several years, and strong statistical evidence is submitted in its favor. The existence of such a model argues cogently against the validity of the strongly efficient and semi-strongly efficient forms of the random walk model.

More specifically, I shall demonstrate that the investing public's response to surprising quarterly earnings—that is, earnings widely divergent from the estimates—is *not* by any means reflected instantaneously in stock prices, as demanded by the strongly efficient and semi-strongly efficient models, but is a continuing process that may go on for months. During this period of adjustment, there are opportunities for substantial profits. This discussion is limited to the effect of earnings alone because it is the sole factor characterizing all corporations that can be treated statistically in a meaningful manner.

The following procedure was used to test the semi-strongly efficient market assumption:

1. Quarterly earnings projections for some 1,500 stocks were obtained from investment services and brokerage houses* over two periods of time, from 1 August 1969 to 1 September 1971 and from 1 September 1971 to 15 May 1973. For each company, the highest estimate was compared with the actual earnings reported by the corporation in its quarterly report in the *Wall Street Journal*. The percentage change from the projection was calculated. Companies were then separated into six categories: I, those showing better-than-expected earnings of 20 percent of more; II, those with better-than-expected earnings between 10 and 19 percent; III, 0 to 9 percent; IV, those showing worse-than-expected earnings of 1 to 9 percent; V, 10 to 19 percent; and VI, 20 percent or more worse than expected.

2. The price of each stock was recorded as of the opening of the stock market on the second business day following the announcement of quarterly earnings and again, approximately three months later, at the opening of the stock market on the second business day following the succeeding announcement of quarterly earnings. For each stock, the percentage change in price over the time interval between quarterly earnings reports was calculated along with the percentage change in the Value Line Composite geometric average of all the stocks followed over the same period.

3. For all stocks in each group, the percentage change in the price of each stock was plotted against the corresponding percentage change in the composite average. For each group, the mean percentage change in price and the number of stocks performing better or worse than average was determined.

4. Three tests for the detection of significant deviation from the semi-strongly efficient markets model were applied.

Stocks in Groups I and II are considered to have reported surprisingly high earnings, those in Groups V and VI surprisingly low earnings. If a semi-strongly efficient market exists, there should be no apparent differences in the price actions of stocks in the various groups in the period following the release of earnings; if the market is only weakly efficient, stocks in Groups I and II should show the best performance, stocks in Groups V and VI the worst.

A word on the earnings estimates. They are prepared by financial analysts who maintain close relations with the companies concerned and who should, therefore, be in the best position for forecasting (aside from the officers of the company, who usually do not give out earnings projections). I assume these estimates represent the thinking of investors in the great majority of cases, so that when a company reports earnings much higher or lower than the estimate, it is a

---

*Sources were *The Value Line Investment Survey*, *Standard & Poor's Stock Guide*, and the brokerage firm of Merrill Lynch, Pierce, Fenner and Smith.

surprise. Further considerations of estimates vis-a-vis earnings will be given in the next chapter.

The results for the period 1 August 1969 to 1 September 1971 are exhibited in Figure 13-1, each point of which depicts the price of a stock relative to the market average of that group of stocks for which quarterly earnings 20 percent or more better-than-expected were reported (Group I). The y-axis measures the percentage change in price of a stock in the interval between successive quarterly earnings reports; the x-axis measures the percentage change in the composite average over the same time. The $45°$ diagonal divides those stocks which outperformed the market from those that did not. Those points lying above the x-axis represent stocks increasing in price over the approximately three-month period; those points below the x-axis show stocks declining in price. Bull markets over these quarterly intervals occurred to the right of the y-axis and bear markets to the left. The dashed lines in the first and third quadrants indicate points lying off scale. Graphs obtained for the other stock groups were similar, except that the clouds of points settle lower relative to the diagonal.

Figure 13-2 features the results for each of the six stock groups plus the total sample and shows the number of stocks in each group, the mean price change for the group, and the number of stocks in each group performing better and worse than the average. The "Expectation" row gives the range of results to be expected if a person blindly picks a sample of this group size from the total sample and observes the number doing better than the average. It will be discussed later.

Figure 13-3 is a frequency distribution of the percentage price changes for the sample points of Group I in our first time period. Also shown is a normal curve with a mean of 5.9 and a standard deviation of 17, which parameters were computed from the data. Our distribution deviates from the normal curve in a manner similar to the data of Fisher and Lorie for the returns on stocks from 1926 to 1960.

During the two-year period under examination, stocks in our total sample outperformed the market average in 55 percent of the quarterly intervals, with those stocks reporting better-than-expected earnings doing better than the market in over 60 percent of the intervals. The mean percentage gain in price over the quarterly intervals decreased monotonically from +5.9 percent for Group I stocks to -2.5 percent for Group VI. Changes caused by cash dividend payments were neglected, but stock dividends were taken into account. It is estimated that the cash dividends increase the mean percentage gain by about 1 percent. Commissions on the actual purchase and sale of stocks were also neglected. They can, however, be a significant cost, especially for small amounts of low-priced stocks.

Figures 13-4 and 13-5 display similar results for the period 1 September 1971 to 15 May 1973. During this period, the market averages did not show nearly as

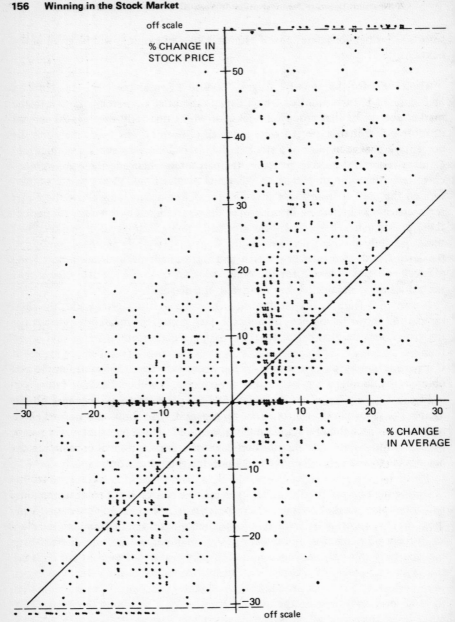

Figure 13-1. Percentage Changes in Stock Prices Relative to the Value Line Composite Average for Those Stocks Reporting 20 Percent or More Better-than-expected Earnings for Time Intervals between Successive Quarterly Earnings Reports, 1 August 1969 to 1 September 1971

Figure 13-2. Price Performance of Stocks by Group, 1 August 1969 to 1 September 1971

Group	I	II	III	IV	V	VI	Total
Number of stocks	981	732	1907	1440	960	2260	8280
Mean price change	+5.9%	+2.9%	+1.4%	−0.2%	−1.2%	−2.5%	+0.4%
Number of stocks performing better than the market	605 (62%)	484 (66%)	1157 (61%)	829 (58%)	536 (56%)	945 (42%)	4556 (55%)
Number of stocks performing equal to or worse than the market	376 (38%)	248 (34%)	750 (39%)	611 (42%)	424 (44%)	1315 (58%)	3724 (45%)
Expectation	540 ±28	403 ±24	1049 ±36	792 ±34	528 ±30	1243 ±40	

drastic three-month swings as those in the two years up till 1 September 1971; the average price change for all three-month intervals was down 0.7 percent compared to the 0.4 percent increase in the earlier period.

The semi-strongly efficient markets model of the stock market denies the possibility of segregating a given sample of stocks with respect to their future performance on the basis of published information. A person choosing blindly should do as well as an expert guided by all publicly available knowledge. Therefore, if our results can be shown to be statistically significant—that is, if a person choosing blindly would have little chance of achieving the discrimination displayed in these results—the model will have failed a critical test.

Three tests have been applied to the data. The first evaluates the probability of selecting blindly from our 8,280 sample points of the first time period a group of 981 stocks of which 62 percent outperform the market average, our Group I. Since 55 percent of the stocks in our total sample outperformed the market, it is most likely that in any blind selection of stocks from the total population 55 percent, or 540, will outperform the market. The standard deviation for this sampling process is given by

$$\text{s.d.} = \sqrt{981 \times 0.55 \times 0.45} \sqrt{1 - (981/8280)} = 14$$

(where the factor $\sqrt{1 - (981/8280)}$ allows for sampling without replacement). Such a standard deviation implies that there is less than a 5-percent probability of selecting more than 540 + 28 or less than 540 - 28 stocks in a random sample of 981 stocks drawn from our total population of 8,280. This range of two stan-

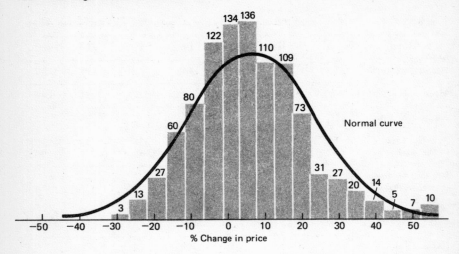

Figure 13-3. Distribution of Percentage Price Changes of Group I Stocks, 1 August 1969 to 1 September 1971

dard deviations for each of the six groups is given in the "Expectation" row of Figure 13-4. A similar analysis applies to the results of Figure 13-5 for our second time period. In both tables, the totals for Groups I, II, and III fall far above the indicated ranges, those for Groups IV and V inside, and for Group VI far below. It must be concluded that, contrary to the semi-strongly efficient markets hypothesis, discrimination among stocks as to future performance is possible on the basis of comparing actual quarterly earnings with estimated earnings.

The second test, known as the "t" test, estimates the significance of the difference in the mean price changes for two groups. Two samples are assumed drawn at random from the same parent population, in this case the 8,280 price changes of our first period and the 9,401 of our second period, each sample containing the same number of points as one of our six stock groups, and "t" values calculated. For each pair of groups, "t" fell in the range between five and ten, implying that there is much less than one chance in a hundred of a person picking blindly from the parent population and selecting groups with as large differences in the means as found in our six groups. On the basis of this test, the conclusion of the previous paragraph is reinforced.

The third test is the "ballot problem" test. Here, two groups, say Groups I and II, are chosen blindly from a parent population and ordered from highest to lowest percentage price change. Corresponding pairs are then matched to see which is the greater. For two groups containing the same number of elements n, the probability $p(k)$ of obtaining k or more leads for one group over the other

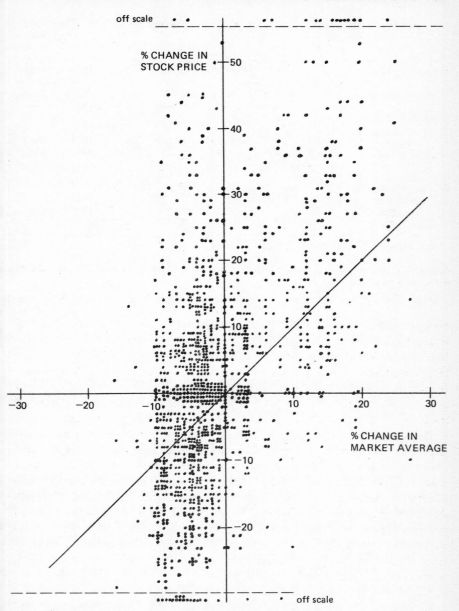

Figure 13-4. Percentage Changes in Stock Prices Relative to the Value Line Composite Average for Those Stocks Reporting 20 Percent or More Better-than-expected Earnings for Time Intervals between Successive Quarterly Earnings Reports, 1 September 1971 to 15 May 1973

Figure 13-5. Price Performance of Stocks by Group, 1 September 1971 to 15 May 1973

Group	I	II	III	IV	V	VI	Total
Number of stocks	1193	683	2158	1682	1161	2524	9401
Mean price change	+3.7%	+2.4%	+0.6%	−1.4%	−2.3%	−3.5%	−0.7%
Number of stocks performing better than the market	680 (57%)	394 (58%)	1189 (55%)	842 (50%)	551 (47%)	1001 (40%)	4657 (50%)
Number of stocks performing equal to or worse than the market	513 (43%)	289 (42%)	969 (45%)	840 (50%)	610 (53%)	1523 (60%)	4744 (50%)
Expectation	597 ±32	342 ±26	1079 ±40	841 ±36	581 ±32	1262 ±44	

when both groups are selected blindly from a parent population of $2n$ elements is

$$p(k) = \frac{n - k + 1}{n + 1}$$

Thus, if all 981 percentage price changes of stocks in Group I of our first period led the corresponding price changes of stocks in another group of 981 elements, the probability of achieving this result by blind chance is

$$p(981) = \frac{981 - 981 + 1}{981 + 1} = \frac{1}{982}$$

or 1 chance in 982. According to the semi-strongly efficient markets hypothesis, a person would have negligible likelihood of accomplishing a feat such as this without inside information. For both our Group I stocks from the two time periods, Group I led each of the other groups in every match. And since no inside information was available, we must assume that the semi-strongly efficient stock market does not exist. Because no two of the groups have the same number of elements, the matches of the percentage price changes were cut when one group was exhausted. The probabilities are somewhat different from those calculated by the formula, but not far removed. For Group I stocks, it is even less likely for a person to achieve the separation relative to Groups III, IV, V, and VI by chance. The greater numbers of stocks in these latter groups furnish higher probabilities of catching big winners. The same treatment applied to Groups II, III,

IV, and V always yielded a $p(k)$ much less than 1 percent. Again, we are forced to affirm the existence of late-breaking, available information enabling an investor to choose from the total population of stocks those apt to do best.

Practically speaking, what these results suggest to Mr. Average Investor is that he should confine his investments to Group I and Group II stocks, those reporting quarterly earnings 10 percent or more better than expected, and he should buy them soon after the release of the report to the press. There is no guarantee of capital gains, unfortunately; a given single purchase may end up anywhere along the distribution of Figure 13-3. Just where it might end up is unpredictable in the same way that the final position in a single random walk experiment is unpredictable. But because the curve for Group I stocks is heavily biased toward higher price changes, the investor is much more likely than not to profit over the next three months to the next earnings report. The bias is so strong that a number of lucky investors will realize gains of 10 percent and more for this period.
It should be noted from Figures 13-1 and 13-4 that much depends on the course of the market's action in the three months following the surprising earnings report. If the market as a whole turns down, an investor is more apt to lose than win even with Group I stocks, although his average loss will be less than that of the market averages. By contrast, in a rising market, his chances of loss are small, while the prospect of large capital gains is very bright. Any prophet who thinks himself capable of foretelling the twists and turns of the stock market should easily amass a fortune by investing only in bull markets. We shall return to the practical aspects of investment in the next chapter.

Our results argue forcibly against the semi-strongly efficient and, *a fortiori*, the strongly efficient models of the stock market. A major consequence of this demonstration is that better-than-average performance in the selection of stocks is possible on the basis of public information. Furthermore, the door is open to the study of the effect of other changes in parameters that affect the stock market, notably interest rates and dividend policy. Little work has been done in these areas as yet.

14
BEAT THE STREET

Defendit numerus!
There is safety in numbers.

Anonymous

Putting into practice a system of stock selection based on surprising earnings embodies a number of problems, procedural and otherwise, which will now be dealt with. At the beginning, let us clearly understand the foundational pillars on which our system rests: (1) The stock market will in the future remain a favorable game, which implies that our economy will remain reasonably free and government growth will be limited. A glance at the cloud of points graphs in the last chapter (Figs. 13-1 and 13-4) should convince anybody that the odds are against an investor making profits in bear markets by buying stocks reporting surprisingly high earnings, and similarly in bull markets for investors short selling stocks reporting surprisingly low earnings. (See the appendix to this chapter for an explanation of short selling.) Since nobody has been able to forecast future bull and bear markets with any measure of reliability, we must fall back on the ever-rising stock market as the basis of profitability. Our system will accumulate profits at a rapid rate in rising markets and keep losses to a minimum in falling markets. That is all that can be asked. A gloom-and-doom speculator may wish to assume the opposite, that the United States will indeed commit suicide and the stock market is headed toward zero. He will continually sell short on surprisingly low earnings, and, should his scenario work out, reap large gains. Of course, if our free society disappears, he may find himself without his money like the rest of us. (2) Earnings are the sole factor of importance for predicting the future behavior of stocks, at least until somebody is able to demonstrate the influence of another factor in a statistically significant way. Like many other pseudo-scientific fields, economics and finance are beset with witchcraft, with supposed sages making all sorts of extravagant claims on the basis of very superficial knowledge and data. So few of them recognize their efforts as little more than searching for patterns in a random walk, much like the chartists in the stock market. The investor in stocks, as well as the investor in horseflesh, must close his mind and heart to all such gobbledegook. The lesson is not easily learned.

We begin with a sampling of quarterly earnings estimates that are to be compared with actually reported earnings. Which leads into the first problem: How are earnings estimates obtained? The best method would be for company presidents to release their forecasts to the public, but they are rarely inclined to do so. Every once in a while, however, short items appear in the *Wall Street Journal* that should be noted, like this one in the 3 November 1977 edition under the caption, "Amcord Raises Its Estimate For Full-Year Earnings": "NEWPORT BEACH, Calif.—Amcord Inc. said that based on record earnings for the third quarter and nine months, it boosted its full-year earnings estimate.

"The cement, metal buildings and leisure products company said it projects earnings for the year of $2.10 a share up from its previous estimate of $1.80 a share."

The article further stated that nine-month net income reached $1.96. Subtracting $1.96 from $2.10 gives $.14, the company's estimate for the last quarter. Without any further ado, if the $.14 estimate is 10 percent or more above previously available projections, the stock should be considered for purchase. This is obviously the case here. Amcord closed at 12$\frac{3}{4}$ on the day of this news release and at 13$\frac{3}{8}$ on 20 January 1978 (as this was being written), a 4.9-percent gain compared to a 3-percent loss in the Dow-Jones Industrial Average over this period. In addition, the company paid a $.20 dividend in December.

Do-it-yourself is another method. Although this approach is not practical for the application of our system of stock selection, some knowledge of the techniques employed by financial officers and analysts to derive earnings estimates can prove helpful. Accordingly, we sketch the means by which the earnings of Eastman Kodak for each of the quarters of 1978 are estimated. It will become immediately evident that the game is just the random walk in a new guise: each step involves a choice between many alternatives with the final outcome dependent on a series of random events. The stock market adopts the mean of thousands of estimates by individual investors as a basis for setting stock prices.

Step 1: Guess the gross national product for 1978. This is the dollar value of the total output of goods and services in the United States and depends sensitively on political, economic, and international considerations. For a company like Eastman Kodak with about 40 percent of its sales transacted outside the country, the GNP's of other countries will also be needed but will be neglected here. For the United States, we estimate a GNP of $2.1 trillion for 1978, up about 10 percent from 1977. Presumably, Kodak's sales are correlated to this figure and, indeed, over the last few years, its sales have held at about .311 percent of the GNP.

Step 2: Taking account of new product introductions, price competition, currency translations, gain or loss of market share for its products, guess Kodak's total sales for 1978. Let us suppose that they will be .311 percent of our estimated GNP of the United States, or $6.531 billion.

Step 3: Again gazing into our crystal ball, we must decide how much of the sales dollars can be brought down to the bottom line where the net earnings are shown. The cost of goods sold, depreciation, selling and administrative expenses, research and development costs, interest payments on debt, and income taxes must all be subtracted from sales. There may be adjustments for dividends and interest received from other corporations, for nonrecurring capital gains and losses, write-offs, inventory accounting, and deferred costs. Looking at statistical summaries for prior years and "adjusting for trends," we arrive at a figure of $751.1 million for the net earnings of Eastman Kodak for 1978.

Step 4: Dividing the estimated net earnings by the 161.6 million common shares Kodak is expected to have outstanding gives $4.65 as the earnings per share expected in 1978. If a company has outstanding an issue of preferred stock, dividends paid on the preferred must first be subtracted from the net earnings before division by the number of common shares.

Step 5: Apportion the $4.65 per share over the four quarters of the year considering past years' quarterly earnings trends and any new information available. Our breakdown follows: first quarter, $.70; second quarter, $1.00; third quarter, $1.35; fourth quarter, $1.60.

Step 6: Find out if these estimates are "in the ballpark" by telephoning a financial officer of Eastman Kodak and asking. Although a specific number will not be revealed, a "yes" or "no" answer may be expected.

Generating earnings estimates is obviously a lot of work and hardly conducive to our purposes. We are looking for surprising events and these are likely to be rare events. To find even one surprising report, we should have on hand fifty, a hundred, and maybe more estimates, and obtaining them on our own is beyond the limits of capacity. So why not simply subscribe to some investment service that performs all the above steps and markets them at a reasonable charge?

The service whose estimates I shall use in this chapter is *The Value Line Investment Survey*. It furnishes on a continuing basis estimates as well as comment and statistical arrays of data on over 1,500 companies. Quarterly earnings for the past several years are shown at the lower left hand side of the one page devoted to each company in a box entitled "Earnings Per Share." Also appearing in the box are estimated earnings for future quarters in *italics*. The latter are the numbers of interest.

Once a set of earnings estimates has been obtained, it is only necessary to compare them with the earnings actually reported by companies at the end of each quarter. These are best found in the *Wall Street Journal*, which contains by far the most complete and error-free financial information of any newspaper, not to mention its superior general interest articles and editorial page. There are corporate earnings reported every day, and these are displayed under a heading "Digest of Corporate Earnings Reports." Several examples illustrate the nature of the reporting, all of them from the issue of 28 October 1977:

1. Arkansas Louisiana Gas (N)

Quar Sept 30:	1977	1976
Revenues	$104,047,639	$83,703,783
Net income	8,217,081	6,887,063
Shr earnings:		
Net income	.64	.54
12 months:		
Revenues	439,083,202	356,252,942
Net income	47,136,788	42,314,114
Shr earnings:		
Net income	3.74	3.36

This is a report from the Arkansas Louisiana Gas Company, whose shares are listed on the New York Stock Exchange (N), for the quarter ending 30 September 1977. Also shown are figures for the corresponding quarter of 1976. In the quarter the company derived revenues of $104,047,639 from its operations (the company is primarily a natural gas utility whose sales of services are called "revenues" as distinct from "sales" of a product) and net income of $8,217,081. Earnings per share were $.64 versus $.54 for the 1976 quarter. There follow figures for the twelve-month period ending September 30. The only number of interest to us is the $.64 share earnings for the quarter.

2. Lockheed Corp. (N)

Quar Sept 25:	1977	1976
Sales	$811,600,000	$729,300,000
Net inco	21,900,000	9,100,000
Avg shrs	13,611,000	12,117,000
Shr earnings (primary)		
Net inco	1.50	.75
Shr earnings (fully diluted)		
Net inco	1.34	.70

9 months	1977	1976
Sales	2,483,100,000	2,429,400,000
Net inco	47,400,000	31,300,000
Avg shrs	13,383,000	11,987,000
Shr earnings (primary)		
Net inco	3.22	2.61
Shr earnings (fully diluted)		
Net inco	2.88	2.38

Although Lockheed released results for the nine-month period ending 25 September as well as for the third quarter, we examine only the quarterly figures. This report is more complicated than the one from Arkansas Louisiana Gas because the number of Lockheed shares outstanding increases with time—from an average of 12.117 million in the third quarter of 1976 to an average of 13.611 million in the third quarter of 1977—and because earnings are reported on two different bases, primary and fully diluted. The reason behind the expanding amount of common stock is the existence of other types of investment instruments which are convertible into common stock at the option of the holder. In Lockheed's case, there are warrants, which may be exchanged for common stock up to a certain date upon payment of a predetermined price, and debentures convertible into common stock at a fixed price of $72.50 per share. Primary share earnings are obtained when net income is divided by the average number of shares outstanding plus what are known as common stock equivalents, or those instruments convertible into stock whose price moves in tandem with the price of the stock. With Lockheed's stock price well in excess of the exercise price of the warrants (there are $7.00 and $10.00 warrants which permit holders to obtain Lockheed stock well under the current market price of about $14.00 per share), it is likely that all warrants will be converted into stock, and the primary earnings per share allow for this eventuality. On the other hand, the conversion price of the debentures is so far above the stock price that conversion is unlikely (at the $1,000 face value of the debenture, only 13.79 shares would be obtained by conversion), but the fully diluted earnings allow for even this possibility. When comparing estimated with actual earnings, the bases of the two calculations must be the same. Value Line estimates for Lockheed earnings are on a primary basis.

3. Schlumberger Ltd. (N)

Quar Sept 30:	1977	1976
Revenues	$543,289,000	$440,077,000
Net inco	106,865,000	79,240,000

Quar Sept 30:	1977	1976
Avg shrs	85,725,000	a85,954,000
Shr earns:		
Net inco	1.24	.92

a—Adjusted for three-for-two stock split in December 1976.

Here again, the basis for calculating earnings per share is the average number of shares outstanding over the reporting period. The non-appearance of primary and fully diluted earnings indicates that Schlumberger has no convertible securities outstanding. However, the amount of stock may still change: It may decrease if a company buys in its own stock or it may increase if stock is issued to take over another company or if officers exercise stock purchase options. The share earnings in this case is simply obtained by dividing the net income by the average number of shares.

One additional feature is present, the stock split as explained in the footnote. In December 1976, Schlumberger issued free to its stockholders one extra share for each two shares held, increasing the total number of shares by 50 percent. This action did nothing to improve the lot of the stockholders since corporate assets and earnings were unaffected. However, the earnings per share decreased because the same earnings that existed before the split must now be divided by 1.5 times more shares. At the same time, the price of the stock decreases by the same factor. In this way, all statistics are kept on a comparable basis.

When a corporation releases an earnings report after a stock split has occurred, an investor comparing estimated with actual earnings per share must make sure that the estimate was prepared using the new share total. If it was not, he must adjust the old estimate and the old price: Simply divide both by the factor by which the number of shares was increased. In the event of a three-for-two split (or its equivalent, a 50 percent stock dividend), divide the old estimate and price by 1.5. If Schlumberger's estimated earnings per share were $1.86 before the split, the new figure is $1.86 ÷ 1.5 = $1.24; if the price was $90, the adjusted price is $60. The following table lists some common stock splits, their equivalent stock dividends (either term may be used), and the appropriate dividing factor:

Stock split	Stock dividend	Dividing factor
101-for-100	1%	1.01
102-for-100	2%	1.02
105-for-100	5%	1.05
110-for-100	10%	1.10
3-for-2	50%	1.5
2-for-1	100%	2

The same considerations apply if a company sells new stock to the public in order to raise money.

4. Washington Post Co. (A)

13 wk Oct 2	1977	1976
Revenues	$101,928,000	$85,840,000
Net income	6,611,000	3,524,000
Avg shares	8,317,000	a9,006,000
Shr earns (com and com equiv):		
Net income	.79	a.39

39 weeks:		
Revenues	309,444,000	264,848,000
Net income	22,453,000	b15,052,000
Avg shares	8,545,000	a9,034,000
Shr earns (com and com equiv):		
Net income	2.63	a1.67

a—Adjusted to reflect a two-for-one stock split paid in December 1976.

b—Includes a gain from the sale of a radio station in February 1976 of $1,800,000.

Shares of The Washington Post Company are traded on the American Stock Exchange (A), and the reporting period is for the thirteen weeks ending 2 October. The number of shares has decreased since 1976 because of purchases by the company of its own stock. Share earnings are based on common stock and equivalents, which for this corporation indicates the existence of two classes of stock: Class A, which is not publicly traded; and Class B, which is. Footnote a shows that 1976 figures were adjusted for a two-for-one stock split in December 1976. Footnote b reveals a capital gain of $1.8 million was realized in February 1976 from the disposal of a radio station. When comparing estimates with actual earnings, the investor must know whether or not the estimate makes allowance for any capital gains or losses that the company may incur. If it does not, the actual earnings must be adjusted downward or upward for a capital gain or loss respectively. There also may be extraordinary credits or charges to income from a tax loss carry-forward or a write-off of discontinued operations which may have to be taken into account.

5. Katy Industries Inc. (N)

Quar Sept 30	1977	1976
aSales	$41,200,000	$40,756,000
Inco cnt op	4,052,000	3,389,000
Loss dis op	201,000	355,000
Income	3,851,000	3,034,000
Extrd cred	212,000	646,000
Net income	4,063,000	3,680,000
Avg shrs	4,764,573	4,736,256
Shr earns:		
Inco cnt op	.75	.61
Income	.70	.54
Net income	.75	.68
Shr earns (fully diluted):		
Inco cnt op	.50	.43
Income	.48	.38
Net income	.51	.46

a—From continuing operations, excludes operations of Missouri-Kansas-Texas Railroad Co.

Sales reported by Katy Industries are from continuing operations only and losses from the 97 percent owned railroad are not consolidated. Three kinds of income are displayed: (1) income from continuing operations amounting to $.75 per share for 1977's third quarter; (2) income of $.70 per share which includes a loss from operations discontinued during the quarter; and (3) net income of $.75 which includes an extraordinary credit not explained in the *Journal* digest. Estimates are usually made for continuing operations and tend to exclude non-recurring gains and losses, but they should be checked for such exclusions. If Value Line estimates are used, a call to the analyst will clear up any confusion.

Now that we know how to obtain both earnings estimates and actual earnings reports, all that is left is to compare them and pick out those stocks with surprising earnings. This is now done specifically for the period between July and November 1977, the latest available at the time of writing. Earnings reports from companies whose second quarter of 1977 ends in June were screened to select those with actual second quarter earnings 10 percent or more higher than the estimate of The Value Line. These stocks promise to be the best performers over the next several months according to our earlier results. The screening process itself takes practice: the investor must keep in mind all stocks for which he has estimates as he scans the *Journal's* Digest of Earnings Reports, comparing each stock's earnings with the estimate. The 10 percent dividing line is an easy one to use for mental calculations. Earnings are released every day, and at quarter's end, the number of reports reaches flood proportions. Some investors may wish to limit the number of companies followed, depending on the amount of time at their disposal.

Figure 14-1 tabulates information on estimated and actual earnings for these high expectation stocks and also data to display their subsequent performance. Because more than 250 stocks out of the 1,600 screened came in with earnings 10 percent or more higher than expected, I have arbitrarily limited the data to those 59 companies that reported for the second quarter on or before 21 July. This sample suffices for our purposes. The columns of Figure 14-1 specify the following details:

Column   1—the stock symbol (the corresponding company names are shown in the appendix to this chapter)

Column   2—the earnings estimated for the second quarter of 1977 by The Value Line ("d" before the earnings indicates a deficit)

Column   3—the actual earnings reported by the company in the *Wall Street Journal* for the second quarter (adjusted to the same basis as the estimate if necessary)

Column   4—the percentage difference between estimated and actual earnings $\left(\dfrac{\text{actual earnings} - \text{estimated earnings}}{\text{estimated earnings}} \times 100 \right)$

Column   5—the closing price on the day the earnings report appeared in the *Wall Street Journal*

Column   6—the closing price on the day the subsequent earnings report appeared in the *Wall Street Journal* approximately three months later

Column   7—the percentage change in price $\left(\dfrac{\text{Final price} - \text{initial price}}{\text{initial price}} \times 100 \right)$

Column   8—the percentage change in the Dow-Jones Industrial Average

Column   9—the month and day of the first report

Column 10—the month and day of the subsequent report

Any investor may expect this table to represent a fair sampling of what to expect should he decide to use this system of stock selection. He has ample opportunity to buy on the day the earnings report appears and, likewise, time to sell on the day the subsequent report appears near that day's closing price.

The time interval for our illustration of the workings of the system was a rather unfortunate one for most investors. The Dow-Jones Industrial Average

Figure 14-1. Performance Data for Stocks Reporting Second Quarter 1977 Earnings 10 Percent or More Higher than Expected

Stock	Est. Earns. per Share	Actual Earns. per Share	% Over Estimate	Initial Closing Price	Final Closing Price	% Change	% Change DJIA	Time Interval	
AL	$1.00	$1.23	+23.0%	$27\frac{7}{8}$	$23\frac{1}{4}$	−16.6%	−12.4%	7/21	10/21
AALS	.90	1.07	+18.9	$46\frac{3}{4}$	$47\frac{7}{8}$	+2.4	−10.8	7/20	10/18
ACD	1.42	2.22	+56.3	$48\frac{1}{2}$	$42\frac{3}{4}$	−11.9	−9.2	7/14	10/17
AAC	.70	.94	+34.3	$13\frac{5}{8}$	$12\frac{5}{8}$	−7.3	−13.0	7/21	10/25
AMB	1.30	1.55	+19.2	$46\frac{3}{4}$	$42\frac{1}{8}$	−9.9	−12.4	7/21	10/21
AHS	.45	.51	+13.3	$24\frac{3}{4}$	$24\frac{1}{8}$	−2.5	−11.7	7/20	10/19
AD	1.85	2.43	+31.4	$57\frac{1}{2}$	54	−6.1	−11.5	7/19	10/26
AII	.55	.65	+18.2	$10\frac{3}{8}$	$11\frac{5}{8}$	+12.0	−11.0	7/21	10/18
BNF	.41	.48	+17.1	10	$8\frac{1}{4}$	−17.5	−12.4	7/21	10/21
BF	1.52	2.07	+36.2	$21\frac{3}{8}$	$21\frac{1}{2}$	+0.6	−11.7	7/20	10/19
CAO	.20	.32	+60.0	$4\frac{1}{8}$	$5\frac{7}{8}$	+42.4	−8.6	7/2	9/27
CRT	.80	.94	+17.5	$25\frac{3}{4}$	$24\frac{1}{4}$	−5.8	−9.7	7/15	10/13
CSN	.93	1.12	+20.4	$28\frac{1}{8}$	$28\frac{3}{8}$	+0.9	−10.7	7/19	10/18
CWE	.40	.44	+10.0	$31\frac{3}{4}$	29	−8.7	−12.1	7/19	10/21
CAX	.85	1.03	+21.2	$22\frac{3}{8}$	$21\frac{1}{4}$	−5.0	−11.7	7/20	10/19
CNF	.95	1.09	+14.7	$23\frac{3}{4}$	$23\frac{1}{2}$	−1.1	−11.6	7/21	10/20
ZB	1.15	1.29	+12.2	35	$32\frac{3}{4}$	−6.4	−9.5	7/19	10/11
DIA	1.10	1.34	+21.8	$30\frac{3}{8}$	$28\frac{3}{8}$	−6.6	−9.3	7/15	10/14
DC	.40	.45	+12.5	$12\frac{7}{8}$	$10\frac{1}{4}$	−20.4	−11.7	7/20	10/19
DOR	.67	.97	+44.8	$16\frac{3}{8}$	$17\frac{1}{2}$	+6.9	−10.8	7/20	10/18
DD	2.90	3.28	+13.1	121	109	−9.9	−10.7	7/19	10/18
ETN	1.55	1.71	+10.3	$42\frac{1}{2}$	$38\frac{1}{8}$	−10.3	−12.2	7/20	10/21
FSD	.55	.86	+56.4	$29\frac{1}{8}$	32	+9.9	−12.7	7/19	10/25
FWF	.46	.63	+37.0	$9\frac{7}{8}$	11	+11.4	−11.4	7/20	10/20
FNM	.62	.70	+12.9	$16\frac{3}{4}$	$15\frac{7}{8}$	−5.2	−7.9	7/14	10/11
FBD	.20	.31	+55.0	$9\frac{1}{2}$	$7\frac{1}{8}$	−25.0	−11.6	7/21	10/20
FFI	1.07	1.27	+18.7	25	$23\frac{1}{2}$	−6.0	−8.7	7/12	10/12
FBOS	.40	.73	+82.5	$20\frac{1}{4}$	17	−16.0	−10.8	7/19	10/17
FRM	.66	.93	+40.9	$13\frac{1}{2}$	$9\frac{7}{8}$	−26.9	−11.7	7/20	10/19
FO	1.05	1.25	+19.0	$19\frac{1}{4}$	$18\frac{7}{8}$	−1.9	−11.4	7/20	10/20
GPU	.35	.45	+28.6	$21\frac{1}{8}$	20	−5.3	−10.8	7/18	10/26
GP	.60	.66	+10.0	$30\frac{1}{8}$	$26\frac{5}{8}$	−11.6	−10.8	7/20	10/18
GLB	1.20	1.45	+20.8	$35\frac{3}{4}$	44	+23.1	−12.0	7/20	11/4
GWW	.52	.59	+13.5	$29\frac{3}{4}$	28	−5.9	−12.4	7/21	10/21
GWF	1.05	1.22	+16.2	$24\frac{1}{8}$	$21\frac{7}{8}$	−9.3	−8.7	7/13	10/12
ICX	1.10	1.43	+30.0	$26\frac{7}{8}$	$22\frac{1}{2}$	−16.3	−12.7	7/19	10/25
INX	.25	.29	+16.0	$27\frac{3}{4}$	$20\frac{1}{2}$	−27.5	−11.4	7/20	10/20
KML	.40	.45	+12.5	$9\frac{3}{8}$	$7\frac{5}{8}$	−18.7	−9.0	7/14	10/14
KSU	1.25	2.07	+65.6	$38\frac{5}{8}$	$32\frac{5}{8}$	−15.5	−11.6	7/21	10/20
KRN	.98	1.10	+12.2	35	$35\frac{1}{2}$	+1.4	−11.6	7/19	10/19
KRA	1.32	1.47	+11.4	$49\frac{5}{8}$	$47\frac{1}{4}$	−4.8	−9.8	7/18	10/14
KR	.95	1.14	+20.0	$27\frac{1}{8}$	$24\frac{1}{4}$	−10.6	−10.5	7/8	10/26

Figure 14-1. (*Continued*)

Stock	Est. Earns. per Share	Actual Earns. per Share	% Over Estimate	Initial Closing Price	Final Closing Price	% Change	% Change DJIA	Time Interval	
MKY	$.36	$.40	+11.1%	$14\frac{1}{2}$	$11\frac{3}{8}$	−21.6%	−11.6%	7/21	10/20
MHP	.35	.41	+17.1	$19\frac{1}{8}$	$18\frac{5}{8}$	−2.6	−10.8	7/19	10/17
MRK	1.00	1.21	+21.0	$56\frac{1}{4}$	$52\frac{1}{4}$	−7.1	−11.9	7/21	10/19
MUN	.12	.29	+141.7	$18\frac{5}{8}$	$17\frac{5}{8}$	−5.4	−11.6	7/21	10/20
NCR	.95	1.29	+35.8	$40\frac{1}{4}$	40	−0.6	−9.3	7/15	10/14
NG	.60	.71	+18.3	$16\frac{1}{2}$	16	−3.0	−11.7	7/20	10/19
OVT	.97	1.63	+68.0	21	$19\frac{3}{8}$	−7.7	−11.4	7/20	10/20
OCF	1.60	1.87	+16.9	$69\frac{1}{8}$	65	−6.0	−9.8	7/18	10/14
MO	1.25	1.42	+13.6	$58\frac{5}{8}$	$60\frac{1}{2}$	+3.2	−10.7	7/19	10/18
PEG	.62	.69	+11.3	$25\frac{5}{8}$	$23\frac{5}{8}$	−7.8	−13.0	7/21	10/24
ROH	1.03	1.25	+21.4	$38\frac{3}{8}$	$29\frac{1}{2}$	−23.1	−11.7	7/20	10/19
SFF	1.50	1.77	+18.0	$41\frac{1}{2}$	$36\frac{3}{8}$	−12.3	−12.4	7/21	10/21
SO	.37	.45	+21.6	18	$17\frac{1}{2}$	−2.8	−12.1	7/19	10/21
STO	.65	.72	+10.8	$13\frac{3}{4}$	$11\frac{3}{4}$	−14.5	−11.7	7/20	10/19
SVU	.70	.83	+18.6	25	$26\frac{3}{8}$	+5.5	−6.7	7/1	10/3
TFB	.90	1.04	+15.6	29	$26\frac{7}{8}$	−7.3	−12.4	7/21	10/21
WSN	.75	.92	+22.7	24	$21\frac{3}{4}$	−9.4	−11.3	7/19	10/20

declined sharply, 11.1 percent, and only 12 of our 59 stocks went up, about one in five, a figure also valid for all 253 stocks that showed second quarter earnings 10 percent or more better than expected. However, fully 42 of our 59 stocks performed better than the DJIA and the average price change was a 6.2 percent decline. Dividends amounted to about 1.5 percent, making the return −4.7 percent for the three-month period, less than half the DJIA. The statistical tests that were administered in the last chapter yield the same results when applied to the 1977 data, supporting once again the weakly efficient market hypothesis. But as I mentioned earlier, it is very unlikely that anybody using the system will profit in a severe bear market. All that can be hoped for is to limit losses and await a turnaround.

Breaking the figures down into Group I (stocks reporting 20 percent or more better-than-expected earnings) and Group II (stocks with 10 percent to 19 percent better-than-expected earnings) gives the following tabulation:

	Number of stocks up in price	Number of stocks down in price	Average price change	Change in DJIA
Group I	7	20	−4.8%	−11.3%
Group II	5	27	−7.3%	−10.9%

As was the case in our 1969–1973 results, Group I stocks again did best. But even they could not buck the drastic deterioration of the market over this three-month period. My recommendation to investors is to initiate an investment by purchasing only Group I stocks and hold on to them so long as their earnings in subsequent reports are 10 percent or more better than expected. The reasons behind this suggestion arise from considerations of commissions and taxes, to be discussed below.

Each quarter, roughly 15 percent of the earnings reports will exceed projections by 10 percent or more, and 7 percent of the total will be Group I stocks. An investor following 100 stocks may expect on average 7 Group I stocks to appear, one following 1,600 stocks may find 110. Which are to be bought? Alas, for at this point I can be of no further help. Just one more factor to aid in choosing the best from our set of better-than-average performing stocks and we could all get rich very quickly, even in bear markets. But I have not been able to find the magic factor, and one probably does not exist. Quality, price-to-earnings ratios, β-coefficients (a dubious measure of risk employed by analysts)—none of these aspects of a company's stock is of any avail. And, of course, we should not expect them to be in a weakly efficient market. An investor must make his selections from the set of stocks with surprising earnings and trust to the random walk for above-average performance. In a normally rising stock market, profits will be more than satisfactory.

Diversification is essential to smooth over the up-and-down fluctuations in stock prices. A prudent investment procedure is to divide investment capital into equal portions and invest a roughly constant amount of money in each "signal" stock that comes along until no more is left. A portfolio of three stocks is a good start, and ten or twenty would assure the investor of realizing the superior return characteristic of this group.

More venturesome readers may wish to leverage their investments by buying on "margin," which is a technique wherein up to half the money used to purchase a stock may be borrowed from the brokerage firm through which business is done or from a bank. Suppose an investor buys 100 shares of General Motors at $60 per share for a cost of $6,000 (neglecting commissions, which are discussed below). He decides to put up $3,000 of his own money and borrow $3,000. Should GM then appreciate to $70, his profit would be $1,000. Had he bought 50 shares outright with his $3,000, his profit would have amounted to only $500. Using margin he made $33\frac{1}{3}$ percent on his capital compared to $16\frac{2}{3}$ percent on an outright purchase. The other side of the coin is a greater chance of loss. If GM had declined to $50, the loss would have been $1,000, or $33\frac{1}{3}$ percent on the invested capital, compared to only $500 had the stock not been margined. Margin buying increases the chances for profit at the cost of greater risk. In a favorable game like the stock market, it should be used by the aggressive investor seeking capital gains, especially under the new tax law, which

permits deductions against earned income of up to $3,000 a year for capital
losses and indefinite loss carry-forwards.

When to sell? Immediately on the next earnings report if the company has
lower-than-expected earnings. Even before that time, an investor should exercise
continuous supervision over the earnings prospects of his stocks by perusing the
Wall Street Journal for the appearance of any items revising projections downward and keeping up to date with his investment service. Sell on any downward
revisions of earnings estimates and don't be afraid to take losses. They can be
made up in stocks offering better prospects.

Other than for reduced earnings, taxes and commissions are two reasons for
not rushing to sell. Any profits from stocks held one year or less are added onto
and taxed as regular income. They drive the investor into higher tax brackets
where higher rates are in effect. It usually pays to hold stocks if possible more
than a year so as to take advantage of the lower capital gains tax rates whereby
"only" 50 percent of the profits add on to income up to a maximum tax of
25 percent. (There are certain "preferences" to be complied with by investors
with large profits that increase this tax substantially. Our government seems
bent on destroying the efficiency of the marketplace with its confiscatory tax
policies).

Regular brokerage commissions also eat into profits. The small investor can
figure on paying 2 percent to buy and 2 percent to sell, for a loss of 4% of his
invested capital almost before he starts, and even these rates may go up in the
near future. Because commissions favor large investors, they can count on
charges half as much. The use of a discount broker will reduce rates by another
half, and such firms should be used. They do everything the regular broker does
except for providing investment advice. This is really an advantage.

Do not sell for any reason other than the prospect of reduced earnings.
Especially do not sell because of subjective feelings that the market is too high
or because it looks like the bottom will drop out. Many brokers play on these
fears near the bottom of a long decline in the hopes of getting commissions.
"Blood money" is the name for this type of business. Just remember, when you
feel bluest, everyone else probably feels the same. By the time you take action
to sell, everyone has sold who intended to and the market is ready for a rise.
All too often, the biggest rallies begin after breathtaking sinking spells. There is
nothing more disheartening than to watch a stock skyrocket in price after it has
been sold.

In contrast, many "signal" stocks act well from the moment of purchase. And
the temptation is strong to nail down profits after a substantial rise. After all, is
a stock as "safe" at 200 as it was at 25? Is the current price, however high, the
sole measure of value? My answer to both these questions is an unqualified
"yes." Do not be shaken out of a stock because the price seems too high. Never

orget that other people are buying at 200, and there is no reason, as long as earnings prospects are improving, that the stock could not go much higher. Too many investors lose the greatest part of possible capital gains by shying away from dizzying heights. Once in a while, a stock may retrace all its gain, but more often than not, truly fantastic flyers will carry into the clouds. Do not let go until a sell signal is given.

On occasion, some investors are privy to inside information about a company and its competitors. If such information includes estimated earnings, I would use it as dictated by the system: If previous earnings estimates are revised upward by 10 percent or more, consider the stock for purchase; if downward, no matter how slightly, sell. Do not use it as I once did with the Control Data Corporation. Late in 1966, the earnings projections of this company were upgraded sharply. Actually, although the percentage increase was enormous, the total predicted was only about $.50 a share for 1967. Unfortunately, before acting on these revised earnings estimates, I talked to friends of mine in both 3M and Control Data about the latter company's prospects. The opinion was unanimous: only slow growth could be expected for Control Data. On the basis of this expert advice, I let the stock go. And go it did, up over 150. The lesson clear: Trust the earnings figures and nothing else.

Many investors may wish to sell as soon as a company reports earnings in line with or slightly better than expectations and to buy stocks with better prospects. The suitability of such a program can only be determined on an individual basis. For an investor enjoying low commission charges and tax rates, that is the way to go.

In conclusion, we take a look at the performance of the stocks in Figure 14-1 after the third quarter earnings reports were released. First, those stocks reporting 10 percent or more higher-than-expected earnings for the third quarter of 1977 comprise Figure 14-2. Having reported surprisingly high earnings twice in a row, these should be the best stocks to own according to our way of thinking, and they lived up to expectations. Their performance from the day of release of third quarter earnings in October or November 1977 to 12 January 1978 (the date of this writing) far outpaced the Dow-Jones Industrial Average, which continued its sharp drop of the previous three months. Of the seventeen stocks listed in Figure 14-2, eleven outperformed the DJIA and ten of them actually went up in price. Their average price rose 2.5 percent compared to a 4.4 percent decline in the DJIA. Again, buying on surprisingly high earnings paid off.

Of the stocks in Figure 14-2, the original Group I stocks, those that reported earnings 20 percent or more better than expected for the second quarter, far outperformed the corresponding Group II stocks in the period to 12 January 1978: The average price change of Group I stocks was an increase of 9.8 percent,

Figure 14-2. Performance Data to 12 January 1978 for Stocks Reporting Second and Thir Quarter 1977 Earnings 10 Percent or More Higher Than Expected

Stock	Est. Earns. per Share Oct–Nov	Actual Earns. per Share Oct–Nov	% Over Estimate	Price 1/12/78	% Price Change Since Oct–Nov	% Price Change DJIA Since Oct–Nov	% Price Change Since Jly	% Price Change DJIA Since Jly
*AL	$1.00	$1.32	+32.0%	$24\frac{1}{8}$	+3.8%	−3.7%	−13.5%	−15.6%
*AAC	.61	.85	+39.3	$13\frac{3}{4}$	+8.9	−3.0	+0.9	−15.6
AHS	.40	.47	+17.5	$24\frac{7}{8}$	+3.1	−4.2	+0.5	−15.4
*BF	.70	1.12	+60.0	$31\frac{3}{8}$	+45.9	−4.2	+46.7	−15.4
*CAO	.29	.40	+37.9	$7\frac{1}{8}$	+21.3	−6.8	+72.7	−14.9
CRT	1.07	1.24	+15.9	$20\frac{1}{8}$	−17.0	−4.9	−21.8	−14.1
CNF	1.15	1.28	+11.3	$22\frac{1}{8}$	−5.9	−4.5	−6.8	−15.6
*FWF	.45	.53	+17.8	$8\frac{1}{4}$	−25.0	−4.5	−16.5	−15.4
FO	1.15	1.55	+34.8	$19\frac{1}{8}$	+1.3	−4.5	−0.6	−15.4
GP	.62	.71	+14.5	25	−6.1	−5.2	−17.1	−15.4
*GLB	1.91	2.45	+28.3	44	0	−4.0	+23.1	−15.4
KML	d.10	.09	+∞	$6\frac{7}{8}$	−9.8	−5.4	−26.7	−13.8
*KSU	1.25	1.44	+15.2	$39\frac{1}{4}$	+20.3	−4.5	+1.6	−15.6
*MUN	.98	1.11	+13.3	$17\frac{3}{4}$	+0.7	−4.5	−4.7	−15.6
PEG	.70	.78	+11.4	22	−6.9	−3.0	−14.1	−15.6
TFB	1.70	1.96	+15.3	$29\frac{1}{2}$	+9.8	−3.7	+1.7	−15.6
*WSN	.85	.97	+14.1	$24\frac{1}{2}$	+12.6	−4.5	+2.1	−15.3

*Indicates a Group I stock from Figure 14-1 on the basis of second quarter earnings.

whereas Group II stocks showed a 3.9 percent decline. These results, part of larger body of data, lie behind my suggestion to initiate purchases with Group stocks and hold onto them so long as they report earnings 10 percent or mor higher than expected.

In the period from the July 1977 earnings report to 12 January 1978, marke by a drastic erosion in the DJIA of 15.3 percent, thirteen of these stocks be tered the "Dow" and only four fared worse. Eight went up and nine down, bt the average price increased 1.6 percent. Unfortunately, we as investors coul not have expected to do this well because we had no way of knowing in Jul which of those stocks would report higher-than-expected earnings in October c November.

Figure 14-3 exhibits the performance of those stocks reporting slightly highe than-expected earnings in the third quarter. Twelve of the nineteen bettere the DJIA (eight went up in price) while showing an average price decline c 2.4 percent in the period from October–November to 12 January 1978. Ove the July-to-January interval, their average decline was 6.7 percent.

Finally, Figure 14-4 lists those stocks reporting disappointing earnings for th third quarter. They did surprisingly well in the October–November-to-January period, fifteen of twenty-three bettering the Dow, although not as well as the stocks of Figure 14-2. Nine went up and the average price increased 2.4 percent, mainly due to two takeover situations. It appears that the poor third quarter earnings may have been anticipated, judging from the very steep declines in the three months following the July report. For the July to January period, only three of these stocks went up in price and the average loss was 9.1 percent.

The results of this chapter coupled to those presented in my book *Beating the Street* imply the persistence of the weakly efficient nature of the stock market over a thirteen-year period from 1965 to 1978. Most likely this property is permanent, rooted as it is in the inertial essence of all large institutions. That it will persist into the indefinite future is a basic assumption of the system.

In exploiting weak efficiency for profit, we have thus far confined our attention to common stocks. Other investment instruments, such as convertible bonds and convertible preferred stock which may be converted into common stock,

Figure 14-3. Performance Data to 12 January 1978 for Stocks Reporting Second Quarter 1977 Earnings 10 Percent or More Higher than Expected and Third Quarter 1977 Earnings 0 to 9 Percent Higher than Expected

Stock	Est. Earns. per Share Oct–Nov	Actual Earns. per Share Oct–Nov	% Over Estimate	Price 1/12/78	% Price Change Since Oct–Nov	% Price Change DJIA Since Oct–Nov	% Price Change Since Jly	% Price Change DJIA Since Jly
AALS	$.95	$1.01	+6.3%	45¾	−4.4%	−5.2%	−2.1%	−15.4%
AMB	1.40	1.47	+5.0	41⅛	−2.4	−3.7	−12.0	−15.6
CSN	1.25	1.34	+7.2	29⅜	+3.5	−5.2	+4.4	−15.3
CAX	.80	.86	+7.5	20⅝	−2.9	−4.2	−7.6	−15.4
DD	2.77	2.91	+5.1	109½	+0.5	−5.2	−9.5	−15.3
ETN	1.45	1.50	+3.4	34⅛	−10.5	−3.7	−19.7	−15.4
FSD	.75	.76	+1.3	28⅝	−10.5	−3.0	−1.7	−15.3
FFI	1.36	1.46	+7.4	26⅜	+12.2	−5.6	+5.5	−13.8
GPU	.72	.73	+1.4	20½	+2.5	−4.3	−3.0	−14.6
GWW	.58	.62	+6.9	28	0	−3.7	−5.9	−15.6
ICX	1.05	1.09	+3.8	22⅞	+1.7	−3.0	−14.9	−15.3
INX	.28	.29	+3.4	16¼	−19.3	−4.5	−41.4	−15.4
KRN	.78	.84	+7.7	36¾	+3.5	−4.2	+5.0	−15.4
MHP	.75	.76	+1.3	17¼	−7.4	−5.1	−9.8	−15.4
NCR	1.14	1.24	+8.8	37¼	−6.9	−5.4	−7.5	−14.1
OVT	1.02	1.11	+8.9	19¾	+1.9	−4.5	−6.0	−15.4
OCF	2.11	2.21	+4.7	61	−6.2	−5.4	−11.8	−14.6
MO	1.49	1.57	+5.4	56⅜	−6.8	−5.2	−3.8	−15.3
SVU	.72	.76	+5.6	27⅞	+5.7	−8.7	+11.5	−14.8

Figure 14-4. Performance Data to 12 January 1978 for Stocks Reporting Second Quarter 1977 Earnings 10 Percent or More Higher than Expected and Third Quarter 1977 Earnings Lower than Expected

Stock	Est. Earns. per Share Oct–Nov	Actual Earns. per Share Oct–Nov	% Over Estimate	Price 1/12/78	% Price Change Since Oct–Nov	% Price Change DJIA Since Oct–Nov	% Price Change Since Jly	% Price Change DJIA Since Jly
ACD	$1.20	$.81	−32.5%	38¼	−10.5%	−5.1%	−21.1%	−13.8%
AD	2.06	1.88	−8.7	54½	+0.9	−4.3	−5.2	−15.3
AII	.47	.38	−19.1	11⅛	+4.5	−5.2	+7.2	−15.6
BNF	.55	.41	−25.5	9½	+15.2	−3.7	−5.0	−15.6
CWE	1.08	1.04	−3.7	27⅝	−4.7	−3.7	−13.0	−15.3
ZB	1.24	1.13	−8.9	32⅜	−1.1	−6.5	−7.5	−15.3
DIA	1.10	1.08	−1.8	26⅞	−5.3	−5.4	−11.5	−14.1
DC	.25	.02	−92.0	12	+17.1	−4.2	−6.8	−15.4
DOR	.75	.49	−34.7	21¼	+21.4	−5.2	+29.8	−15.4
FNM	.64	.62	−3.1	14⅞	−6.3	−6.5	−11.2	−13.8
FBD	.35	.02	−94.3	12⅛	+70.2	−4.5	+27.6	−15.4
FBOS	.15	.12	−20.0	15	−11.8	−5.1	−25.9	−15.4
FRM	.37	.22	−40.5	9¼	−6.3	−4.2	−31.5	−15.4
GWF	1.27	1.26	−0.8	19½	−10.9	−5.6	−19.2	−13.8
KRA	1.50	1.42	−5.3	43¾	−7.4	−5.4	−11.8	−14.6
KR	1.25	1.17	−6.4	25⅝	+5.7	−4.3	−5.5	−14.3
MKY	.37	.32	−13.5	12	+5.5	−4.5	−17.2	−15.6
MRK	.95	.92	−3.2	54⅛	+3.6	−4.2	−3.8	−15.4
NG	.82	.81	−1.2	14	−12.5	−4.2	−15.2	−15.4
ROH	1.85	.71	−61.6	29	−1.7	−4.2	−24.4	−15.4
SFF	1.50	1.36	−9.3	36¼	−0.3	−3.7	−12.7	−15.6
SO	.83	.75	−9.6	17⅛	−2.1	−3.7	−4.9	−15.3
STO	.73	.48	−34.2	10⅞	−7.4	−4.2	−20.9	−15.4

have been ignored. The usually greater yields of these securities is more than offset by a lack of leverage, and their consequent smaller percentage price changes are not conducive to aggressive investing. They will not be considered in this book. Instead, we turn to the newest game in town, one that should appeal to the inveterate gambler interested in maximum leverage, in the chance of making large profits form limited capital at the cost of greater probability of ruin. It is the options market, and its workings are taken up in the next chapter.

APPENDICES TO CHAPTER 14

I: Short Selling

Ordinarily, a person buys a stock, hoping it will go up in price, and sells at some later date. During the period in which he owns the stock, he is said to be "long" of the stock. However, the stock exchanges make it possible to reverse this procedure. A person may sell a stock that he does not own, hoping it will go down in price, and buy it back at a later time. During the period between these two times, he is said to be "short" of the stock, and the selling process is known as *selling short*. If the stock goes down after selling short, the speculator can buy it back at a lower price. He thereby makes a profit which is the difference between the selling price and the buying price, less commissions. If the stock goes up after selling short and he buys it back at a higher price, there is a loss. When a stock is bought back after a short sale, the short sale is said to be *covered*.

What actually goes on is this: If you tell your broker to sell 100 shares of General Motors short, he will borrow the shares from some other investor and sell them. Your account is then credited with the proceeds from the sale. When you cover, the stock is returned to its owner. While you are short, you must pay the owner of the shares any dividends that accrue. It is also necessary to put up with your broker a sum of money that depends on the margin rates in existence at the time. If the margin requirement is 50 percent, you must put up 50 percent of the selling price of the stock.

II. Stock Symbols of Companies Listed in Figure 14-1

AL	Alcan Aluminium Ltd.
AALS	Alexander & Alexander Services (traded over-the-counter)
ACD	Allied Chemical
AAC	Amcord
AMB	American Brands
AHS	American Hospital Supply
AD	Amsted Industries
AII	Automation Industries
BNF	Braniff International
BF	Budd Company
CAO	Carolina Freight Carriers
CRT	Certain-teed Corporation
CSN	Cincinnati Bell
CWE	Commonwealth Edison
CAX	Conrac Corporation
CNF	Consolidated Freightways
ZB	Crown Zellerbach
DIA	Diamond Shamrock
DC	Dictaphone Corporation
DOR	Dorr-Oliver

DD	Du Pont
ETN	Eaton Corporation
FSD	Falcon Seaboard
FWF	Far West Financial
FNM	Federal National Mortgage
FBD	Fibreboard Corporation
FFI	Financial Federation
FBOS	First Boston (over-the-counter)
FRM	First Mississippi
FO	Flintkote
GPU	General Public Utilities
GP	Georgia Pacific
GLB	Globe-Union
GWW	Grainger (W.W.)
GWF	Great Western Financial
ICX	IC Industries
INX	Inexco Oil
KML	Kane-Miller
KSU	Kansas City Southern Industries
KRN	Knight-Ridder Newspapers
KRA	Kraft
KR	Kroger Company
MKY	Mary Kay Cosmetics
MHP	McGraw-Hill
MRK	Merck & Company
MUN	Munsingwear
NCR	NCR Corporation
NG	National Gypsum
OVT	Overnite Transportation
OCF	Owens-Corning Fiberglas
MO	Philip Morris
PEG	Public Service Electric & Gas
ROH	Rohm & Haas
SFF	Santa Fe Industries
SO	Southern Company
STO	Stone Container
SVU	Super Valu Stores
TFB	Taft Broadcasting
WSN	Western Company North America

15
THE OPTIONS MARKET

Give me a lever long enough
And a prop strong enough.
I can single-handed move the world.

Archimedes

16 And Laban had two daughters: the name of the elder was Leah, and the name of the younger was Rachel.

17 Leah was tender eyed, but Rachel was beautiful and well favoured.

18 And Jacob loved Rachel; and said, I will serve thee seven years for Rachel thy younger daughter.

19 And Laban said, It is better that I give her to thee, than that I should give her to another man: abide with me.

20 And Jacob served seven years for Rachel; and they seemed unto him but a few days, for the love he had to her.

This biblical excerpt from Genesis 29 marks the first recorded transaction involving a business option.*† For the price of seven years of his labor, Jacob bought the right to marry Rachel, the option exercisable only after completion of his service. Under the terms of this contract, Jacob was the option buyer; he risked seven years of his labor for the reward of marriage to Rachel if he so chose at the expiration date of the option. Laban was the option writer: he guaranteed for a consideration of seven years' service the right of Jacob to marry Rachel. Had Jacob refused to marry Rachel at the end of the stipulated time, Laban would still have had the benefit of Jacob's labor for seven years.

Options first came into common use during the seventeenth century tulipmania in Holland, when wild speculation sometimes brought several thousands of dollars for a single tulip bulb. As in today's commodity markets, a merchant quoted prices on tulip bulbs for future delivery to customers and bought what are known as *call* options to protect himself from future price fluctuations. These options entitled him to buy at a designated price the bulbs needed for later sale up until a specified date in the future. If in the meantime prices declined below the option price, the option became worthless. But then the mer-

---

*A. Reinach, *The Nature of Puts and Calls* (New York: The Bookmailer, 1961).

†For a more detailed account of the options market, see P. Sarnoff, "An Empirical Examination of the Options Market," *Yearbook of Business*, ser. 11, vol. 4 (Hempstead: Hofstra University School of Business, 1977).

chant was able to purchase the required bulbs at lower market prices. If bulb prices went up, he exercised the option to obtain the bulbs. In this manner, he assured himself of having bulbs to sell at prices that would bring satisfactory profits no matter what course the market took. The option writer has the bulbs to sell if called on or can get them, for which service he receives an agreed on option fee known as the premium. The premium is his whether or not the option is exercised.

On the production side of the market, tulip growers also sought to protect themselves. In the months preceding the harvest of the tulip crop, prices were high, whereas prices usually fell sharply after the harvest. By purchasing a *put* option, a grower could take advantage of prevailing prices and ensure himself of a profit regardless of future price fluctuations. The put option enabled him to sell bulbs for future delivery at a fixed price until a stipulated future date. If prices declined during the option period, he exercised the put. If prices rose, he left the put unexercised and sold his produce at the higher market price. In its action, the option market thus serves not only to protect businessmen from the vagaries of the future, but also to smooth out price fluctuations in the marketplace.

The options market in stocks brings together the buyer and writer of stock options. For a negotiated premium, the buyer of an options contract (*call*) acquires the right to purchase 100 shares of a stock at a fixed price (the *striking price*) for a specified length of time, after which the option expires. He hopes that the market value of the underlying stock rises above the striking price before expiration day. If that happens, he can exercise the option and sell the stock at the higher market price. His return is the sale price of the stock less the cost of the stock less the premium less borkerage commissions. In today's market, however, options are infrequently exercised. With the commencement of operations of the Chicago Board Options Exchange in 1973, and many others since then, most options buyers simply sell listed options when they desire. If the premium has gone up since purchase of the contract, they realize a profit whether or not the underlying stock is above or below the striking price; if the premium has gone down, there is a loss. The person buying the option at this point is either establishing a new position as an option holder or is a writer closing out his position. On expiration day, all outstanding contracts between buyers and writers are matched and washed out except for those that buyers wish to exercise.

The principal advantage in buying a call option is leverage. For a fraction of the cost of actually purchasing the underlying shares, the buyer may benefit greatly from a price increase. The risk is limited to the premium (plus commission), while the reward may be a profit many times the size of the investment. Very large percentage gains are possible. We are going to calculate the expectation in this options market for our Group I stocks in some illustrative examples, but first let us see how transactions in options are displayed in the news media.

In the *Wall Street Journal,* option information including closing prices, number of contracts bought, striking prices, expiration months, and the closing prices of the underlying stock is tabulated under the heading "Listed Options Quotations." Presently, options are traded on the Chicago Board Options Exchange, the Pacific Exchange, the American Exchange, the Philadelphia Exchange, and the Midwest Exchange. A sample from the Chicago Board gives the results of trading in Eastman Kodak options on 2 February 1978:

Option & Price	Apr Vol	Apr Last	Jul Vol	Jul Last	Oct Vol	Oct Last	N.Y. Close
Eas Kd 45	597	$2\frac{3}{8}$	152	$3\frac{1}{2}$	118	$4\frac{3}{8}$	$45\frac{5}{8}$
Eas Kd p 45	801	$1\frac{3}{4}$	96	$2\frac{3}{16}$	15	$2\frac{7}{8}$	$45\frac{5}{8}$
Eas Kd 50	620	$\frac{5}{8}$	472	$1\frac{9}{16}$	153	$2\frac{5}{16}$	$45\frac{5}{8}$
Eas Kd p 50	424	$4\frac{3}{4}$	128	$5\frac{1}{4}$	7	$5\frac{1}{2}$	$45\frac{5}{8}$
Eas Kd 60	52	$\frac{1}{8}$	21	$\frac{1}{4}$	16	$\frac{9}{16}$	$45\frac{5}{8}$
Eas Kd p 60	157	$14\frac{3}{8}$	5	14	1	$14\frac{3}{8}$	$45\frac{5}{8}$
Eas Kd 70	6	$\frac{1}{16}$	b	b	b	b	$45\frac{5}{8}$

b—No option offered

There are twenty-one different options listed, twelve call options with different striking prices (45, 50, 60, 70) and expiration dates (April, July, October), and nine put options (labeled by *p*) with different striking prices of 45, 50, and 60 and the same expiration months as the calls. The precise expiration date is the Saturday immediately following the third Friday of the expiration month. Reading across the top line, we see the name of the company (abbreviated to Eas Kd) and the striking price (45) under the heading "Option & Price." Next is the volume (Vol) of options contracts traded having an April expiration month (597) with the last or closing price at $2\frac{3}{8}$. The person buying this last call on 2 February 1978 paid $2\frac{3}{8}$ ($2.375) for each share of underlying stock. Contracts are usually for 100 shares of underlying stock so that this last call cost the purchaser $237.50 plus commission. He has bought the right to purchase 100 shares of Eastman Kodak at $45 a share until the expiration date of the contract in April. His hope is that the premium of $2\frac{3}{8}$ will rise in price by then to a value more than $2\frac{3}{8}$ plus commission, thus enabling him to sell at a profit.

Expiration dates further in the future are available at greater cost. Continuing across the top line, we come to a July expiration option that last sold at $3\frac{1}{2}$ and then an October expiration with a last sale at $4\frac{3}{8}$. Finally, the day's closing price of the underlying stock on the New York Stock Exchange is quoted, this being $45\frac{5}{8}$. These options are termed "in-the-money" since the striking price is less than the closing price of the underlying shares.

Considering the April 45 call option, the purchaser has gained the right to share in any major advance in the price of Eastman Kodak stock that may take place before the April expiration at nominal cost. Should Eastman Kodak advance to 50, the option would sell at over 5 (how much over depends on the proximity of expiration day) and he would more than double his money. If he had bought the stock outright and laid out $4,562.50 plus commission for it, his profit would have been only about $400, or less than 10 percent on his investment. By the same token, if Eastman Kodak goes down below 45, his entire investment could be wiped out. But he may lose much more on an outright purchase. The options game thus takes on much of the character of horse betting with both huge percentage gains and 100 percent losses frequently occurring.

The second line shows the trading details for an Eastman Kodak put option with a striking price of 45. There were 801 April 45 put options traded and the closing price was $1\frac{3}{4}$. The buyer of this last put paid $175 for the right to sell 100 shares of Eastman Kodak at a price of $45 per share up until expiration day. He hopes the price of Eastman Kodak stock sinks, which will increase the price of the put above what he paid for it. As stock prices decline, put prices increase. If Eastman Kodak stock goes up in price, he loses his original investment of $175. Should Eastman Kodak stock decline to 40, he more than doubles his money, for the put will sell at a price greater than 5, again depending on the proximity of expiration day.

The remaining lines show a wide variety of other options. Note the lower option prices when the striking price is higher than the market price of the underlying shares in the case of calls (the call is "out-of-the-money" in these instances) and the exact reverse in the case of puts.

On 20 October 1975, the Du Pont Company released a report of surprisingly high earnings for the quarter ending September 30, more than 20 percent above expectations, causing the stock to move up $2\frac{3}{4}$ points to $116\frac{5}{8}$ that day. On October 21, the report appeared in the *Wall Street Journal,* and at the close on October 23, the price was $120\frac{1}{2}$. The stock looked like an excellent buy to me but being almost fully invested at the time and not wanting to sell anything, I was without the money for an outright purchase. On October 23, I decided to buy options on Du Pont stock and accordingly acquired 10 April 140 calls at a price of $3\frac{1}{2}$. For $3,500 (each of the 10 contracts cost $350) I had received the

right to buy 1,000 shares of Du Pont at a price of $140 per share until the April
expiration day. The calls were "out-of-the-money" since the striking price of
140 was above the market price of the stock. They had moved upward from $3\frac{3}{8}$
to $3\frac{1}{2}$ while the stock price advanced from $113\frac{7}{8}$ on the release of the earnings
report to $120\frac{1}{2}$. By 20 January 1976, the stock had risen to $142\frac{1}{2}$ and the April
140 calls were selling at $7\frac{1}{4}$. If I had closed out my position by selling the calls,
my profit would have been over 100 percent of my original investment, which
was made at a call price of $3\frac{1}{2}$. In the meantime the stock price was up from
$120\frac{1}{2}$ to $142\frac{1}{2}$, a 15 percent gain.

At this point, Du Pont came out with another surprisingly good earnings
report, this one for the quarter ended December 31, and I decided to hold on.
On January 23, the stock closed at $148\frac{1}{2}$ and the April 140 call at $12\frac{1}{4}$. Now,
with the market price above the striking price, any gain in the stock price is
almost fully reflected, point for point, in the call price and the percentage gains
to holders of the call are enormous. Of course, any losses in the price of the
stock translate into huge percentage losses in the call price.

The stock price peaked at 161 and the call at 21 in late January, from which
point the stock began a gradual decline for no apparent reason. I finally sold the
10 calls three days before expiration when the stock price reached 146 and the
call price 6. It was a shame to see such fantastic gains wiped out, but I still had
done very well on a percentage basis.

What was the expectation on this investment? A good idea can be obtained
with the help of Figure 13-3 in Chapter 13, which displays the distribution of
three-month percentage price changes for Group I stocks in the time period 1
August 1969 to 1 September 1971. If we assume this graph represents typical
behavior for Group I stocks over any three-month interval, we can calculate the
probability of a given percentage price change of the stock in a future three-
month interval following the release of a surprisingly high earnings report. As an
example, note from the graph that 73 out of the total of 981 stocks climbed 20
percent (actually a small range around 20 percent is used). The probability of a
20 percent appreciation is then near 73/981 or 7 percent. The probability of a
30 percent appreciation is 27/981 or 3 percent, and so on. Multiplying each of
these probabilities for percentage price changes of the stock by the reward in the
form of the corresponding price change of the call and adding gives us our three-
month expectation in the usual manner:

$$E = p_1(c_1 - c_0) + p_2(c_2 - c_0) + p_3(c_3 - c_0) + \cdots$$

where the p's are the probabilities of given percentage price changes of the
underlying stock over the next three months, c_0 is the original cost of the call,
and the other c's are the call prices corresponding to the various stock prices.

There is a problem in forecasting the relationship between the stock price and the call price. At the end of three months, this Du Pont April 140 call has value even if the stock price has not reached the striking price because there are still three months to go before expiration date. Various models have been put forth to relate the call price to the stock price, none particularly successful. A better way is to simply look at the market prices of other listed calls on the same stock with expiration dates three months away and different striking prices. For Du Pont, a three-month call on the stock when it sells near the striking price is about 4 percent of the striking price. When Du Pont stock sells at 140, we should therefore expect the call to sell at about $5\frac{1}{2}$. When Du Pont stock sells at 10 percent below the striking price, or at 126, the call sells at about 1.2 percent of the striking price or $1\frac{3}{4}$. As the stock price rises well above the striking price, the call price approaches the difference of the two prices. Other values of the call price may be obtained by interpolation. The following table correlates the prices of the stock and the Du Pont April 140 calls:

Stock price	Percent above $120\frac{1}{2}$	Probability of occurrence	Call price	Call price less $3\frac{1}{2}$ (cost)
Less than 121	0 or less	439/981	0	$-3\frac{1}{2}$
126	5%	136/981	$1\frac{3}{4}$	$-1\frac{3}{4}$
133	10%	110/981	$3\frac{1}{2}$	0
140	16%	109/981	$5\frac{1}{2}$	2
144	20%	73/981	8	$4\frac{1}{2}$
150	25%	31/981	12	$8\frac{1}{2}$
156	30%	27/981	17	$13\frac{1}{2}$
162	35%	20/981	22	$18\frac{1}{2}$
168	40%	14/981	28	$24\frac{1}{2}$
174	45%	5/981	34	$30\frac{1}{2}$
180	50%	7/981	40	$36\frac{1}{2}$
190	75%	10/981	50	$46\frac{1}{2}$

Using the expectation formula and the table,

$$E = \frac{439}{981}\left(-3\frac{1}{2}\right) + \frac{136}{981}\left(-1\frac{3}{4}\right) + \frac{110}{981}(0) + \frac{109}{981}(2) + \frac{73}{981}\left(4\frac{1}{2}\right)$$

$$+ \frac{31}{981}\left(8\frac{1}{2}\right) + \frac{27}{981}\left(13\frac{1}{2}\right) + \frac{20}{981}\left(18\frac{1}{2}\right) + \frac{14}{981}\left(24\frac{1}{2}\right)$$

$$+ \frac{5}{981}\left(30\frac{1}{2}\right) + \frac{7}{981}\left(36\frac{1}{2}\right) + \frac{10}{981}\left(46\frac{1}{2}\right)$$

$$E = +1.00$$

The expectation of profit from holding this call option three months was one dollar for every three and a half dollars risked, or a percentage gain of almost 29 percent. This expectation is typical for Group I stocks. Again this number is only the mean of a random walk, and wide swings either way are to be expected in any one investment. Also, commissions have been neglected, and these can amount to several percent of the investment.

In contrast, another investment in options turned into a 100-percent loss. On 23 February 1976 just after a surprisingly high earnings report, I bought International Harvester April 30 calls at a price of $\frac{7}{8}$, when the stock was selling at $27\frac{7}{8}$. Unfortunately, the stock never reached the striking price of 30 and sank to 26 by expiration date. The options lapsed unexercised and I lost the original investment of $87.50 per contract.

From my limited data, the options game appears to be favorable for Group I stocks as far as calls are concerned, but the probability of ruin is very high. A down market in the next three months can erase the total investment. Then, too, the number of plays is limited. Although options exist for about 250 stocks, surprisingly high earnings in these companies occur much more infrequently than the results of Chapter 14 led us to believe. The reason lies in the character of the stocks, many of which are staid old blue chips which rarely show surprising earnings. Put options are of too recent a vintage for the accumulation of sufficient data with which a determination of an expectation can be made. Those investors interested in writing options should confine their activities to the stocks of Groups IV, V, and VI. For Mr. Average Investor, anxious to amass wealth rapidly on limited capital, the options market offers great potential at high risk, providing he limits his activities to calls on Group I stocks.

PART IV
CONCLUSION

16
AMASSING
A FORTUNE?

As a cousin of mine once said about money, money is always there but the pockets change; it is not in the same pockets after a change, and that is all there is to say about money.

Gertrude Stein

For those of my readers who may have gained a presumptuous and purely amateurish conviction of superiority over the marketplace, a word of caution. All I can do in this book is to lay a firm theoretical foundation for winning practice and to clarify the procedures with some examples where sufficient satisfactory research happens to exist. What I cannot do is initiate the reader bent on amassing a fortune into the realities of the marketplace. Financial transactions under pressure introduce wholly new aspects largely unappreciated by the uninitiated. Each market has its own particular jargon, mechanisms, and strategies to cope with. There are such matters as the size of investments, allocation of resources, probability of ruin, costs, taxes, profit margins, time, and mental and physical wear and tear to worry about. In short, the risks, frustrations, hardships, and torment encountered in managing a business enterprise are the rule, and one's aptitude for handling these affairs is largely unpredictable. Too often do the probabilities fade from view under adversity, to be replaced by irrational, emotional responses. Winning is a random walk with a positive expectation, and runs of good luck as well as bad can occur when least expected. Failure to adhere to standard operating procedure may whipsaw the fortune hunter into disaster, into situations where he gambles when he should not and does not gamble when he should. It is easy to be led astray; it is hard to win.

Some considerations of importance pertaining to our two primary market studies remain, in particular, allocation of resources, size of investment, and probability of ruin. Always the first decision must be: How much in the way of financial and time resources should be allocated to the battle? For a person starting a new business, the answer is obvious—100 percent. For Mr. Average, who wishes to keep risks to a minimum by holding onto a good job while venturing into a weakly efficient market in the hope of substantially augmenting his income, all variations are possible. The decision must be a personal one.

At the racetrack, there are limitations on the size of an investment imposed by the nature of the pari-mutuel market and the probability of ruin, the chance

of losing all of one's starting capital. As we have learned, the greater the amount
of money wagered on a horse, the lower the odds or the less the return. Now
suppose a racing fan spots a favorable betting opportunity and places a bet. Because of his bet, the return on his horse, should it win, will be lower than it
would otherwise have been. How much lower depends on the ratio of his bet to
the total amount in the win pool. A substantial lowering of the profit margin en-
sues for bets in excess of 2 percent of the win pool. If a number of people at the
same track all use the same valid system, the profit margin on this kind of investment could vanish.

Figure 16-1 displays the deterioration of return in a number of representative
situations for a 17 percent take and is to be interpreted in the following manner:
The left column gives some representative dollar odds o on the system horse calculated without the system bet. In other words, these are the odds on the horse
if no bet were placed by the system player. The top row indicates the size of the
bet with respect to the total amount of money in the win pool b/M, where b is
the amount of the system bet and M the amount of money in the win pool. For
example, the column headed by .001 shows that the system bet was $1/1000$ of
the total amount of money in the win pool. The various numbers in the table
give the reductions in dollar odds in pennies caused by the system bet. As is easily seen from the table, the odds drop increases significantly as the ratio b/M and
the odds increase. An investor must be more careful about making large bets on
second and third choices than favorites. A wager amounting to 10 percent of the
win pool will reduce the odds on a 3/1 horse to 2/1.

Before saying anything more about the size of the investment, let us consider
one other limitation, the probability of ruin. In any game of chance, even a favorable one, there exists a probability of losing starting capital in a long losing
streak before increasing it to some predetermined amount. This probability of
ruin depends on the size of the bet (assuming flat bets) relative to total starting
capital, the final amount of money to be amassed, and the expected win percentage and return. Its magnitude may be obtained from the theory of the gen-

Figure 16-1. Reduction of the Dollar Odds in Pennies as a Function of the Ratio of the
Amount Bet to the Total Amount of Money in the Win Pool b/M and the Odds o.

Dollar Odds o	b/M .001	.005	.01	.02	.1
1	.3¢	1.3¢	2.7¢	5.3¢	22.5¢
1.5	.5	2.5	4.8	9.4	38.4
2	.8	3.8	7.5	14.5	57.5
3	1.5	7.4	14.4	27.8	102.4
4	2.5	12.2	23.6	44.8	157.4

eralized random walk (sequential sampling).* Applying these considerations to our system, a prudent maximum bet for an investor wishing to increase his starting capital 100 times is $\frac{1}{20}$ of his starting capital, and this figure is an approximate value covering favorites, second choices, and third choices using average odds of 8/5, 7/2, and 9/2 respectively. The calculation leads to a probability of ruin of less than 1 percent; there is less than one chance in a hundred of an investor losing his money before attaining his goal. If he desires to stretch $1,000 into $100,000, his bet should be a constant $50 for a starting capital of $1,000. Larger bets with the same starting capital may help reach the goal faster at the cost of a greater probability of ruin.

Returning to the pari-mutuel limitation, we can now understand that a system bet not only lowers the odds, but by doing so increases the probability of ruin. Again, the amount of risk to be borne must be a personal decision. My best judgment is not to exceed 2 percent of the win pool for favorite bets and $\frac{1}{2}$ percent for second and third choice bets. At large tracks in New York and California where win pools run into hundreds of thousands of dollars, $2,000 flat bets should be a satisfactory maximum. Such a sum necessitates a starting capital pool of $40,000. At other tracks, much smaller maximum bets are called for. Should these limits be exceeded because too many people are using the system, the profit margin may vanish.

Now let us see what a seasoned bettor well versed in the intricacies of the system may expect to win. Bearing in mind that the figures are the means of a random walk, we calculate the expectation of gain for a week's attendance (six days) at the races. In the 54 races run during the week, 18 bets on favorites (1 out of three races), 8 bets on second choices (1 out of 7 races), and 4 bets on third choices (1 out of 13 races) are expected. Based on the 1,242-race sample of Chapter 10, our bettor should realize roughly a 50-percent return on favorite bets, 100 percent on second choice bets, and 150 percent on third choice bets. If he makes flat wagers of $50, his investment on favorites for the week is $900 on which he should realize a profit of $450. On second choices, his investment is $400 on which a profit of $400 should develop. And on third choices, his investment is $200 on which he should make $300. Summing up, he can expect a profit of $1,150 for his week's work, over 75 percent of the amount bet.

These profits are breathtaking and admittedly hard to believe. Again I must stress these are average figures and severe fluctuations are to be expected. From my experience with the 6,000-race sample published in *Horse Sense*, profits

*See William Feller, *An Introduction to Probability Theory and Its Applications* (New York: John Wiley, 1957), Ch. 14.

should develop as expected so long as the percentage of winning favorites at a meeting is above 30 percent. On any dip below 30 percent, deficit operations may arise. A small percentage of winning favorites at a meeting points to the public's inability to handicap properly. Whatever the reason, it wreaks havoc on a system that depends on knowledgeable public betting for its success. Fortunately, the favorite win percentage infrequently drops below 30 percent.

The prospects for winning in the pari-mutuel market, as in every other market, are fading because of rising taxes on winners. From a microeconomic point of view, pari-mutuel taxes creep persistently higher steadily reducing the return to investors. A high 10 percent when enabling legislation was first passed in the 1930s, the takes have almost doubled since then for regular betting and more than doubled on exotic wagers. Their near confiscatory levels have sharply curtailed growth in racetrack attendance and betting and, in many areas, declines have set in. From a macroeconomic viewpoint, the inflation tax hamstrings the wealth seeker at the races. There is no inflation in win probabilities to lessen the difficulty in picking winners, yet the reward continually loses value as inflation cheapens the dollar. The win probability of a two-to-one favorite is the same today as ten years ago, but that two-dollar profit from a one-dollar bet (if the horse wins) is worth only half as much in terms of what can be bought with it. Any attempt to compensate for the diluted reward by wagering a larger amount only reduces the return still further because of the stagnant win pools. The racing fan is being squeezed into oblivion between greedy state legistatures and a spendthrift Congress.

And how simple the remedy! All that must be done is to make it possible for people to win. A reduction of the pari-mutuel tax to 7 percent (to be used mainly for covering operating expenses of the track) makes the game favorable to favorite players and much less onerous to longshot players. Those investing on all the post favorites would actually realize profits on average and horse betting would become a desirable investment. The public would quickly grasp the new nature of the game and flock to the races in droves. Present racetracks could not possibly handle the demand and track managements would be relieved of their mounting financial burdens. Even the states, which have had to give up more and more of their share of the take to keep the tracks in operation, might benefit from the 1 percent or 2 percent of the pools left to them. In contrast, if the reduction in take does not come about, it is only a question of time before the race tracks founder on the rocks of inflating operating costs.

Although both the pari-mutuel and stock markets are basically weakly efficient markets, their outward features are decidedly different. Next to the time-compressed excitement and vaulting capital changes characteristic of the pari-mutuel market, the stock market with its endless stream of small price movements appears a staid affair indeed. But according to an investor's aptitude, each market has its advantages and disadvantages: Stock market business is conducted a telephone line away from the arena and on an intermittent basis, while the pari-mutuel market demands one's immediate and continual presence. The stock game can be played with much more capital because of an almost negligible probability of ruin. Small though the percentage changes in capital may be on a daily basis, actual gains and losses probably dwarf one day's transactions at the races for even a moderate-sized portfolio. Unlike the limitation imposed by the pari-mutuel market on the amount wagered, no individual investor should experience any problem in buying and selling all the stock he desires, except possibly for thinly traded issues with small capitalizations (number of shares).

The profit margin to be expected from system operations in the stock market depends on the behavior of the general market. Some idea of the correlation may be gained by "eye-balling" the best straight line through the cloud-of-points graphs of Chapter 13, Figures 13-1 and 13-4, one line for the bull markets to the right and one line for the bear market to the left. (One line for each type market is necessitated by the discontinuity at the origin arising because of the better-than-average performance of these stocks in both bull and bear markets). Any point on the lines correlates a percentage change in the market average (shown along the horizontal axis) with the average percentage change in the system's Group I stocks (shown along the vertical axis). Better lines can be drawn by what is known as a "least-squares" fit and yields the following correlation for the two graphs of Group I stocks (earnings 20 percent or more better than expected):

Bull markets

$$y = 1.2x + 5.2$$

Bear markets

$$y = 1.0x + 3.5$$

In the above, y is the average percentage change in Group I system stocks corresponding to a percentage change in the market average x over a three-month period. Figure 16-2 shows the correlation for various values of the percentage change in the market average. Note that the breakeven point for Group I stocks occurs for a decline in the market average of 3.5 percent. This is a sizable decrease for a three-month period and although not a rare event, is not too common. In most quarters, market action can be expected to be much better, and given the pronounced bias of Group I stocks to the upside, substantial profits are obtainable. If the action of the market from 1926 to 1976 is extrapolated into the future, we may anticipate an increase in the market average of about 1 percent per quarter or roughly 4 percent per year. From Figure 16-2, Group I stocks should ap-

Figure 16-2. Correlation between Percentage Price Changes in the Market Average and the Percentage Price Changes in Group I Stocks over a Three-Month Period.

Percentage Change in Market Average x	Average Percentage Change in Group I Stocks y
+20%	+29%
+10	+17
+5	+11
+1	+6.4
−1	+3
−3.5	0
−5	−2
−10	−7
−20	−17

preciate on average 6.4 percent every three months, which amounts to 28 percent per year compounded quarterly.

There are of course fluctuations around this 1 percent per quarter increase in the market average to be expected and some of them will be of great magnitude. But for us, the swings are beneficial. On downward slides, losses will not occur until a 3.5 percent decline in the market average sets in and will be limited thereafter, while on upward swings, very large gains will materialize. A market average swing from +5 percent in one quarter followed by a −5 percent swing in the next, which leaves the broad market almost unchanged, should result in a +9.7 percent average appreciation for Group I stocks in the six months. The aggressive investor using margin can double profits with relatively little added risk. In general, it is best to consider only Group I stocks. However, there are times when stocks falling into the Group II category report truly surprising earnings, as evidenced by comments in the news media. There should be no hesitation in acquiring them in these cases.

The stock market is much more sensitive to political developments than the pari-mutuel market. And at this time the prognosis is not good, not as long as the wealth of the country is diverted away from the growth of our means of production and into the growth of government. We still live in a democracy, however, and I have great faith that the citizenry will awaken to the bureaucratic dangers confronting the country and take appropriate action. Already, a noticeable swing back to a reliance on the random walk of free market mechanisms is in evidence. The movement promises to mushroom as our understanding matures and our standard of living declines. Watch for the dawn! When it comes, a vastly underpriced stock market will become the preferred vehicle to a fortune. Not only will the boom make many of you rich, but it will contribute mightily to the well-being and security of our great country. A happy stock market makes for a happy country.

The fate of an adventurer seeking his fortune in a weakly efficient market rests on many unknowns. No doubt, there are some who will use the information acquired from this book to increase their capital substantially. And there are others who will, sadly, lose money. On one point only do I have a prediction. It is that the returns garnered by my readers in their future pursuits will constitute a normal distribution, with an expectation above what it would have been had they remained oblivious of the science of winning. Where on the curve a person may fall, no one can say; all one can do is trust in the random walk and try.

Good luck!

BIBLIOGRAPHY

Ainslie, Tom. *Ainslie's Complete Guide to Thoroughbred Racing.* New York: Simon & Schuster, Trident Press, 1968.

Brealey, Richard A. *An Introduction to Risk and Return from Common Stocks.* Cambridge: MIT Press, 1969.

Cootner, Paul, ed. *The Random Character of Stock Market Prices.* Cambridge: MIT Press, 1964.

Engel, Louis. *How to Buy Stocks.* New York: Bantam Books, 1972.

Feller, William. *An Introduction to Probability Theory and Its Applications*, vol. 1. 3d ed. New York: John Wiley, 1968.

Friedman, Milton and Schwartz, Anna. *A Monetary History of the United States 1867-1960.* Business Cycles Series, no. 12. Princeton: Princeton University Press, 1963.

Graham, Benjamin; Dodd, David L.; and Cottle, Sidney. *Security Analysis.* 4th ed. New York: McGraw-Hill, 1962.

Heisenberg, Werner. *Physics and Philosophy: The Revolution in Modern Science.* New York: Harper & Row, 1958.

Leffler, George L., and Farwell, Loring C. *The Stock Market.* 3d ed. New York: Ronald Press, 1963.

Morgenstern, Oskar and von Neumann, John. *Theory of Games and Economic Behavior.* Rev. ed. Princeton: Princeton University Press, 1953.

Parratt, Lyman G. *Probability and Experimental Errors in Science: An Elementary Survey.* New York: John Wiley, 1961.

Scarne, John. *Scarne's Encyclopedia of Games.* New York: Harper & Row, 1973.

Scott, Marvin B. *The Racing Game.* Chicago: Aldine, 1968.

Thorp, Edward O. *Beat the Dealer.* Rev. ed. New York: Random House, Vintage Books, 1966.

Wallis, W. Allen, and Roberts, Harry V. *Statistics: A New Approach.* New York: The Free Press, 1956.

Wilson, Allan N. *The Casino Gambler's Guide* rev. ed. New York: Harper & Row, 1970.

APPENDIX A

A NEW AND IMPROVED SYSTEM OF PARI-MUTUEL BETTING

The new system presented here differs from the one in the main text principally in its use of the morning line as a proxy for historical information, the past performances of the horses, as distinguished from privileged or late-breaking information represented by the closing post odds. It assumes that the on-track expert, the oddsmaker, evaluates the horses at least as well if not better than other handicappers and has the most influence with the public. Aside from the necessary changes in the symmetry rules, the procedure for uncovering a favorable bet is the same as presented in Chapter 10.

I shall first present the new system - symmetry rules, definitions and tabular material - in a compact, algebraic form that is unambiguous and programmable. The language is symbolic and it must, of course, be learned. Numerous examples follow that illustrate the betting method. The system was developed on a data base of 3000 races and tested on a fresh sample of 1800 races. I continue to test the rules on new samples for possible shifts in betting habits.

I should emphasize that it is not necessary to employ a computer to apply the system. With practice, a system bet should be recognizable in a matter of seconds. Mastering the system is not easy, but neither is taking money away from other people.

There are 9 symmetry rules, each containing several subdivisions. In each, the target, the horse being considered for a bet and designated by "F", is compared to another horse designated by "O". If any subdivision of a rule applies, the two horses are considered "similar". When that occurs, a certain number of points based on O's closing odds accrue to the target. F is then to be compared to the other horses in the race, one at a time. If a sufficient point score results, the target F is to be bet.

Each subdivision of a symmetry rule describes a situation where the target horse is probably underbet. Those in which "B" is used point to target horses that are being bet much more strongly than warranted by the past performances. But for just that reason, not strongly enough. There may be late-breaking information not fully discounted by the public. The use of "B" by itself is not sufficient to yield profitable results, which indicates that many bettors are fully aware of any deviations of the post odds from the morning line and bet indiscriminately on such horses.

The symmetry rules requiring the target horse to have a shorter morning line than the other contenders point to races in which the others have been assigned morning lines not in keeping with apparently good past performances. For what he and I think are good reasons, the oddsmaker has disregarded the record. But because of the good records, the public seems to bet too strongly on these other contenders. And that makes the target a more favorable bet.

SYMMETRY RULES

I. a) B x Flrc < Olrc x Olrf 1, 2, 3 x (Flrf 1, 2 + Olrf 1E)
   b) B x Flrc < Olrc x [(Olrf 1 x FP S_1, =, s) + (Olrf 2, 3 x FP =, s)]
   c) B x Flrc < Olrc x OD x (Flrf 1, 2, esl + FP =,s)
   d) B x Flrc < Olrc x Olrf 4 x Oprf 3 x (Flrf 1, 2, esl + FP =, s)
   e) B x Flrc < Olrc x Z x [FP N_s, W_s + (Flrf 1, 2 esl x FP s) + (FDD' x Flrf < Olrf)]
   f) B x Flrc < Olrc x Flrf 1, 2, esl x FM N_s, W_s
   g) B x FL x Flrf 3 x FR x OD
   h) B x FL x Flrf 1, 2, 3 x FR x (FP S_1, =, s + Z)
   i) B x FL x [FM W_s + (Flrf 1E x FM N_s) + (Flrf 1E x Fprf 1E x FM s)]

   j) B x Flrc = Olrc x Olrf 1, 2, 3<1 x (FM N_1, S_1, =, s + FD)
   k) B x Flrc = Olrc x OD x FM s
   l) B x Flrc = Olrc x OD x Flrf < Olrf x Flrf 1,2,3<1l,esl
   m) B x Flrc = Olrc x OD' x Flrf < Olrf x Fesl x FP N_s, W_s
   n) B x Flrc = Olrc x OD' x FD x FM N_1, S_1, =, s x (Fesl + FP N_s, W_s)
   o) B x Flrc = Olrc x OD x FD x (Fesl + FP N_s, W_s)
   p) B x Flrc = Olrc x Flrf = Olrf x FM N_s, W_s
   q) B x Flrc = Olrc x FDD' x (Flrf < Olrf + FM s)

   r) B x FH x Flrc > Olrc x Olrf 1, 2, 3<1l x FM s
   s) B x FH x Flrc > Olrc x OD x FM N_s, W_s
   t) B x FH x Flrc > Olrc x OD x Flrf < Olrf x Flrf 1,2,3<1l,esl x FP S_1, =, s
   u) B x FH x Flrc > Olrc x OD' x Flrf < Olrf x Fesl x FP N_s, W_s
   v) B x FH x Flrc > Olrc x OD' x FD x Fesl x FM s
   w) B x FH x Flrc > Olrc x OD x FD x Fesl x FM N_1,S_1, =, s
   x) B x FH x Flrc > Olrc x Flrf = Olrf x FM W_s
   y) B x FH x Flrc > Olrc x Olrf 1, 2, 3 x FDD'

   z) B x FH x FDD' x [(Olrf 1, 2 x FP S_1, =, s) + (Olrf 3, 4 x FP W_s)]
   z') B x FH x FDD' x (Oesl* + Oslow)
   z") B x FH x Flrf 1, 2, 3 x Fprf 1, 2, 3 if any x Fesl x (Olrf 1 + Oesl* + Oslow) x FP s

II. a) Olrf 1, 2 x FM W_s ~ FP N_s, W_s
   b) Olrf 1, 2 x (Flrf 1 + Oesl) x FM W_s ~ FP S_s
   c) Olrf 1, 2 x (Flrf 1, 2 + Oesl) x FM W_s ~ FP =
   d) Olrf 1, 2 x Flrc <= Olrc x FM W_s ~ FP S_l, =, s

   e) Olrf 1E* x FMN_s ~ FP N_s, W_s
   f) Olrf 1E* x (Flrf 1,2 + Oesl) x FM N_s ~ FP =, S_s
   g) Olrf 1E* x Flrc <= Olrc x FM N_s ~ FP S_l, =, s

   h) Oprf 1, 2 x Flrf 1, 2 x FM W_s ~ FP W_s
   i) Oprf 1, 2 x Flrc < Olrc x Flrf 1E x FM W_s ~ FP =, s
   j) Oprf 1, 2 x Flrc = Olrc x FD x FM W_s ~ FPs
   k) Oprf 1, 2 x FL x Flrf 1E x FM W_s ~ FP S_l, =, s

   l) Oprf 1E x Flrf 1E x Fprf 1E x FM N_s, W_s ~ FP W_s
   m) Oprf 1E x Flrc < Olrc x Flrf 1E x FM N_s, W_s ~ FP =,s
   n) Oprf 1E x Flrc = Olrc x FD x Flrf 1E x FM N_s, W_s ~ FP s

III. F raced O in one of the last two races of each x Z x (Flrf 1 + Olrf 1) x FR x
   a) Y x FT x FM S_s ~ FP s
   b) Y x FT' x FM S_s ~ FP =
   c) Y x Olrf >= Flrf x (OD + Flrf 1, 2, 3, esl) x (FM S_s ~ FP =, s
                                     + FM N_s ~ FP N_s, W_s + FM W_s ~ FP N_s, W_s)
   d) (F 1>, 2>, < + OD + Oeslt + Oslowt) x FM N_s ~ FP W_s
   e) (F 1>, 2>, < + OD + Oeslt + Oslowt) x FM W_s ~ FP N_s, W_s
   f) (OD + Oeslt + Oslowt + F<) x B x FM s
   g) B x Flrf>Olrf x FP N_s, W_s
   h) B x F 2p-2l behind RWS x Flrf >Olrf x F raced O in last two of each x FP S_l, =, s
   i) B x F 3p-3½l behind RWS x Flrf > Ol x F raced O in last two of each
   j) B x F 2p-2l behind RWS x Flrf >Olrf x F raced O in last two of each x FP N_s, W_s
   k) F raced O in last two of each x [FM N_s, W_s ~ FP =, s
                                     + (OD x FM N_s, W_s ~ FP S_l, =, s)]

IV. Flrc < Olrc x Fprc < Oprc x Flrf <= Olrf x Fprf <= Oprf x (FM S_s ~ FP S_l, =, s
                                     + FM s ~ FP N_s, W_s)

V. Flrc <= Olrc x Fprc <= Oprc x Flrf <= Olrf x Fprf <= Oprf x (FM N_s ~ FP N_s, W_s
                                     + FM W_s ~ FP W_s)

VI. a) FL x Flrf <= Olrf x (OD + $\underline{FD}$ + Oesl) x Z x FM s ~ FP S_1
    b) FL x Flrf <= Olrf x Z x FM s ~ FP =, s
    c) FL x Flrf < Olrf x FM s ~ FP N_s, W_s
    d) FL x Flrf = Olrf x (ODD' + $\underline{FD}$) x FM s ~ FP N_s, W_s
    e) FL x (Oprf 1E + Olrf 2, 3<1l) x $\underline{Flrf\ 1E^*}$ x FM S_s ~ FP s
    f) FL x Olrf 3, 4 x Oprf 1, 2, 3 x $\underline{Flrf\ 1E^*}$ x FM N_s, W_s ~ FP s
    g) FL x (Oprf 1E + Olrf 2, 3<1l) x FM N_s, W_s ~ FP s
    h) FL x Olrf 2, 3 x Oprf 1, 2 x FM s ~ FP N_s, W_s
    i) FL x Olrf 3 x $\underline{Flrf\ 1E^*}$ x FM W_s ~ FP s

VII. a) OR x $\underline{FJ}$ x [(Olrf 1, 2 x $\underline{Flrf\ 1,\ 2}$) + (Olrf 1, 2, 3 x $\underline{Flrf\ 1,\ 2,\ 3}$)]
                                                    x FM s ~ FP S_1, =, s
     b) OR x $\underline{FR}$ x (OD x $\underline{FD}$) x FM N_s, W_s ~ FP s
     c) OR x $\underline{FR}$ x [(OD x $\underline{FD}$) + (Olrf 1, 2 x $\underline{Flrf\ 1,\ 2}$) + (Olrf 3 x $\underline{Flrf\ 1,\ 2,\ 3}$)]
                                                    x FM s ~ FP s
     d) OJ x Oesl* x ($\underline{FR}$ + Fslow) x $\underline{F(HxD)}$ x FM s ~ FP =, s
     e) OJ x Oesl x $\underline{FR}$ x (FM N_s ~ FP W_s + FM W_s ~ FP N_s, W_s)
     f) OR x B x FM s

VIII. a) OJ x (Olrf 1, 2, 3, 4, esl + $\underline{Flrf\ 1,\ 2,\ 3}$) x $\underline{FR}$ x FM W_s ~ FP =, s
      b) OJ x (Olrf 1, 2, 3, 4, esl + $\underline{Flrf\ 1,\ 2,\ 3}$) x $\underline{FJ}$ x Flrc <= Olrc x FMW_s ~ FP S_1, =, s
      c) OJ x (ODD' + $\underline{FD}$) x $\underline{FR}$ x FM W_s ~ FP W_s

      d) OJ x (ODD' + FD) x Flrc <= Olrc x FM W_s ~ FP N_s, W_s
      e) OJ x (ODD' + $\underline{FD}$) x Flrc <= Olrc x $\underline{FR}$ x FM W_s ~ FP =, s

IX. F or O a first-time starter (fts)
    a) Ofts x $\underline{Ffts}$ x B x [($\underline{FD}$ x FP =, s) + ($\underline{Flrf\ 1,\ 2}$ x FP W_s)]
    b) Ofts x Ffts x B x FP S_1, =, s
    c) Ffts x B x [Olrf 1, 2 + (Oprf 1, 2 x FP =, s)]
    d) Ffts x B x OD' x FP W_s
    e) Ffts x B x OJ x FP W_s
    f) Ffts x OR x FM s ~ FP s
    g) Ffts x OD x OJ x FM s ~ FP s

SYMBOL	DEFINITION
x	and
+	or
,	or
~	to
<	lower than or worse than
<=	lower than or equal to or worse than or equal to
>	higher than or better than
>=	higher than or equal to or better than or equal to
F	target horse
O	other horse
B	ratio of F post odds win probability to O post odds win probability divided by ratio of F morning line win probability to O morning line win probability is greater than or equal to 1.60 (see B-table and following discussion). B is a measure of the deviation of the post odds from the morning line.
lrc	last race class
lrf	last race finish
prc	previous race class
prf	previous race finish
1E	first place finish and won by 2 or more lengths
X	not X (all underlined clauses are "not" clauses)
M	morning line odds
P	closing post odds
l	lengths ahead of 2nd place finisher if won or lengths behind winner if lost
esl	early speed last - 1, 2 at ¼-mile and ½-mile calls in last race (not in races <5f)
esl*	esl and finished 1, 2, 3, 4 (not in races <5f)
slow	slow start last - in last race, second half of the field at the pre-stretch call, but not for 3 in 5-horse race, 4 in 7-horse race, 5 in 9-horse race, 6 in 11-horse race, 7 in 13-horse race, *and* lrf 1, 2, 3, 4
D	lrf 1, 2, 3<1l + prf 1, 2
D'	lrf 3, 4, esl + prf 3, 4
DD'	D or D'
Z	ODD' + FDD'
FP =	target's closing post odds equal to other's closing post odds

FP s	target's closing post odds shorter than other's closing post odds
S_l	F odds longer than O odds and strong betting pattern - ratio of O win probability to F win probability <1.44 (see Table of Betting Patterns)
N_l	F odds longer than O odds and normal betting pattern - ratio of O win probability to F win probability 1.44 - 1.77 (see Table of Betting Patterns)
S_s	F odds shorter than O odds and strong betting pattern - ratio of F win probability to O win probability < 1.44 (see Table of Betting Patterns)
N_s	F odds shorter than O odds and normal betting pattern - ratio of F win probability to O win probability 1.44 - 1.77 (see Table of Betting Patterns)
W_s	F odds shorter than O odds and weak betting pattern - ratio of F win probability to O win probability > 1.77 (see Table of Betting Patterns)
FL	lower class of O last two races > than higher class of F last two races (for one-time starters, use last race twice)
FH	lower class of F last two races > than higher class of O last two races (for one-time starters, use last race twice)
f	furlong
J	today's race one or more furlongs shorter or longer than last two races (if one-time starter, use last race twice). Consider all races at 1½ miles and over of equal length. Today's race may be shorter than the last and longer than the previous and vice versa.
R	J x (esl*+slow)
Y	F beat O in latest race together
RWS	relative weight shift between F and O - 3 pounds = 1l
eslt	early speed in latest race together
slowt	slow in latest race together and finished 1, 2, 3, 4
T	F beat O by one or two places and (<2l ahead RWS + Oeslt)
T'	F beat O by one or two places and finished behind O RWS
F 1>, 2>, <	F one place better or two places better or behind O in latest race together
F 2p-2l	F two or more places and >= 2l RWS behind O in latest race together
F 3p-3½	F three or more places and >= 3½l RWS behind O in latest race together
class	class ordering from high to low - stake grade I, stake grade II, stake grade III, name handicap, overnight handicap in order of purse value (hcp), allowance in order of purse value (alw), maiden special weight in order of purse value if known (Msw), claiming races in order of claiming prices (Clm), maiden claiming races in order of claiming prices (MCl). Starter races (designated by "s" after the claiming price) are higher in class than claiming races of the same price but lower than claiming races of a higher price.

GENERAL RULES

1) For pari-mutuel takes between and including 15% and 17%, consider only those horses at closing post odds <= 8/1. These horses are called "contenders". A point score >= 46.5 points is required for a bet. For a pari-mutuel take of 18% or 18.1%, consider only those horses at closing post odds <= 7/1 and require a point score of 50.5 points for a bet. I would advise against playing at courses with higher takes.
2) Use only Symmetry Rule III and not any other rule when F raced O in one or two of the last two races of each.
3) Use only Symmetry Rule IX and not any other rule when either F or O or both are first-time starters.
4) Always use the original morning line when scratches occur and ignore the changes.
5) Use the new morning line when a race is switched from turf to dirt.
6) If a disqualification occurred in the past performances, use the revised finish.
7) If any subdivision of any Symmetry Rule applies, F is similar to O.
8) Note that Symmetry Rules II, IV, V, VI, VII, and VIII all require F to have shorter morning line odds than O.
9) Note that "B" appears in all subdivisions of Symmetry Rule I. A "B" >= 1.6 demands a substantial change in the closing post odds of F and/or O from the morning line. Whenever the morning line of F is equal to or longer than the morning line of O, B must be satisfied for similarity to be possible.

Table I: System points corresponding to post odds

Post odds	Points	Post odds	Points
4/5	55	5/2	28.5
1	50	3	33
6/5	45	7/2	22
7/5	42	4	20
3/2	40	9/2	18
8/5	38	5	16.5
9/5	36	6	14
2	33	7	12.5
		8	11

Table II: Betting patterns (All odds to $1 unless otherwise indicated)

Odds	Strong	Normal	Weak
3/5	4/5 - 6/5	7/5 - 9/5	2 and longer
4/5	1 - 8/5	9/5 - 2	5/2 "
1	6/5 - 9/5	2 - 5/2	3 "
6/5	7/5 - 2	5/2	3 "
7/5	3/2 - 2	5/2 - 3	7/2 "
3/2	8/5 - 5/2	3	7/2 "
8/5	9/5 - 5/2	3 - 7/2	4 "
9/5	2 - 3	7/2	4 "
2	5/2 - 3	7/2 - 4	9/2 "
5/2	3 - 4	9/2 - 5	6 "
3	7/2 - 9/2	5 - 6	7 "
7/2	4 - 5	6	7 "
4	9/2 - 6	7	8 "
9/2	5 - 6	7 - 8	10 "
5	6 - 7	8	10 "
6	7 - 8	10	12 "
7	8	-	-
8	10	12	15 "
10	12	15	20 "
12	15	20	25 "
15	20	25	30 "

Table III. B-table: For given FM and OM, the FP and OP are the required post odds for B >=1.6. OM is given in the left hand column. The first odds in the table are FP and the second odds are OP (FP-OP). Any other odds combination, (FP'-OP'), has B>1.6 if FP'<=FP and OP'>=OP for any given (FP-OP). Because the post odds are approximate, the midpoints of the range are used in the calculation.

FM 3/5

OM	FP-OP			
3/5	3/5-9/5	4/5-2	6/5-5/2	
4/5	3/5-2	4/5-5/2	6/5-3	
1	3/5-5/2	1-3	6/5-7/2	
6/5	3/5-5/2	4/5-3	1-7/2	6/5-4
7/5	3/5-3	4/5-7/2	1-4	6/5-9/2
8/5	3/5-7/2	4/5-4	1-9/2	7/5-5

9/5	3/5-7/2 4/5-9/2 6/5-5
2	3/5-4 4/5-9/2 1-5
5/2	3/5-5 1-6 6/5-7 8/5-8
3	3/5-6 1-7 6/5-8
7/2	4/5-7 1-8
4	3/5-7 4/5-8
9/2	3/5-8

FM 4/5

OM	FP-OP
3/5	3/5-7/5 4/5-8/5 1-2 3/2-5/2
4/5	3/5-9/5 4/5-2 6/5-5/2
1	3/5-2 1-5/2 6/5-3 3/2-7/2
6/5	4/5-5/2 1-3 6/5-7/2 3/2-4
7/5	3/5-5/2 4/5-3 1-7/2 7/5-4 8/5-9/2
8/5	3/5-3 4/5-7/2 1-4 7/5-9/2 8/5-5 9/5-6
9/5	3/5-3 4/5-7/2 1-4 6/5-9/2 3/2-5 9/5-6
2	3/5-7/2 4/5-4 1-9/2 6/5-5 8/5-6 9/5-7 2-8
5/2	3/5-9/2 1-5 6/5-6 8/5-7 9/5-8
3	3/5-5 1-6 6/5-7 3/2-8
7/2	3/5-6 1-7 6/5-8
4	3/5-6 4/5-7 1-8
9/2	3/5-7 4/5-8
5	3/5-8

FM 1

OM	FP-OP
3/5	3/5-6/5 4/5-7/5 1-8/5 7/5-2 9/5-5/2 2/3
4/5	3/5-7/5 4/5-9/5 1-2 3/2-5/2 95-3
1	3/5-9/5 4/5-2 6/5-5/2 3/2-3 9/5-7/2
6/5	3/5-2 1-5/2 6/5-3 8/5-7/2
7/5	3/5-2 4/5-5/2 1-3 7/5-7/2 8/5-4
8/5	3/5-5/2 4/5-3 1-7/2 7/5-4 8/5-9/2
9/5	4/5-3 1-7/2 6/5-4 3/2-9/2 9/5-5
2	3/5-3 4/5-7/2 1-4 6/5-9/2 8/5-5
5/2	3/5-7/2 4/5-9/2 6/5-5 3/2-6 95-7 2-8
3	3/5-9/2 4/5-5 6/5-6 3/2-7 95-8
7/2	3/5-5 4/5-6 6/5-7 3/2-8
4	3/5-6 1-7 6/5-8
9/2	3/5-6 4/5-7 1-8
5	3/5-7 4/5-8
6	3/5-8

FM 6/5

OM	FP-OP
3/5	3/5-1 4/5-6/5 1-7/5 6/5-8/5 7/5-9/5 8/5-2 2-5/2
4/5	3/5-6/5 4/5-3/2 1-9/5 7/5-2 8/5-5/2 2-3
1	3/5-3/2 4/5-9/5 1-2 3/2-5/2 9/5-3
6/5	3/5-9/5 4/5-2 6/5-5/2 3/2-3 9/5-7/2 2-4
7/5	3/5-2 1-5/2 6/5-3 8/5-7/2 9/5-4 2-9/2
8/5	3/5-2 4/5-5/2 1-3 7/5-7/2 8/5-4 9/5-9/2 2-5
9/5	3/5-5/2 4/5-3 6/5-7/2 3/2-4 8/5-9/2 9/5-5
2	3/5-5/2 4/5-3 1-7/2 6/5-4 3/2-9/2 9/5-5 2-6
5/2	3/5-7/2 4/5-4 1-9/2 3/2-5 9/5-6 2-7
3	3/5-4 4/5-9/2 1-5 3/2-6 9/5-7 2-8
7/2	3/5-9/2 4/5-5 6/5-6 3/2-7 9/5-8
4	3/5-5 4/5-6 6/5-7 3/2-8
9/2	3/5-6 1-7 6/5-8
5	3/5-6 4/5-7 1-8
6	3/5-8

FM 7/5

OM	FP-OP
3/5	3/5-4/5 4/5-1 1-6/5 6/5-7/5 7/5-8/5 8/5-9/5, FP s
4/5	3/5-1 4/5-6/5 1-3/2 6/5-9/5 8/5-2 9/5-5/2 2-3 5/2-7/2 3-4
1	3/5-6/5 4/5-3/2 1-9/5 6/5-2 8/5-5/2 9/5-3 2-7/2 5/2-4 3-9/2
6/5	3/5-3/2 4/5-9/5 1-2 3/2-5/2 9/5-3 2-7/2 5/2-9/2
7/5	3/5-9/5 4/5-2 6/5-5/2 3/2-3 9/5-7/2 2-4 5/2-5 3-6 4-7 9/2-8
8/5	3/5-2 1-5/2 7/5-3 8/5-7/2 9/5-4 2-9/2 5/2-5
9/5	3/5-2 4/5-5/2 1-3 7/5-7/2 8/5-4 9/5-9/2 2-5 5/2-6
2	3/5-5/2 1-3 6/5-7/2 3/2-4 8/5-9/2 2-5 5/2-6 3-7 7/2-8
5/2	3/5-3 4/5-7/2 1-4 7/5-9/2 8/5-5 2-6 5/2-8
3	3/5-7/2 4/5-4 1-9/2 6/5-5 8/5-6 9/5-7 2-8
7/2	3/5-4 4/5-9/2 1-5 7/5-6 8/5-7 95-8
4	3/5-9/2 4/5-5 1-6 3/2-7 8/5-8
9/2	3/5-5 4/5-6 6/5-7 3/2-8
5	3/5-6 1-7 6/5-8
6	3/5-7 4/5-8
8	1/2-8

208

FM 8/5

OM	FP-OP
3/5	FP =, s
4/5	3/5-4/5 4/5-1 1-7/5 6/5-3/2 3/2-9/5 9/5-2 2-5/2 5/2-3 3-7/2
1	3/5-1 4/5-7/5 1-8/5 6/5-9/5 3/2-2 9/5-5/2 2-3 5/2-7/2 3-4
6/5	3/5-6/5 4/5-8/5 1-9/5 6/5-2 8/5-5/2 9/5-3 2-7/2 5/2-4 3-9/2
7/5	3/5-3/2 4/5-9/5 1-2 7/5-5/2 8/5-3 9/5-7/2 2-4 5/2-9/2 3-5 7/2-6 9/2-7
8/5	3/5-9/5 4/5-2 6/5-5/2 3/2-3 9/5-7/2 2-4 5/2-5 3-6 4-7 9/2-8
9/5	3/5-2 1-5/2 7/5-3 8/5-7/2 9/5-4 2-9/2 5/2-5 3-6 7/2-7 4-8
2	3/5-2 4/5-5/2 6/5-3 3/2-7/2 8/5-4 9/5-9/2 2-5 5/2-6 3-7 7/2-8
5/2	3/5-5/2 4/5-3 1-7/2 6/5-4 3/2-9/2 9/5-5 2-6 5/2-7 3-8
3	3/5-3 4/5-7/2 1-4 6/5-9/2 3/2-5 9/5-6 2-7 5/2-8
7/2	3/5-7/2 4/5-4 6/5-5 8/5-6 9/5-7 2-8
4	3/5-4 1-5 6/5-6 8/5-7 9/5-8
9/2	3/5-9/2 4/5-5 1-6 7/5-7 8/5-8
5	3/5-5 4/5-6 6/5-7 3/2-8
6	3/5-6 4/5-7 1-8
8	3/5-8

FM 9/5

OM	FP-OP
3/5	4/5-3/5 1-4/5 6/5-1 7/5-6/5 3/2-7/5 8/5-3/2 9/5-8/5 2-2 5/2-5/2 3-3
4/5	FP =, s
1	3/5-1 4/5-6/5 1-7/5 6/5-8/5 7/5-9/5 8/5-2 2-5/2 5/2-3 3-4 7/2-9/2 4-5
6/5	3/5-6/5 4/5-7/5 1-8/5 6/5-9/5 3/2-2 9/5-5/2 2-3 5/2-7/2 3-9/2 7/2-5
7/5	3/5-7/5 4/5-8/5 1-9/5 6/5-2 8/5-5/2 9/5-3 2-7/2 5/2-4 3-5
8/5	3/5-3/2 4/5-9/5 1-2 7/5-5/2 8/5-3 9/5-7/2 2-4 5/2-9/2 3-5
9/5	3/5-9/5 4/5-2 6/5-5/2 3/2-3 9/5-7/2 2-4 5/2-5 3-6 4-7 9/2-8
2	3/5-9/5 4/5-2 1-5/2 7/5-3 8/5-7/2 9/5-4 2-9/2 5/2-5 3-6 7/2-7 4-8
5/2	3/5-5/2 1-3 6/5-7/2 3/2-4 8/5-9/2 2-5 5/2-6 3-7 7/2-8
3	3/5-3 4/5-7/2 6/5-4 7/5-9/2 8/5-5 2-6 5/2-7 3-8
7/2	3/5-7/2 4/5-4 1-9/2 7/5-5 9/5-6 2-7
4	3/5-4 4/5-9/2 1-5 3/2-6 9/5-7 2-8
9/2	3/5-9/2 4/5-5 6/5-6 8/5-7 9/5-8
5	4/5-5 1-6 7/5-7 8/5-8
6	3/5-6 1-7 6/5-8
8	3/5-8

FM 2

OM	FP-OP
3/5	4/5-3/5 1-4/5 7/5-1 8/5-6/5 9/5-3/2 2-9/5 5/2-2 3-5/2 7/2-3 4-7/2 9/2-4
4/5	FP =, s
1	3/5-4/5 4/5-1 1-6/5 6/5-7/5 7/5-8/5 8/5-9/5 9/5-2 2-5/2 5/2-3 3-7/2 7/2-4
6/5	3/5-1 4/5-6/5 1-3/2 6/5-8/5 7/5-9/5 8/5-2 9/5-5/2 2-3 5/2-7/2 3-4 7/2-9/2
7/5	3/5-6/5 4/5-7/5 1-8/5 7/5-2 9/5-5/2 2-3 5/2-4 3-9/2 7/2-5 9/2-6 5-7
8/5	3/5-7/5 4/5-8/5 6/5-2 8/5-5/2 9/5-3 2-7/2 5/2-4 3-5 4-6 9/2-7 5-8
9/5	3/5-3/2 4/5-9/5 1-2 7/5-5/2 8/5-3 9/5-7/2 2-4 5/2-9/2 3-5 7/2-6 4-7 9/2-8
2	3/5-9/5 4/5-2 6/5-5/2 3/2-3 9/5-7/2 2-4 5/2-5 3-6 4-7 9/2-8
5/2	3/5-2 4/5-5/2 1-3 7/5-5/2 8/5-4 9/5-5/2 2-5 5/2-6 3-7 7/2-8
3	3/5-5/2 4/5-3 1-7/2 7/5-4 8/5-9/2 9/5-5 2-6 5/2-7 3-8
7/2	3/5-3 4/5-7/2 1-4 6/5-9/2 8/5-5 9/5-6 2-7 5/2-8
4	3/5-7/2 4/5-4 1-9/2 6/5-5 8/5-6 9/5-7 2-8
9/2	3/5-4 4/5-9/2 1-5 3/2-6 9/5-7 2-8
5	3/5-9/2 4/5-5 6/5-6 3/2-7 9/5-8
6	3/5-5 4/5-6 1-7 7/5-8
8	3/5-7 4/5-8

FM 5/2

OM	FP-OP
3/5	6/5-3/5 3/2-4/5 8/5-1 9/5-6/5 2-7/5 5/2-9/5 3-2
4/5	4/5-3/5 6/5-4/5 3/2-1 8/5-6/5 9/5-7/5 2-8/5 5/2-2 3-5/2 7/2-3 9/2-7/2 5-9/2
1	FP=,s 6/5-1 7/5-6/5 3/2-7/5 8/5-3/2 9/5-8/5
6/5	FP=,s
7/5	3/5-4/5 4/5-1 1-6/5 6/5-3/2 7/5-8/5 3/2-9/5 9/5-2 2-5/2 5/2-3 3-7/2 7/2-4 4-9/2 9/2-5 5-6 6-7 7-8
8/5	3/5-1 4/5-6/5 1-3/2 6/5-9/5 8/5-2 9/5-5/2 2-3 5/2-7/2 3-4 7/2-9/2 4-5 9/2-6 5-7 6-8

210

9/5 3/5-6/5 4/5-7/5 1-8/5 7/5-2 9/5-5/2 2-3 5/2-4 3-9/2 7/2-5 9/2-6
     5-7
2   3/5-7/5 4/5-8/5 1-9/5 6/5-2 8/5-5/2 9/5-3 2-7/2 5/2-4 7/2-5 4-6
     9/2-7 5-8
5/2 3/5-9/5 4/5-2 6/5-5/2 3/2-3 9/5-7/2 2-4 5/2-5 3-6 4-7 9/2-8
3   3/5-2 4/5-5/2 6/5-3 3/2-7/2 8/5-4 9/5-9/2 2-5 5/2-6 3-7 7/2-8
7/2 3/5-5/2 4/5-3 6/5-7/2 3/2-4 8/5-9/2 9/5-5 2-6 5/2-7 3-8
4   3/5-3 4/5-7/2 6/5-4 7/5-9/2 8/5-5 2-6 5/2-7 3-8
9/2 3/5-3 4/5-7/2 1-9/2 3/2-5 9/5-6 2-7 5/2-8
5   3/5-7/2 4/5-4 1-9/2 6/5-5 8/5-6 9/5-7 2-8
6   3/5-9/2 4/5-5 6/5-6 3/2-7 9/5-8
8   3/5-6 4/5-7 6/5-8
10   3/5-7 4/5-8

FM 3

OM	FP-OP
3/5	3/2-3/5 9/5-4/5 2-1 5/2-7/5 3-9/5 7/2-2 9/2-5/2 5-3 6-4 7-9/2 8-5
4/5	6/5-3/5 3/2-4/5 9/5-1 2-7/5 5/2-8/5 3-2 7/2-5/2 9/2-3 5-7/2 6-9/2
	7-5 8-6
1	1-3/5 6/5-4/5 3/2-1 8/5-6/5 9/5-7/5 2-8/5 5/2-2 3-5/2 4-3 9/2-7/2
	5-4 6-5 7-6 8-7
6/5	4/5-3/5 1-4/5 6/5-1 3/2-6/5 8/5-7/5 9/5-3/2 2-9/5 3-5/2 7/2-3
	4-7/2 9/2-4 5-9/2 7-6 8-7
7/5	FP=,s 3/2-7/5
8/5	FPs
9/5	3/5-4/5 4/5-6/5 1-7/5 6/5-8/5 3/2-9/5 9/5-2 2-5/2 5/2-3 3-7/2
	7/2-9/2 4-5 5-6 6-7 7-8
2	3/5-1 4/5-6/5 1-3/2 6/5-9/5 8/5-2 9/5-5/2 2-3 5/2-7/2 3-4 7/2-9/2
	4-5 9/2-6 5-7 6-8
5/2	3/5-7/5 4/5-8/5 6/5-2 3/2-5/2 9/5-3 2-7/2 5/2-4 3-5 4-6 5-8
3	3/5-9/5 4/5-2 6/5-5/2 3/2-3 9/5-7/2 2-4 5/2-5 3-6 4-7 9/2-8
7/2	3/5-2 4/5-5/2 6/5-3 3/2-7/2 9/5-4 2-5 5/2-6 7/2-7 4-8
4	3/5-5/2 1-3 6/5-7/2 3/2-4 8/5-9/2 2-5 5/2-6 3-7 7/2-8
9/2	3/5-5/2 4/5-3 1-7/2 6/5-4 3/2-9/2 9/5-5 2-6 5/2-7 3-8
5	3/5-3 4/5-7/2 1-4 6/5-9/2 8/5-5 9/5-6 2-7 5/2-8
6	3/5-7/2 4/5-9/2 6/5-5 3/2-6 9/5-7 2-8
8	3/5-5 4/5-6 6/5-7 3/2-8
10	3/5-6 4/5-7 1-8
12	3/5-8

FM 7/2

OM	FP-OP
3/5	9/5-3/5 2-4/5 5/2-1 3-7/5 7/2-8/5 4-2
4/5	3/2-3/5 9/5-4/5 2-1 5/2-7/5 3-9/5 7/2-2 9/2-5/2
1	6/5-3/5 3/2-4/5 9/5-1 2-6/5 5/2-8/5 3-2 4-5/2 9/2-3 5-7/2
6/5	1-3/5 6/5-4/5 3/2-1 9/5-6/5 2-3/2 5/2-2 3-5/2 4-3
7/5	4/5-3/5 1-4/5 7/5-1 8/5-6/5 9/5-3/2 2-9/5 5/2-2 3-5/2 7/2-3 4-7/2 9/2-4
8/5	FP=,s 7/5-6/5 3/2-7/5 8/5-3/2 9/5-8/5
9/5	FP=,s
2	FPs
5/2	3/5-6/5 4/5-7/5 1-8/5 6/5-9/5 3/2-2 9/5-5/2 2-3 5/2-7/2 3-9/2 4-5 9/2-6 5-7 6-8
3	3/5-7/5 4/5-8/5 1-2 3/2-5/2 9/5-3 2-7/2 5/2-9/2 3-5 4-6 9/2-7 5-8
7/2	3/5-9/5 4/5-2 6/5-5/2 3/2-3 9/5-7/2 2-4 5/2-5 3-6 4-7 9/2-8
4	3/5-2 1-5/2 6/5-3 3/2-7/2 9/5-4 2-9/2 3-6 7/2-7 4-8
9/2	4/5-5/2 1-3 6/5-7/2 3/2-4 9/5-9/2 2-5 5/2-6 3-7 7/2-8
5	3/5-5/2 4/5-3 1-7/2 7/5-4 8/5-9/2 9/5-5 2-6 5/2-7 3-8
6	3/5-3 4/5-7/2 1-4 6/5-9/2 3/2-5 9/5-6 2-7 5/2-8
8	3/5-9/2 4/5-5 6/5-6 3/2-7 9/5-8
10	4/5-6 1-7 6/5-8
12	3/5-7 4/5-8

FM 4

OM	FP-OP
3/5	2-3/5 5/2-1 3-6/5 7/2-7/5 4-8/5 9/2-2 5-5/2
4/5	9/5-3/5 2-4/5 5/2-6/5 3-7/5 7/2-9/5 4-2 5-5/2
1	3/2-3/5 9/5-4/5 2-1 5/2-7/5 3-9/5 7/2-2 9/2-5/2
6/5	6/5-3/5 8/5-4/5 9/5-1 2-6/5 5/2-8/5 3-2 4-5/2
7/5	1-3/5 7/5-4/5 8/5-1 9/5-6/5 2-3/2 5/2-9/5 7/2-5/2 4-3 9/2-7/2
8/5	4/5-3/5 1-4/5 7/5-1 8/5-6/5 9/5-7/5 2-8/5 5/2-2 3-5/2 7/2-3 4-7/2 9/2-4
9/5	FP=,s 4/5-3/5 1-4/5 6/5-1 3/2-6/5 8/5-7/5 9/5-8/5 2-9/5 7/2-3 4-7/2 9/2-4
2	FP=,s
5/2	3/5-4/5 4/5-6/5 1-7/5 6/5-8/5 3/2-9/5 9/5-2 2-5/2 5/2-3 3-7/2 7/2-9/2 9/2-5 5-6 6-7 7-8
3	3/5-6/5 4/5-7/5 1-8/5 7/5-2 9/5-5/2 2-3 5/2-4 3-9/2 7/2-5 9/2-6 5-7
7/2	3/5-7/5 4/5-9/5 1-2 3/2-5/2 9/5-3 2-7/2 5/2-9/2 3-5 7/2-6 9/2-7

212

5-8

4	3/5-9/5	4/5-2	6/5-5/2	3/2-3	9/5-7/2	2-4	5/2-5	3-6	4-7 9/2-8
9/2	3/5-2	1-5/2	6/5-3	8/5-7/2	9/5-4	2-9/2	3-6	7/2-7	4-8
5	3/5-2	4/5-5/2	1-3	7/5-7/2	8/5-4	9/5-9/2	2-5	5/2-6	3-7 7/2-8
6	4/5-3	1-7/2	6/5-4	3/2-9/2	9/5-5	2-6	5/2-7	3-8	
8	3/5-4	4/5-9/2	1-5	3/2-6	9/5-7	2-8			
10	3/5-5	1-6	6/5-7	8/5-8					
12	3/5-6	4/5-7	1-8						
15	3/5-8								

FM 9/2

OM	FP-OP
3/5	2-3/5 5/2-4/5 3-1 7/2-6/5 4-7/5 9/2-8/5 5-2 6-5/2 7-3
4/5	2-3/5 5/2-1 3-6/5 7/2-3/2 4-9/5 9/2-2 5-5/2 6-3 7-7/2
1	9/5-3/5 2-4/5 5/2-6/5 3-3/2 7/2-9/5 4-2 9/2-5/2 5-3 6-7/2
6/5	3/2-3/5 9/5-4/5 2-1 5/2-7/5 3-9/5 7/2-2 9/2-5/2 5-3 6-4
7/5	6/5-3/5 8/5-4/5 9/5-1 2-6/5 5/2-8/5 3-2 4-5/2 9/2-3 5-7/2 6-4
8/5	1-3/5 7/5-4/5 8/5-1 9/5-6/5 2-7/5 5/2-9/5 3-2 7/2-5/2 4-3 9/2-7/2 5-4
9/5	4/5-3/5 6/5-4/5 3/2-1 8/5-6/5 9/5-7/5 2-8/5 5/2-2 3-5/2 7/2-3 9/2-7/2 5-4
2	4/5-3/5 1-4/5 6/5-1 3/2-6/5 9/5-3/2 2-9/5 5/2-2 3-5/2 7/2-3 4-7/2 9/2-4 5-9/2 6-5 7-6 8-7
5/2	FPs
3	3/5-1 4/5-6/5 1-7/5 6/5-8/5 7/5-9/5 2-5/2 5/2-7/2 3-4 7/2-9/2 4-5 5-6 6-8
7/2	3/5-6/5 4/5-3/2 1-9/5 7/5-2 8/5-5/2 2-3 5/2-4 3-9/2 7/2-5 9/2-6 5-7
4	3/5-3/2 4/5-9/5 1-2 3/2-5/2 9/5-3 2-7/2 5/2-9/2 3-5 7/2-6 9/2-7 5-8
9/2	3/5-9/5 4/5-2 6/5-5/2 3/2-3 9/5-7/2 2-4 5/2-5 3-6 4-7 9/2-8
5	3/5-2 1-5/2 6/5-3 8/5-7/2 9/5-4 2-9/2 5/2-5 3-6 7/2-7 4-8
6	3/5-5/2 4/5-3 6/5-7/2 3/2-4 8/5-9/2 9/5-5 2-6 5/2-7 3-8
8	3/5-7/2 4/5-4 1-9/2 7/5-5 8/5-6 2-7
10	3/5-9/2 4/5-5 1-6 3/2-7 9/5-8
12	3/5-5 4/5-6 1-7 7/5-8
15	3/5-7 4/5-8

FM 5

OM	FP-OP
3/5	5/2-3/5 3-4/5 7/2-1 4-6/5 9/2-7/5 5-9/5 6-2
4/5	2-3/5 5/2-4/5 3-1 7/2-6/5 4-3/2 9/2-9/5 5-2
1	9/5-3/5 2-4/5 5/2-1 3-6/5 7/2-3/2 4-9/5 9/2-2 5-5/2 6-3
6/5	9/5-3/5 2-4/5 5/2-6/5 3-3/2 7/2-9/5 4-2 9/2-5/2 5-3 6-7/2 7-4
7/5	3/2-3/5 9/5-4/5 2-1 5/2-7/5 3-9/5 7/2-2 9/2-5/2 5-3 6-7/2 7-9/2
8/5	7/5-3/5 8/5-4/5 9/5-1 2-6/5 5/2-8/5 3-2 4-5/2 9/2-3 5-7/2 6-4 7-5 8-6
9/5	1-3/5 7/5-4/5 8/5-1 9/5-6/5 2-7/5 5/2-9/5 3-2 7/2-5/2 4-3 9/2-7/2 5-4 6-9/2 7-5 8-6
2	1-3/5 6/5-4/5 3/2-1 8/5-6/5 9/5-7/5 2-8/5 5/2-2 3-5/2 4-3 9/2-7/2 5-4 6-5 7-6 8-7
5/2	FP=,s 7/5-6/5 3/2-7/5 8/5-3/2 9/5-8/5
3	FPs
7/2	3/5-1 4/5-6/5 1-3/2 6/5-9/5 8/5-2 9/5-5/2 2-3 5/2-7/2 3-4 7/2-9/2 4-5 9/2-6 5-7 6-8
4	3/5-6/5 4/5-3/2 1-9/5 6/5-2 8/5-5/2 9/5-3 2-7/2 5/2-4 3-9/2 7/2-5 4-6 9/2-7 5-8
9/2	3/5-3/2 4/5-9/5 1-2 3/2-5/2 9/5-3 2-7/2 5/2-9/2 3-5 7/2-6 9/2-7 5-8
5	3/5-9/5 4/5-2 6/5-5/2 3/2-3 9/5-7/2 2-4 5/2-5 3-6 4-7 9/2-8
6	3/5-2 4/5-5/2 1-3 7/5-7/2 8/5-4 9/5-9/2 2-5 5/2-6 3-7 7/2-8
8	3/5-3 4/5-7/2 1-4 6/5-9/2 8/5-5 9/5-6 2-7 5/2-8
10	3/5-4 4/5-9/2 1-5 3/2-6 9/5-7 2-8
12	3/5-5 1-6 7/5-7 8/5-8
15	3/5-6 4/5-7 1-8
20	3/5-8

FM 6

OM	FP-OP
3/5	3-3/5 7/2-4/5 9/2-1 5-7/5 6-9/5 7-2 8-5/2
4/5	5/2-3/5 3-4/5 7/2-1 4-6/5 9/2-7/5 5-8/5 6-2 7-5/2 8-3
1	5/2-3/5 3/1 7/2-6/5 4-7/5 9/2-8/5 5-2 6-5/2 7-3 8-7/2
6/5	2-3/5 5/2-4/5 3-6/5 7/2-7/5 4-8/5 9/2-9/5 5-2 6-5/2 7-3
7/5	9/5-3/5 2-4/5 5/2-1 3-7/5 7/2-8/5 4-9/5 9/2-2 5-5/2 6-3 7-7/2 8-4
8/5	8/5-3/5 9/5-4/5 2-1 5/2-6/5 3-3/2 7/2-9/5 4-2 9/2-5/2 5-3 6-7/2 7-4 8-9/2

9/5	3/2-3/5	9/5-4/5	2-1	5/2-7/5	3-9/5	7/2-2	9/2-5/2	5-3	6-4	7-9/2	8-5
2	7/5-3/5	8/5-4/5	9/5-1	2-6/5	5/2-8/5	3-9/5	7/2-2	4-5/2	9/2-3	5-7/2	
	6-4	8-5									
5/2	1-3/5	6/5-4/5	3/2-1	8/5-6/5	9/5-7/5	2-8/5	5/2-2	3-5/2	4-3	9/2-7/2	
	5-4	6-5	7-6	8-7							
3	3/5-3/5	4/5-4/5	6/5-1	7/5-6/5	3/2-7/5	9/5-8/5	2-2	5/2-5/2	3-3		
	7/2-7/2	9/2-4	5-5	6-6	7-7	8-8					
7/2	FPs										
4	3/5-1	4/5-6/5	1-7/5	6/5-8/5	7/5-9/5	8/5-2	2-5/2	5/2-3	3-4	7/2-9/2	
	4-5	5-6	6-7								
9/2	3/5-6/5	4/5-7/5	1-8/5	6/5-9/5	3/2-2	9/5-5/2	2-3	5/2-7/2	3-9/2		
	7/2-5	9/2-6	5-7	6-8							
5	3/5-7/5	4/5-8/5	1-9/5	6/5-2	8/5-5/2	9/5-3	2-7/2	5/2-4	7/2-5	4-6	
	9/2-7	5-8									
6	3/5-9/5	4/5-2	6/5-5/2	3/2-3	9/5-7/2	2-4	5/2-5	3-6	4-7	9/2-8	
8	3/5-5/2	4/5-3	6/5-7/2	3/2-4	8/5-9/2	9/5-5	2-6	5/2-7	3-8		
10	3/5-3	4/5-7/2	1-9/2	3/2-5	9/5-6	2-7	5/2-8				
12	3/5-4	4/5-9/2	1-5	7/5-6	8/5-7	9/5-8					
15	3/5-5	4/5-6	6/5-7	3/2-8							
20	3/5-7	4/5-8									

FM 8

OM	FP-OP							
3/5	9/2-3/5	5-4/5	6-6/5	7-7/5	8-8/5			
4/5	4-3/5	9/2-4/5	5-1	6-7/5	7-9/5	8-2		
1	7/2-3/5	4-4/5	9/2-1	5-6/5	6-8/5	7-2	8-5/2	
6/5	3-3/5	7/2-4/5	4-1	9/2-6/5	5-3/2	6-2	8-5/2	
7/5	5/2-3/5	3-4/5	7/2-1	4-6/5	9/2-7/5	5-9/5	6-2	7-5/2	8-3
8/5	2-3/5	5/2-4/5	3-1	7/2-6/5	4-7/5	9/2-8/5	5-2	6-5/2	7-3	8-7/2
9/5	2-3/5	5/2-4/5	3-6/5	7/2-7/5	4-8/5	9/2-9/5	5-2	6-5/2	7-3	8-7/2
2	9/5-3/5	2-4/5	5/2-1	3-6/5	7/2-3/2	4-9/5	9/2-2	5-5/2	6-3	7-7/2	8-4

5/2 8/5-3/5 9/5-4/5 2-1 5/2-7/5 3-8/5 4-2 9/2-5/2 5-3 6-7/2 7-9/2 8-5
3   6/5-3/5 3/2-4/5 9/5-1 2-6/5 5/2-8/5 3-9/5 4-5/2 9/2-3 5-7/2 6-9/2 7-5 8-6
7/2 1-3/5 6/5-4/5 3/2-1 8/5-6/5 9/5-7/5 2-8/5 5/2-2 3-5/2 4-3 9/2-7/2 5-4 6-5 7-6 8-7
4   4/5-3/5 1-4/5 6/5-1 3/2-6/5 8/5-7/5 9/5-8/5 2-9/5 3-5/2 7/2-3 4-7/2 9/2-4 5-9/2 7-6 8-7
9/2 FP=,s
5   FPs
6   3/5-6/5 4/5-7/5 1-8/5 6/5-9/5 3/2-2 9/5-5/2 2-3 5/2-7/2 3-9/2 4-5 9/2-6 5-7 6-8
8   3/5-9/5 4/5-2 6/5-5/2 3/2-3 9/5-7/2 2-4 5/2-5 3-6 4-7 9/2-8
10   4/5-5/2 1-3 6/5-7/2 3/2-4 9/5-9/2 2-5 5/2-6 3-7 7/2-8
12   3/5-3 4/5-7/2 1-4 7/5-9/2 8/5-5 2-6 5/2-8
15   3/5-4 4/5-9/2 1-5 3/2-6 9/5-7 2-8
20   3/5-5 4/5-6 1-7 7/5-8

FM 10

OM	FP-OP
3/5	5-3/5 6-4/5 7-1 8-6/5
4/5	5-3/5 6-1 7-6/5 8-3/2
1	9/2-3/5 5-4/5 6-6/5 7-3/2 8-9/5
6/5	4-3/5 9/2-4/5 5-1 6-7/5 7-9/5
7/5	7/2-3/5 4-4/5 9/2-1 5-6/5 6-8/5 7-2 8-5/2
8/5	3-3/5 7/2-4/5 4-1 9/2-6/5 5-7/5 6-9/5 7-2 8-5/2
9/5	5/2-3/5 3-4/5 7/2-1 4-6/5 9/2-7/5 5-8/5 6-2 7-5/2 8-3
2	5/2-3/5 3-4/5 7/2-1 4-6/5 9/2-3/2 5-9/5 6-2 7-5/2 8-3
5/2	2-3/5 5/2-4/5 3-6/5 7/2-7/5 4-8/5 9/2-2 5-5/2 6-3 7-7/2 8-4
3	9/5-3/5 2-4/5 5/2-6/5 3-3/2 7/2-9/5 4-2 5-5/2 7-7/2 8-9/2
7/2	3/2-3/5 9/5-4/5 2-6/5 5/2-7/5 3-8/5 7/2-2 9/2-5/2 5-3 6-4 7-9/2 8-5
4	6/5-3/5 3/2-4/5 8/5-1 9/5-6/5 2-7/5 5/2-9/5 3-2 7/2-5/2 9/2-3 5-7/2 6-9/2 7-5 8-6
9/2	1-3/5 6/5-4/5 3/2-1 8/5-6/5 9/5-7/5 2-8/5 5/2-2 3-5/2 4-3 9/2-7/2 5-4 6-5 7-6 8-7
5	4/5-3/5 1-4/5 6/5-1 3/2-6/5 9/5-3/2 2-9/5 5/2-2 3-5/2 7/2-3 4-7/2 9/2-4 5-9/2 6-5 7-6 8-7
6	FPs
8	3/5-6/5 4/5-3/2 1-9/5 7/5-2 8/5-5/2 2-3 5/2-4 3-9/2 7/2-5 9/2-6 5-7

10	3/5-9/5 4/5-2 6/5-5/2 3/2-3 9/5-7/2 2-4 5/2-5 3-6 4-7 9/2-8
12	3/5-2 4/5-5/2 1-3 7/5-7/2 8/5-4 9/5-9/2 2-5 5/2-6 3-7 7/2-8
15	3/5-3 4/5-7/2 1-4 7/5-9/2 8/5-5 2-6 5/2-8
20	3/5-4 1-5 7/5-6 8/5-7 9/5-8

FM 12

OM	FP-OP
3/5	7-3/5 8-4/5
4/5	6-3/5 7-4/5 8-1
1	5-3/5 6-4/5 7-1 8-7/5
6/5	9/2-3/5 5-4/5 6-1 7-6/5 8-8/5
7/5	9/2-3/5 5-1 6-6/5 7-3/2 8-9/5
8/5	4-3/5 9/2-4/5 5-1 6-7/5 7-9/5 8-2
9/5	7/2-3/5 4-4/5 9/2-1 5-6/5 6-8/5 7-2 8-5/2
2	3-3/5 7/2-4/5 4-1 9/2-6/5 5-7/5 6-9/5 7-2 8-5/2
5/2	5/2-3/5 3-4/5 7/2-1 4-6/5 9/2-3/2 5-9/5 6-2 7-5/2 8-3
3	2-3/5 5/2-4/5 3-1 7/2-7/5 4-8/5 9/2-9/5 5-2 6-5/2 7-3 8-7/2
7/2	9/5-3/5 2-4/5 5/2-1 3-7/5 7/2-8/5 4-9/5 9/2-2 5-5/2 6-3 7-7/2 8-4
4	8/5-3/5 9/5-4/5 2-1 5/2-6/5 3-8/5 4-2 9/2-5/2 5-3 6-7/2 7-4 8-5
9/2	7/5-3/5 8/5-4/5 9/5-1 2-6/5 5/2-3/2 3-9/5 7/2-2 4-5/2 9/2-3 5-7/2 6-4 7-9/2 8-5
5	6/5-3/5 3/2-4/5 8/5-1 9/5-6/5 2-7/5 5/2-9/5 3-2 7/2-5/2 9/2-3 5-4 6-9/2 7-5 8-6
6	4/5-3/5 1-4/5 6/5-1 3/2-6/5 9/5-3/2 2-9/5 5/2-2 3-5/2 7/2-3 4-7/2 9/2-4 5-9/2 6-5 7-6 8-7
8	3/5-4/5 4/5-1 1-7/5 6/5-3/2 3/2-9/5 9/5-2 2-5/2 5/2-3 3-7/2 7/2-4 9/2-5 5-6 6-7 7-8
10	3/5-6/5 4/5-8/5 1-9/5 6/5-2 8/5-5/2 9/5-3 2-7/2 5/2-4 3-9/2 7/2-5 4-6 9/2-7 5-8
12	3/5-9/5 4/5-2 6/5-5/2 3/2-3 9/5-7/2 2-4 5/2-5 3-6 4-7 9/2-8
15	4/5-5/2 1-3 6/5-7/2 3/2-4 9/5-9/2 2-5 5/2-6 3-7 7/2-8
20	3/5-7/2 4/5-4 1-9/2 7/5-5 9/5-6 2-7

FM 15

OM	FP-OP
4/5	8-3/5
1	7-3/5 8-4/5
6/5	6-3/5 7-4/5 8-1
7/5	5-3/5 6-4/5 7-1 8-6/5
8/5	5-3/5 6-1 7-6/5 8-3/2
9/5	9/2-3/5 5-4/5 6-1 7-7/5 8-8/5
2	4-3/5 9/2-4/5 5-1 6-6/5 7-3/2 8-9/5
5/2	7/2-3/5 4-4/5 9/2-1 5-6/5 6-8/5 7-2 8-5/2
3	3-3/5 7/2-4/5 4-1 9/2-6/5 5-8/5 6-2 7-5/2 8-3
7/2	5/2-3/5 3-4/5 7/2-6/5 4-7/5 9/2-8/5 5-9/5 6-5/2 8-3
4	2-3/5 5/2-4/5 3-6/5 7/2-7/5 4-8/5 9/2-9/5 5-2 6-5/2 7-3 8-7/2
9/2	9/5-3/5 2-4/5 5/2-1 3-7/5 7/2-8/5 4-9/5 9/2-2 5-5/2 6-3 7-7/2 8-4
5	8/5-3/5 9/5-4/5 2-1 5/2-6/5 3-3/2 7/2-9/5 4-2 9/5-5/2 5-3 6-7/2 7-4 8-9/2
6	6/5-3/5 8/5-4/5 9/5-1 2-6/5 5/2-8/5 3-2 4-5/2 9/2-3 5-7/2 6-4 7-5 8-6
8	4/5-3/5 1-4/5 6/5-1 3/2-6/5 8/5-7/5 9/5-8/5 2-9/5 5/2-5/2 7/2-3 4-7/2 9/2-4 5-9/2 6-6 8-7
10	3/5-4/5 4/5-1 1-6/5 6/5-3/2 7/5-8/5 3/2-9/5 9/5-2 2-5/2 5/2-3 3-7/2 7/2-4 4-9/2 9/2-5 5-6 6-7 7-8
12	3/5-6/5 4/5-3/2 1-9/5 7/5-2 8/5-5/2 2-3 5/2-4 3-9/2 7/2-5 9/2-6 5-7
15	3/5-9/5 4/5-2 6/5-5/2 3/2-3 9/5-7/2 2-4 5/2-5 3-6 4-7 9/2-8
20	3/5-5/2 4/5-3 1-7/2 7/5-4 8/5-9/2 9/5-5 2-6 5/2-7 3-8

FM 20

OM	FP-OP
7/5	8-4/5
8/5	7-3/5 8-4/5
9/5	6-3/5 7-4/5 8-1
2	6-3/5 7-1 8-6/5
5/2	9/2-3/5 5-4/5 6-1 7-6/5 8-3/2
3	4-3/5 9/2-4/5 5-1 6-6/5 7-8/5 8-9/5
7/2	7/2-3/5 4-4/5 9/2-1 5-6/5 6-8/5 7-9/5 8-2
4	3-3/5 7/2-4/5 4-1 5-3/2 6-9/5 7-2 8-5/2

9/2	5/2-3/5	3-4/5	7/2-1	4-6/5	9/2-7/5	5-8/5	6-2	7-5/2 8-3
5	5/2-3/5	3-1	7/2-6/5	4-7/5	9/2-8/5	5-2	6-5/2	7-3 8-7/2
6	9/5-3/5	2-4/5	5/2-1	3-6/5	7/2-3/2	4-9/5	9/2-2	5-5/2 6-3 7-7/2 8-4
8	7/5-3/5	8/5-4/5	9/5-1	2-6/5	5/2-8/5	3-9/5	7/2-2	4-5/2 9/2-3 5-7/2
	6-4 8-5							
10	4/5-3/5	1-4/5	7/5-1	8/5-6/5	9/5-7/5	2-8/5	5/2-2	3-5/2 7/2-3 4-7/2
	9/2-4 5-9/2 6-5 7-6 8-7							
12	FP=,s							
15	3/5-1	4/5-7/5	1-3/2	6/5-9/5	3/2-2	9/5-5/2	2-3	5/2-7/2 3-4 4-5
	9/2-6 5-7 6-8							
20	3/5-9/5	4/5-2	6/5-5/2	3/2-3	9/5-7/2	2-4	5/2-5	3-6 4-7 9/2-8

APPENDIX B

BEATING THE ODDS

The System in Practice

Our first example exhibits the format used to present the needed data. It is the 5th race at Calder Race Course (Crc), Miami, Florida, 27 July 1990, a 6-furlong event for horses entered at a claiming price of $8000. The contenders are listed in order of post position. Since the Florida "take" at the time was 18.1%, only horses going off at post odds <=7/1 are shown. We shall need 50.5 points for a bet on any target horse. The post time odds or the odds as close to post time as possible should be used for the point score. There will be times when a bet becomes a non-bet because of last second changes on the "tote" board and vice versa. Over time, these occurrences should compensate each other.

27Jly90   5-Crc   6f   Clm 8000

Nainette:			111	M5	P5/2					
19Jly90	10-Crc	7f		Clm5000		1	1	1-3/4	115	11
8Jly90	2-Crc	6f		Clm7500		1	1	1-2½	116	8
Crafty Flo:			120	M5/2	P7/2					
19Jly90	7-Crc	6f		Clm10000		1	1	3-5	112	8
29Jun90	6-Crc	6½f		Clm8000		1	1	1-1½	120	9
Pixie Quick:			109	M6	P7/2					
19Jly90	7-Crc	6f.		Clm10000		4	5	4-6¼	111	8
8Jly90	2-Crc	6f		Clm7500		6	6	5-9¼	115	8

Edie Mum:			116	M4	P5						
18Jly90	2-Crc	7f		Clm8500		1	1	3-1		116	8
5Jly90	10-Crc	1		Clm10000	1	1	2	9-17¼		116	10

Ballerina On Ice:			106	M 3	P 4					
18Jly90	2-Crc	7f		Clm8000		4	4	2-1	105	8
12Jly90	2-Crc	6f		Clm5000		4	1	4-2	120	10

La Favorita:			112	M 6	P 5					
19Jly90	10-Crc	7f		Clm5000		10	7	2-3/4	116	11
12Jly90	2-Crc	6f		Clm5000		7	7	2-½	116	10

Nainette, the post favorite in today's race, carries 111 pounds, is assigned a morning line of 5/1 and goes off at 5/2. We shall use only the last two races of each contender. Following along, we have the date of the last race, the number of the race and the track at which it was run, the distance, the class of the race, the position at the ¼-mile call, the position at the ½-mile call, the finish, the lengths ahead if a winner and the lengths behind if a loser, the weight carried, and the number of horses in the race. In sprints - races at under a mile - the ½-mile call is the pre-stretch call. In routes - races at 1 mile or over - there will be one more number inserted between the ½-mile call and the finish and that will be the pre-stretch call (see Edie Mum's 5Jly90 race). The pre-stretch call is used in determining whether a horse is slow.

Now, faced with this enormous amount of data, where do we begin? Almost always, it is best to start with the post favorite as the target horse,"F", and compare it for similarity first to the shorter odds contenders. If no similarity exists, it becomes unlikely that sufficient points can be accumulated with the longer odds horses, and no further work need be done on the race. In applying a rule, every clause separated from the other clauses by "x" (and) must be satisfied. Clauses separated by "+" (or) are contained in parentheses or brackets and only one of them need be satisfied.

Comparing Nainette as F to Crafty Flo as O, note that Symmetry Rule III is excluded since the two horses have not raced each other in their last two races. Note also that Rule IX is excluded since neither is a first-time starter, and that Rules II, IV, V, VI, VII, and VIII are excluded since F's morning line is longer than O's. That leaves only Rule I. Since B appears in every subdivision of Rule I, we must look in the B-table for FM5 and OM5/2. FP5/2 is shorter than OP7/2 and B is satisfied. We can now determine whether a subdivision of Rule I applies.

The class of F is lower than that of O so that only parts a) to i) need be considered. Looking first at a), we see that the first three clauses are satisfied. We know that B is, and Nainette's last race class is lower than Crafty Flo's, and Crafty Flo's last race finish is 3rd.

But one of the "+" clauses in the parenthesis must also apply and neither one does - F finished first in its last race and O did not win its last easily. Therefore, Rule Ia) is not satisfied. Go next to Ib). Here, one of the clauses in the bracket does apply - Olrf is 3 and FP is shorter than OP. Rule Ib) is thus satisfied and the target, Nainette, collects 22 points corresponding to Crafty Flo's closing post odds. We need go no further, but let us look at Ic) for tutorial purposes. Crafty Flo's previous race win implies OD and the term in the parenthesis requiring FP to be equal or shorter applies. Therefore, Rule Ic) is also satisfied. It is commonplace for two or more symmetry rules to be satisfied.

Turning our attention to the next contender, Pixie Quick, we note immediately that Nainette raced this horse in the previous race of both, 8Jly90. Therefore, only Rule III need be considered, and none of the subdivisions can be satisfied. No points here for F.

For the same reasons listed for Crafty Flo, only Rules Ia) to i) need be considered when looking at the next contender, Edie Mum. B is satisfied, and so are subdivisions b) and e). c) is not satisfied because Edie Mum is not OD. In e), note that Z (Olrf 3) holds and that the closing post odds are in the normal betting pattern N_s, FP at 5/2 and OP at 5. Collect 16.5 points corresponding to OP5.

Nainette is similar to the next contender, Ballerina On Ice for exactly the same reasons as Crafty Flo. Rules Ib) and c) are satisfied. Collect 20 points corresponding to OP4.

We now have 58.5 points and Nainette is a likely bet. There is one more consideration that I will attend to after looking at the last contender, La Favorita. Here, both horses raced each other in their last race, and only Rule III applies. And only subdivision a) is satisfied - F beat other O by one place and less than 2 lengths after adjusting for the relative weight shift (none since both are dropping 4 pounds), the morning line pattern is S_s for FM5 and OM6, and FP is shorter than OP. Another 16.5 points for F making the total 75 points.

The final consideration is to determine if there are any other bets in the race. Two or more bets in a race happen infrequently, but if such does occur, pass the race. These races are not profitable, possibly because there is just too much information and all of it cannot be valid. In most races, you can quickly tell if another bet is possible. In our example, we must be a little more careful, but the exercise is instructive.

Consider Crafty Flo as the target, F. Comparing it first with Nainette as O, we see immediately that Rule I is excluded because B cannot be satisfied when FP becomes longer than FM and OP becomes shorter than OM. Rules III and IX are excluded for the usual reasons. Rules IV, V, and VI are excluded because Flrc >Olrc. Rules VII and VIII are excluded because neither OR nor OJ hold. That leaves Rule II and only subdivisions e), f), and g). Olrf1E* holds, but the strong and longer closing odds pattern, FP7/2 versus OP5/2 (S_1), appears only in g) and that subdivision requires Flrc<=Olrc. No points for Crafty Flo.

How about Pixie Quick as O? The two horses raced each other last out and Rule III is to be considered. Crafty Flo beat Pixie Quick by 1¼ lengths, but there is a big relative weight shift (RWS) of 10 pounds against F. Equating 3 pounds to 1 length puts F behind O and T' in Ib) holds. But b) requires a strong and shorter morning line betting pattern (S_s) and the pattern is W_s - 5/2 versus 6. It should be clear that none of the other subdivisions can be satisfied. No points for F.

The points that could be collected for similarity with the three remaining contenders now total 53.5, and we must continue the analysis. Edie Mum - Rules I, II, III, IV, V, and VI are excluded for reasons already given. Rule VIII requires FMW_s which is not the case and it is excluded. That leaves Rule VII and in particular d). Edie Mum is OR because today's race is one or more furlongs shorter than its last two races and it does show early speed, being first at the first two calls in its last race in which it finished third. Crafty Flo is FR and F(HxD) and its morning line is FMs and its post odds FPs. VIId) is clearly satisfied. 16.5 points for Crafty Flo.

Ballerina On Ice - Crafty Flo is not similar to this horse by any of the Rules. No points, and Crafty Flo cannot now be a system bet.

La Favorita - Crafty Flo is similar to this horse by Rule IIb) and no other. 16.5 more points for a total of 33 points and no bet. That still leaves Nainette as the bet.

Whenever dealing with targets that have equal or longer morning lines than other contenders, always remember that B must be satisfied for a bet to be possible. Consider now Pixie Quick as the target, F. We see at once that it cannot be similar to either Nainette or La Favorita for this reason. With Crafty Flo as O, only Rule III can apply and here too B must be satisfied for FM equal to or longer than OM, as it is. a), b), c), d), e), f) and k) are excluded because they all require F to have a shorter morning line than O. B is satisfied, however, making us consider the other subdivisions. None of them applies - IIIg) requires FPN_s, W_s and the others a finish two or more places behind O in their race together rather than one place behind. No points for Pixie Quick here. That leaves only the points from Edie Mum and Ballerina On Ice as possible, not enough for a bet. Again, for tutorial purposes, let us apply the Rules with them as O.

Edie Mum - Only Rule I applies since Pixie Quick's morning line odds are longer than Edie Mum's morning line odds and Rules III and IX obviously do not apply. With Pixie Quick as F, B is satisfied. Since F is FH and Flrc>Olrc, subdivisions r) through y) are the ones to consider. Check to see that none are satisfied.

Ballerina On Ice - Rules It) and w) are satisfied and Pixie Quick is similar to this horse.

None of the other contenders are possible bets, as is easily shown with a little practice. Nainette is the bet in this race and it won. This first example should be mastered before going on.

In subsequent examples, I shall condense the analyses as shown below and any discussion will then follow. All applicable Similarity Rules are indicated.

F:	Nainette	FM 5	FP 5/2		
O:	Crafty Flo	OM 5/2	OP 7/2	Ib, Ic	22 points
O:	Pixie Quick	OM 6	OP 7/2		0 points
O:	Edie Mum	OM 4	OP 5	Ib , Ie	16.5 points
O:	Ballerina On Ice	OM 3	OP 4	Ib, Ic	20 points
O:	La Favorita	OM 6	OP 5	IIIa	16.5 points
	Total points: 75				

F:	Crafty Flo	FM 5/2	FP 7/2		
O:	Nainette	FM 5	FP 5/2		0 points
O:	Pixie Quick	FM 6	FP 7/2		0 points
O:	Edie Mum	FM 4	FP 5	VIId	16.5 points
O:	Ballerina On Ice	FM 3	FP 4		0 points

O: La Favorita   FM 6   FP 5   IIb   16.5 points
Total points 33

    In order to approach the actual race track experience, I have chosen to analyze one complete racing card. The day was unusual in that there were six bets called for, far above the system's average of 1.75 bets per day. It was at Aqueduct Racetrack, 3 March 1993. The take was 17% and 46.5 points are needed for a bet. Examples illustrating the other Similarity Rules follow. Keep in mind that those races in which there is no bet are in the great majority.

3Mar93 1-Aqu 6f Msw

Am Sensational::		117	M 5/2	P 2						
10Feb93	5-Aqu	6f	Msw			7	4	3-6¼	117	8
Maggie Day:		122	M 8/5	P 4/5						
18Feb93	3-Aqu	1⁷⁰	Msw		1	2	2	3-14½	122	8
10Feb93	5-Aqu	6f	Msw			4	2	2-3	122	8
Susan's Candy:		122	M 6	P 8						
11Feb93	1-GS	6f	Msw			8	7	3-5	117	9
20Jan93	5-Aqu	6f	Msw			4	4	4-13¼	122	7
Timed Approach:		122	M 2	P 9/2						
20Dec92	4-Aqu	6f	Msw			3	4	6-18	113	6
30Nov92	6-Aqu	6f	Msw			5	6	5-5	120	9

F: Maggie Day	FM 8/5	FP 4/5		
O: Am Sensational	OM 5/2	OP 2		0 points
O: Susan's Candy	OM 6	OP 8	Ip	11points
O: Timed Approach	OM 2	OP 9/2		0 points

Total points 11

    There is no bet here on Maggie Day or any other contender. The system is telling us that all horses in this race are fairly bet. Therefore, over many bets of this type, you must lose the take. It was clear from the beginning of the wagering that there would be no
bet. Note that B is satisfied for the target compared to Susan's Candy and Timed Approach.

3Mar93 2-Aqu 6f Clm17500

Always Ashley:		117	M 6	P 6					
19Feb93	3-Aqu	6f	Clm17500		6	6	4-2 3/4	117	10
10Feb93	1-Aqu	6f	Clm17500		4	4	2-1 3/4	117	6

I'm a Pickpocket:		112	M 5/2	P 5					
19Feb93	3-Aqu	6f	Clm17500		4	4	1-1½	110	10
3 Feb93	2-Aqu	6f	Clm25000		7	7	6-5½	117	9

Pay for Play:		117	M 3	P 7/5					
24Feb93	2-Aqu	6f	Clm14000		1	1	3-1	117	11
14Feb93	2-Aqu	6f	Clm14000		1	2	3-4¼	117	10

Jocovitch:		113	M 8	P 7/2					
26Mar92	4-Aqu	6½f	Clm45000		4	4	1-3/4	113	8
27Feb92	4-Aqu	6f	Clm35000		5	6	5-9	119	6

Old Ways:		117	M 10	P 8					
24Feb93	7-Aqu	6f	Clm25000		3	4	6-15 3/4	117	8
3Feb93	2-Aqu	6f	Clm25000		2	2	9-11½	112	9

F:	Pay for Play	FM 3	FP 7/5		
O:	Jocovitch	OM 8	OP 7/2	IIa, IId, VIb, VIc	22 points
O:	I'm a Pickpocket	OM 5/2	OP 5	Ia, Ib, Ic , Ie, Ig	16.5 points
O:	Always Ashley	OM 6	OP 6	Ic, Ie, Ig, Ii, VIf	14 points
O:	Old Ways	OM 10	OP 8		0 points
Total points 52.5					

In this race, Pay for Play is the somewhat surprising favorite since it is stepping up in class and facing some competitors with good records. But that is exactly what we are looking for. A surprise means that the horse is being underbet because of a superficially inferior record. Play for Pay is to be bet and it won. You should follow each "x" clause in the Similarity Rules and see that each is satisfied. No other bet is possible in this race.

3Mar93 3-Aqu 1 1/8 MdClm35000

Rubber Rudder: 122   M 6   P 5
18Feb93   9-Aqu   1^{70} MCl30000   4   3   2   5-9   118   10

Heavenly Hooch   118   M 15   P 7
20Feb93   3-Aqu   6f   MCl30000   7   7   6-5½   118   12
31Jan93   3-Aqu   1 1/16 MCl30000   3   4   5   6-17   118   12

Donnacha: 122   M 9/5 P 2
31Jan93   3-Aqu   1 1/16 MCl35000   7   7   8   2-8½   122   12
 4Jan93   4-Aqu   1^{70} MCl35000   7   7   5   2-9¼   122   9

Stand Trial: 118   M 2   P 5/2
18Feb93   9-Aqu   1^{70} MCl30000   8   7   6   4-8 3/4   113   10
20Jan93   2-Aqu   1 1/16 MCl30000   4   4   3   5-8¼   118   9

Big Carouser: 113   M 4   P 2
18Feb93   9-Aqu   1^{70} MCl30000   7   4   3   2-4½   113   10
 8Feb93   1-Aqu   1^{70} MCl30000   7   6   4   3-13   113   9

F: Donnacha   FM 9/5   FP 2
O: Big Carouser   OM 4   OP 2   0 points
O: Stand Trial   OM 2   OP 5/2   0 points
O: Rubber Rudder   OM 6   OP 5   0 points
O: Heavenly Hooch   OM 15   OP 7   0 points
Total points   0

F: Big Carouser   FM 4   FP 2
O: Donnacha   OM 9/5   OP 2   Ib, Ic   33 points
O: Stand Trial   OM 2   OP 5/2   0 points
O: Rubber Rudder   OM 6   OP 5   0 points
O: Heavenly Hooch   OM 15   OP 7   0 points
Total points 33

F: Heavenly Hooch   FM 15   FP 7
O: Donnacha   OM 9/5   OP 2   IIIi   33 points
O: Big Carouser   OM 4   OP 2   0 points
O: Stand Trial   OM 2   OP 5/2   Iq   28.5 points
O: Rubber Rudder   OM 6   OP 5   Iq   16.5 points
Total points 78 points

It should be clear that Rubber Rudder cannot be a bet because B is not satisfied for any of the shorter priced contenders. Even at the long odds of 7/1, Heavenly Hooch is being strongly bet relative to the morning line, this despite a record that shows nothing. Whenever a horse receives such strong betting relative to the morning line, it must be considered. Heavenly Hooch won the race. A system bet at such long odds is a rarity.

3Mar93   4-Aqu 1^{70} Clm50000

Cost Too Much	120	M 7/2	P 2						
20Feb93	1-Aqu	1 1/8	Alw33000	5	5	5	4-1	119	6
15Feb93	7-Aqu	1^{70}	Alw31000	8	7	4	1-3	117	8 ·
Crafty Cash	108	M 5	P 6						
19Feb93	6-Aqu	1 1/16	Clm50000	7	7	6	3-6	112	7
7Feb93	1-Aqu	1 5/8	Hcp47000	5	6	6	4-16½	114	6
I'm Sky High	119	M 5	P 4						
19Feb93	6-Aqu	1 1/16	Clm50000	2	2	2	1-2	117	7
7Feb93	6-Aqu	1 1/8	Clm50000	2	2	5	5-8	117	7
Study Hard	113	M 6	P5						
18Feb93	1-Aqu	1 1/8	Clm35000	6	6	6	1-½	117	7
8Feb93	6-Aqu	1^{70}	Clm35000	5	4	3	3-½	117	5
Will to Reign	117	M4	P5						
20Feb93	1-Aqu	1 1/8	Alw33000	4	3	3	5-2	117	6
29Jan93	8-Aqu	1 1/16	Alw33000	2	3	3	3-4	117	6
Northern Teller	108	M 6	P 6						
7Feb93	6-Aqu	1 1/8	Clm47500	1	1	1	3-5	115	7
31Jan93	6Aqu	6f	Alw41000		3	2	6-5½	110	7

F: Cost Too Much	FM 7/2	FP 2			
O: Crafty Cash	OM 5	OP 6	Iu	14 points	
O: I'm Sky High	OM 5	OP 4		0 points	
O: Study Hard	OM 6	OP 5		0 points	
O: Will to Reign	OM 4	OP 5	IIIa	16.5 points	
O: Northern Teller	OM 6	OP 6		0 points	
Total points 30.5					

F: I'm Sky High	FM 5	FP 4		
O: Cost Too Much	OM 7/2	OP 2		0 points
O: Crafty Cash	OM 5	OP 6		0 points
O: Study Hard	OM 6	OP 5		0 points
O: Will to Reign	OM 4	OP 5		0 points
O: Northern Teller	OM 6	OP 6	IIIa	14 points
Total points 14				

For most of these comparisons, B clearly cannot be satisfied. Such is the case for most of the other rules as well. Note that the I'm Sky High-Northern Teller comparison satisfies Rule IIIa because the large relative weight shift (RWS) in favor of the latter brings the horses together in their common race. No bet here. I'm Sky High, the second choice, won.

3Mar93 5-Aqu 6f Msw

Coly		116	M 7/2	P 9/2						
20Feb93	5-Aqu	6f	Msw			8	7	3-2¼	116	12
3Jan93	6-Aqu	6f	Msw			9	8	5-2½	116	11

Queen's Over Seven		121	M 4	P 5/2						
22Dec92	4-Aqu	6f	MCl45000		10	2	2-3		113	12
28Nov92	8-Aqu	1	NYStallion	5	3	2	4-7½		112	7

Scoutingforkisses		121	M 4	P 6						
15Feb93	5-Aqu	1 1/16	Msw		4	2	1	6-12	116	11
5Feb93	7-Aqu	1 1/16	Msw		1	1	1	2-4	121	8

Sugarpro   121   M 8   P 3/2
First-time starter

F: Sugarpro	FM 8	FP 3/2		
O: Queen's Over Seven	OM 4	OP 5/2	IXc	28.5 points
O: Coly	OM 7/2	OP 9/2	IXd	18 points
O: Scoutingforkisses	OM 4	OP 6	IXc, IXe	14 points
Total points 60.5				

Rule IX must be used here because Sugarpro is a first-time starter. None of the other choices is a possible bet. Sugarpro, although bet down strongly, lost. Queen's Over Seven won.

3Mar93 6-Aqu 1^{70} Alw29000

Koluctoo Jimmy Al		117	M 2	P 6/5					
15Feb93	6-Aqu	6f	Alw27000		6	5	3-3¼	122	6
4Feb93	3-Aqu	6f	Msw		5	2	1-1½	122	11

Acting Admiral		119	M 5	P 7/2					
14Feb93	3-Aqu	1 1/16	Msw	9	9	9	1-hd	122	12

Twice the Debt		117	M 5/2	P 6					
19Feb93	7-Aqu	1 1/16	Alw29000	2	4	3	2-5½	119	9
22Jan93	3-Aqu	1^{70}	Msw	1	1	1	1-5	122	5

Nine Holes		117	M 5	P 4					
19Feb93	7-Aqu	1 1/16	Alw29000	6	6	5	3-6½	117	9
28Jan93	9-Aqu	1^{70}	Alw29000	3	3	3	2-3/4	117	5

F: Koluctoo Jimmy Al	FM 2	FP 6/5			
O: Acting Admiral	OM 5	OP 7/2	IIa		22 points
O: Twice the Debt	OM 5/2	OP 6	Ia, Ib, Ic, Ie		14 points
O: Nine Holes	OM 5	OP 4	IIh, IIi, IIk, VIb, VId, VIf, VIh,		20 points
			VIi		

Total points 56

The favorite, Koluctoo Jimmy Al, was the bet and it won.

3Mar93 7-Aqu 6f Alw27000

Little Annie O		116	M 9/2	P 6					
28Jan93	7-Aqu	6f	Alw27000		Did not finish			116	9
14Jan93	3-Aqu	6f	MCl35000	1	1	1-10½	122	12

Princesse Niner		111	M 3	P 3					
19Feb93	8-Aqu	6f	SpringVic		3	4	4-1½	116	7
29Jan93	3-Aqu	6f	Msw		3	2	1-2	116	11

Saucy Charmer		118	M 4	P 6/5	

229

8Feb93	5-Aqu	6f	Msw		1	1	1-2	121	6

Six Way's 116 M 6 P 9/2

28Jan93	7-Aqu	6f	Alw27000		7	6	4-2	116	9
17Jan93	7-Aqu	6f	Alw27000		4	3	3-nk	116	8

F:	Saucy Charmer	FM 4	FP 6/5		
O:	Princesse Niner	OM 3	OP 3	Ic, Ie	25 points
O:	Six Way's	OM 6	OP 9/2	Ib, Id, Ie	18 points
O:	Little Annie O	OM 9/2	OP 6	Ic, Ie	14 points
Total points 57					

No other choice is a possible bet. Saucy Charmer is to be bet and it won.

3Mar93 8-Aqu 6f Alw34000

Appealing Tracy 117 M 6 P 9/2

17Feb93	1-Aqu	6f	Clm50000	2	4	6-5½	117	6
5 Feb93	8-Aqu	6f	Alw30000	5	3	3-2 3/4	117	5

Explosive One 117 M 8/5 P 2

5Feb93	8-Aqu	6f	Alw30000	1	1	2-nk	119	5
21Jan93	8-Aqu	6f	Alw28000	2	1	1-1¼	119	10

Regal Conquest 117 M 10 P 5/2

18Feb93	8-Aqu	6f	Alw34000	6	6	3-1¼	117	7
25Nov93	5-Aqu	7f	Clm90000	2	2	5-9	118	6

Penny's Buck 117 M 2 P 9/2

7Dec92	8-Aqu	6f	Alw34000	1	1	3-1¼	117	5
25Nov92	5-Aqu	7f	Clm85000	1	1	1-4	116	6

Vermont 117 M 5 P 7/2

18Feb93	8-Aqu	6f	Alw34000	1	1	4-1¼	117	7
31Jan93	6-Aqu	6f	Alw41000	2	1	2-ns	115	7

F:	Explosive One	FM 8/5	FP 2		
O:	Regal Conquest	OM 10	OP 5/2		0 points
O:	Vermont	OM 5	OP 7/2	IIi, IIk, VIf	22 points
O:	Appealing Tracy	OM 6	OP 9/2	IIIe	18 points

O: Penny's Buck   OM 2   OP 9/2   0 points
Total points 40

F: Regal Conquest	FM 10	FP 5/2		
O: Explosive One	OM 8/5	OP 2	It	33 points
O: Vermont	OM 5	OP 7/2		0 points
O: Appealing Tracy	OM 6	OP 9/2		0 points
O: Penny's Buck	OM 2	OP 9/2	IIIg, IIIh, IIIi	18 points

Total points 51

Regal Conquest is to be bet, but it finished second to Vermont. Betting to place is not nearly as profitable as betting to win, and all betting should be confined to win only.

3Mar93 9-Aqu 6f Msw

Always Trying	121	M 8	P 2					
First-time starter								
African Hope	121	M 2	P 2					
10Feb93	9-Aqu	6f	Msw	7	10	3-4	121	12
16Jan93	6-Aqu	6f	Msw	3	1	3-1	121	11
Winning the Day	121	M 5	P 3					
18Oct92	3-Bel	6½f	MCl50000	3	2	6-16	117	12
14Sep92	3-Bel	6f	Msw	9	1	5-2½	117	14

F: Always Trying	FM 8	FP 2	
O: African Hope	OM 2	OP 2	0 points
O: Winning the Day	OM 5	OP 3	0 points

Total points 0

Rule IX must be used here because Always Trying is a first-time starter. Although B is satisfied, none of the subdivisions apply and there is no bet in this race. The race was won by Winning the Day.

The betting on this day was rather successful. However, let me warn you that it will rarely be so good. You can expect one or two bets a day and close to 50% winners. Even with such a high winning percentage, the fluctuations can be severe. It is not unusual to go for a week or two and lose money. Favorable betting situations develop randomly - there can be streaks of winners, streaks of losers, streaks of many bets and streaks of few bets. We shall see later that about half the days are profitable. On rare days, there are three or four bets that all lose. Let us go on to other examples.

14Jun93 1-Bel 7f Clm35000

Old Ways		115	M 3	P 5					
30May93	1-Bel	6f	Clm25000		7	6	4-5½	117	7
16May93	1-Bel	6f	Clm17500		3	3	1-4 3/4	122	7
Carr's Pleasure		112	M 7/2	P 9/5					
2Jun93	1-Bel	1 1/16	Clm45000	4	4	1	4-6 3/4	108	7
23May93	1-Bel	7f	Clm35000		2	1	2-2½	112	7
Top the Record		117	M 5/2	P 2					
30Apr93	6-Aqu	7f	Clm35000		6	7	7-10½	117	8
10Apr93	2-Aqu	6f	Clm25000		5	6	2-3¼	117	6
Ocean Splash		115	M 4	P 5					
23May93	1-Bel	7f	Clm35000		4	5	3-8½	117	7
16Apr93	9-Aqu	6f	Alw27500		7	8	8-11	119	8

F:	Carr's Pleasure	FM 7/2	FP 9/5		
O:	Top the Record	OM 5/2	OP 2		0 points
O:	Old Ways	OM 3	OP 5		0 points
O:	Ocean Splash	OM 4	OP 5	Iu	16.5 points
	Total points 16.5				
F:	Top the Record	FM 5/2	FP 2		
O:	Carr's Pleasure	OM 7/2	OP 9/5	IV	36 points
O:	Old Ways	OM 3	OP 5	It, VIIf	16.5 points
O:	Ocean Splash	OM 4	OP 5		0 points
	Total points 52.5				

In comparing Carr's Pleasure as F with Top the Record as O, note that the former's morning line odds are longer than the latter's and that B is not satisfied. Carr's

Pleasure, then, cannot be similar to Top the Record by Rule I or any other rule. Since there are not enough points associated with the other two contenders, Carr's Pleasure is no bet. Even if B were satisfied by Top the Record's closing odds going to 5/2, Rule I is still not satisfied.

Because Top the Record is the morning line favorite, Rule I and all the other rules must be checked. Top the Record is the bet and it won.

14Jun93 2-Bel 1 1/16 Msw

Running On E		114	M 6	P 4	(coupled with Wegotasecret)				
22May93	6-Hia	6f	Msw		6	7	3-11	113	12

Wegotasecret		114	M 6	P 4	(coupled with Running On E)				
10Jun93	5-Bel	1 1/16	Msw	8	11	14	12-33	114	14
14May93	9-Bel	6f	Msw	10	10	9-32		115	10

Nasdoria		114	M 9/2	P 5					
22Nov92	6-Aqu	7f	Msw		4	3	6-15	117	10
2Nov92	4-Aqu	7f	Msw		3	2	2-10	117	7

Spike Heel		114	M 6	P 5					
25Feb93	5-Aqu	1 1/16	Msw	7	7	7	4-15	121	8
13Jan93	5-Aqu	1^{70}	Msw		3	3	3 7-13	121	8

Sea Ballad		114	M 3	P 6
First-time starter				

Russian Tango		114	M 2	P 8/5					
19Mar93	3-GP	7f	Msw		6	5	4-11	120	12
24Feb93	6-GP	7f	Msw		8	7	3-8½	120	12

Lady Gladiator		114	M 4	P 9/2					
6Jun93	5-Bel	1 1/16	Msw	8	7	6	4-12	114	9
20May93	5-Bel	1 1/16	Msw	5	5	4	4-5¼	115	10

F: Russian Tango	FM 2	FP 8/5		
O: Running On E	OM 6	OP 4	V, VIIIa, VIIIc, VIIId, VIIIe	20 points
O: Wegotasecret	OM 6	OP 4		0 points
O: Nasdoria	OM 9/2	OP 5	IIh, IIj, VIIIa, VIIIc, VIIId, VIIIe	16.5 points
O: Spike Heel	OM 6	OP 5		0 points

O: Sea Ballad   OM 3   OP 6   IXa   14 points
O: Lady Gladiator   OM 4   OP 9/2   0 points
Total points 50.5

There are a number of interesting points to be made here. 1) Running On E is coupled in the betting with Wegotasecret. When that occurs, I generally insist on the target being similar to both horses before assigning points. Here, Russian Tango is not similar to Wegotasecret. However, in a case like this where one part of the entry is obviously the horse to beat, I am satisfied with similarity to the strong horse alone. Things to look for are mention in handicappers' picks and the two jockeys, especially when one is a leading rider and the other more of an exercise boy, as is the case here. 2) In Rule V, whenever one of the horses has raced only once, use that race twice, once for lrc and lrf and once for prc and prf. 3) With so many horses in the race being bet close to the morning line, it is unlikely to find a bet other than on the post favorite. There is no other bet in this race. Russian Tango is the bet and it won.

26Jun92   8-Bel   1   Hcp47000

Won Scent   113   M 6/5 P 1   (coupled with Her She Shawklit)
   1Jun92   7-Bel   1 1/16   Hcp47000   2 2 1 1-1¼   110   3
  25May92   5-Bel   6½f   Alw41000   5 5 5-14   117   5

Her She Shawklit   122   M 6/5 P 1   (coupled with Won Scent)
  20May92   8-Bel   1 1/16   Hcp47000   2 2 1 1-2½   118   6
  29Apr92   8-Aqu   1   Hcp47000   2 3 2 1-3¼   115   5

Bel Ray   111   M 7/2 P 7
  27May92   8-Bel   6½f   Alw41000   4 4 1-hd   117   6
  20May92   8-Bel   1 1/16   Hcp47000   1 1 2 3-4¼   111   6

Haunting   116   M 9/2 P 5
  20Jun92   7-Bel   1 1/16   Hcp47000   6 6 6 6-27   114   6
   2May92   9-Spt   1 1/8   Stk250000   9 10 12 11-10   114   13

Wiggles Law   112   M 3   P 3
   6Jun92   3-Bel   1 1/16   Alw31000   2 1 1 1-10   117   6
  21May92   3-Bel   7f   Clm45000   4 5 2-½   114   7

Richard's Lass   110   M 10   P 5
  20Jun92   7-Bel   1 1/16   Hcp47000   3 3 3 5-4¼   110   6
   3Jun92   1-Bel   1   Clm75000   2 2 1 2-2   112   8

234

F: Won Scent	FM 6/5	FP 1		
O: Bel Ray	OM 7/2	OP 7	Ir, Is, Ix, IIa	12.5 points
O: Haunting	OM 9/2	OP 5		0 points
O: Wiggles Law	OM 3	OP 3	IIa	25 points
O: Richard's Lass	OM 10	OP 5		0 points

Total points 37.5

F: Her She Shawklit	FM 6/5	FP 1		
O: Bel Ray	OM 7/2	OP 7	IIIc, IIIe, IIIf	12.5 points
O: Haunting	OM 9/2	OP 5		0 points
O: Wiggles Law	OM 3	OP 3	IIa	25 points
O: Richard's Lass	OM 10	OP 5		0 points

Total points 37.5

F: Richard's Lass	FM 10	FP 5		
O: Won Scent	OM 6/5	OP 1	Il	50 points
O: Her She Shawklit	OM 6/5	OP 1	Il	50 points
O: Bel Ray	OM 7/2	OP 7	It	12.5 points
O: Haunting	OM 9/2	OP 5		0 points
O: Wiggles Law	OM 3	OP 3		0 points

Total points 62.5

Again, in this race, we have two horses coupled in an entry. Unlike the previous example, however, both are strong horses. Therefore, when considered as the target, both should accumulate sufficient points on their own for a bet. When another horse is the target, it should be similar to both parts of the entry before receiving points. Richard's Lass is similar to both parts of the entry here and receives 50 points (not 100). Richard's Lass is the bet here and it won.

18Mar92   8-Aqu   1   Alw33000

Bridjet Honey		110	M 7/5 P 8/5					
11Mar92	7-Aqu	7f	Alw28000	3	3	1-2	112	5
19Feb92	7-Aqu	6f	Alw27000	4	4	1-hd	115	6

Mezzanotte		117	M 7/2 P 6/5					
6Mar92	8-Aqu	6f	Alw41000	5	4	4-3 3/4	115	5
24Jan92	8-Aqu	1^{70}	Alw33000	4	4	3	4-13	119	5

Catch Chati		117	M 2	P 5/2						
15Feb92	7-Aqu	1 1/16	Alw31000	1	1	1	1-nk	117	7
3Feb92	7-Aqu	1^{70}	Alw31000	2	2	1	2-3/4	117	7

F: Mezzanotte	FM 7/2	FP 6/5		
O: Bridjet Honey	OM 7/5	OP 8/5	Iz"	38 points
O: Catch Chati	OM 2	OP 5/2	Iz"	28.5 points
Total points 66.5				

F: Bridjet Honey	FM 7/5	FM 8/5		
O: Mezzanotte	OM 7/2	OP 6/5		0 points
O: Catch Chati	OM 2	OP 5/2	VIb	28.5 points
Total points 28.5				

In only three cases can a high class horse (FH) like Mezzanotte be similar to lower class horses. These are for Similarity Rules Iz, Iz', and Iz". Mezzanotte satisfies B and all the other conditions for Rule Iz". Catch Chati with longer morning line odds than Bridjet Honey and not satisfying B is an obvious "no bet". Mezzanotte is the bet and won.

14Jly93   1-Crc   5f   Clm6500

Cutapat:		117	M 6	P 5					
27Jun93	9-Crc	6f	Clm14000	5	4	7-5 3/4	115	9
18Jun93	2-Crc	6f	MCl12500	1	1	1-3½	115	12

Hyfits:		117	M 4	P 5					
20Feb93	8-GP	1 1/8	Alw27000	1	1	1	8-8½	112	10
27Jan93	3-GP	1 1/16	Clm 25000	1	1	1	2-3½	116	8

Chiefcooknbotlwshr:		117	M 3	P 2					
26Jun93	1-Crc	6f	Clm10000	1	2	2-4½	119	7
13Jun93	7-Crc	7f	Clm12500	2	2	5-9	119	6

Big Fling:		122	M 8/5	P 1					
1Jly93	4-Crc	6f	Clm10000	1	1	3-2½	122	6
19Jly93	6-Crc	5½f	Hcp15000s	1	2	11-23	115	11

F: Big Fling	FM 8/5	P 1		
O: Chiefcooknbtlwsher	OM 3	OP 2	VIIa, VIIb, VIIc, VIId	33 points
O: Cutapat	OM 6	OP 5	IIh, IIi, Ill, IIm,	16.5 points

O: Hyfits   OM 4   OP 5   Ic, Ie, Ig, Ii, IIh, IIi, IIk, VIIe,
VIIf, VIIIc, VIIId, VIIIe 16.5 points

Total points 66

Big Fling is the only possible bet in this race because none of the other horses can satisfy B. It is the bet but finished second to Cutapat. Note that Fprc is a starter race. Note also that Hyfits shows esl and not esl* so that only the e) part of Rule VII can be applied.

One final example to illustrate more of Rule I. Rules I, II, and III will be those most used.

1Mar90 9-Aqu 1 1/16 Msw

Long Island Sound	121	M 10	P 7					
16Feb90 6-Aqu	1 1/16	Msw		8	4	2	2-7	121	11
31Jan90 5-Aqu	1 1/8	Msw		9	8	6	2-3	121	12
Flying Pegemina	121	M 3	P 7/2					
19Feb90 5-Aqu	1 1/8	Msw		4	4	3	2-hd	121	8
11Feb90 4-Aqu	6f	MCl45000		4	4	3-3½	117	10
Gold N' Ship	121	M 6	P 6					
14Feb90 5-Aqu	6f	Msw		8	7	4-5½	121	9
24Oct89 4-Med	1	Msw		4	4	3	2-3	117	8
Sleek Feet	121	M 5	P 9/5					
27Dec89 4-Aqu	6f	Msw		8	6	5-11	117	12
Another Smiso	121	M 5	P 4					
14Feb90 5-Aqu	6f	Msw		6	5	3-3½	121	9
25Jan90 6-Aqu	6f	Msw		3	4	4-2 3/4	121	9

F: Sleek Feet	FM 5	FP 9/5		
O: Flying Pegemina	OM 3	OP 7/2	Ij, Il, Io, Iq	22 points
O: Another Smiso	OM 5	OP 4	Im, In	20 points
O: Gold N' Ship	OM 6	OP 6	Ik, Il, Io, Iq	14 points
O: Long Island Sound	OM 10	OP 7	Ij, Ik, Il, Io, Iq, IIa, IId, V	12.5 points

Total points 68.5

Here is another example of an unexpected favorite that is obviously being bet on late-breaking information. In this case, the information proved sound and Sleek Feet won.

In conclusion, let me comment on the missing data. I have used in this system only a few of the many factors that decide the outcome of a horse race. Omitted are running times, intervals between races, track conditions, speed ratings and many others. All these I leave to the oddsmaker to handle as best he can. I have little doubt that all of them are reflected in the morning line odds in the best possible way.

APPENDIX C

RESULTS

For testing the system, I sampled 1800 races over 194 racing days at Aqueduct and Belmont Racetracks in New York, Calder and Gulfstream in Florida, and Santa Anita in California. The results were as follows: There were 323 system bets and 179 winners for a win percentage of 55%. Assuming flat bets of $1, the profit amounted to $191 for a return on investment (ROI) of 59%. The frequency of betting is, however, low - about 3 bets every 2 days on average. Most races are fairly bet by a very knowledgeable public. Underestimating their superiority can lead only to disaster. Classifying the results on the basis of the post odds, we obtain the following table:

Odds	Number of bets	Winners	Win %	Profit $1 bets	ROI
3/5	10	7	70	1.2	12%
4/5	22	13	59	1.4	6
1	33	21	64	9.0	27
6/5	36	20	56	8.0	22
7/5	15	7	47	1.8	12
3/2	16	11	69	11.5	72
8/5	27	14	52	9.4	35
9/5	24	15	63	18.0	75
2	57	26	46	21.0	37
5/2	37	23	62	43.5	118
3	15	5	33	5.0	33
7/2	13	8	62	23.0	177
4	4	2	50	6.0	150
9/2	3	2	67	8.0	267
5	7	3	43	11.0	157
6	1	0	0	0	0
7	3	2	67	13.0	433

The profit in the table is actually understated because the lowest possible payout was used. A winner at 5/2, for example, could pay as a profit on a $1 bet as much as $2.80 rather than the $2.50 used above. Moreover, "breakage" has decreased to 5 cents from 10 cents in many places, and that too enhances the profit margin. It is interesting to note the high returns on investment for the longer odds horses. Favorites tend to be overbet today in contrast to the underbet favorites of yesteryear.

Another interesting way to exhibit the results is to show the number of racing days on which a given profit or loss developed, again based on $1 bets to win.

Profit (loss)	No. of days
$ (5)	0
(4)	0
(3)	2
(2)	15
(1)	27
0	57
1	26
2	22
3	20
4	9
5	5
6	6
7	2
8	0
9	2
10	1

We can see that a loss developed on 44 racing days out of the total of 194, or 23%. On 57 of them, or 29%, it was break-even either from no bets or compensating wins and losses. On 93 days, or 48%, there was a profit. All profits and losses were rounded off to $1. There were 37 no-bet days (19%).

I strongly recommend flat betting with amounts equal to one-twentieth of your risk capital. As profits build, so will the amounts of your bets. Varying the betting amounts according to the "Kelly criterion" or other strategies assumes a knowledge of degrees of attractiveness among various bets, which does not exist here. For further considerations on betting amounts, especially as concerns the size of the pari-mutuel betting pools, please refer to the main text.

One final remark on the significance of these results. Assuming the public to be correct in its evaluation of the win probabilities, what is the expected number of winners in a 323-race random sample? To obtain this figure, one must calculate the weighted win probability from the odds and multiply by the number in the sample. The weighted win probability is 30.6% and the number of winners to be expected is 99. This is far below the 179 winners selected by the system. Calculating the standard deviation, we get at the 1% confidence level, 99±25 winners. There is much less than a 1% chance of obtaining by random selection as many winners as the system on this particular sample. The results are highly significant.

APPENDIX D

USING THE SYSTEM IN THE UNITED KINGDOM AND IRELAND

The system as presented in the previous appendices requires the use of a morning line. This is the forecast of the starting odds as made by an on-course oddsmaker who is very familiar with past performances of the entries. It is, therefore, a proxy for the historical record which the system then compares with any late-breaking information as represented by closing odds. Because a morning line as such is unavailable in the U.K and Ireland, I suggest the following betting procedure:

1) As a substitute for the morning line, use the "forecast" odds as published in The Sporting Life, Greyhound Life or The Racing Post.

2) As close to the start of the race as possible, obtain the odds on all the horses or greyhounds in a race, either from the Tote or from the bookmaker. These odds are then the post odds used in the system.

3) Identify a bet using the symmetry rules and past performances in the usual way.

At the present time, I do not know how British and Irish bettors will fare using the system. I can only assume that the results will be comparable to those obtained in the United States. (The publisher would welcome sight of the results of any statistically significant tests on the "U.K." system). The use of "forecast" odds rather than the morning line introduces some uncertainty. In America the use of "probable odds" as published in the newspapers does not work very well. Journalists, it would seem, do not evaluate the past performances nearly as well as the on-course oddsmaker. Whether the "forecast" odds in British newspapers are satisfactory can be tested only by trial.

When betting with the bookmaker, I suggest avoiding those races in which the "take" exceeds 19%, or in terms of the "percentage" (see page 70 in the main text), 123.5%. For races with percentages less than 122%, consider as contenders those horses or greyhounds at post odds of 8/1 or shorter and use a point score of 46.5 for a bet. Between 122% and 123.5%, use 7/1 and 50.5 points. These figures are based on my American experience. Some adjustment may be necessary elsewhere.

For calculating the percentage and the point scores, the following table supplements that appearing in Table I of Appendix A:

Post Odds	Points	Post Odds	Points
2/5	71.5	5/4	44.5
4/9	69	11/8	42
1/2	66.5	13/8	38
4/7	63.5	7/4	36.5
3/5	62.5	15/8	35

Post Odds	Points		Post Odds	Points
4/6	60		9/4	3/1
3/4	57		11/4	26.5
5/6	54.5		11/2	15.5
10/11	52.5		13/2	13.5
11/10	47.5		15/2	12

When using the B-table in Appendix A, use the morning line odds closest to the "forecast" odds

INDEX